IMAGES
of America

The Cove

Panama City's Neighborhood

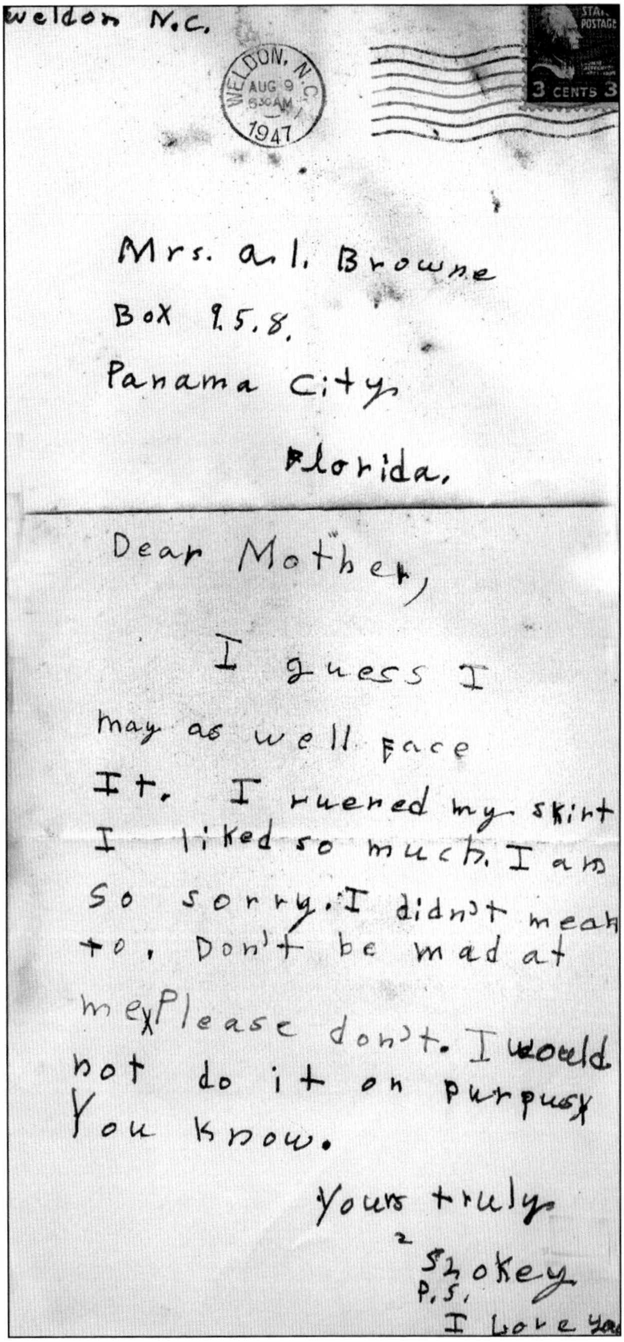

Weldon N.C.

WELDON, N.C. AUG 9 8:30 AM 1947

U.S. POSTAGE 3 CENTS 3

Mrs. a. l. Browne
Box 9.5.8.
Panama City
Florida.

Dear Mother,

I guess I may as well face It. I ruened my skirt I liked so much. I am so sorry. I didn't mean to. Don't be mad at me. Please don't. I would not do it on purpusy you know.

Yours truly
Smokey
P.S.
I Love you

This plaintive missive was sent by 10-year-old Salie Allen Browne, who was in North Carolina, to her mother at their home on Bunker's Cove Road in The Cove. (Courtesy Salie Browne Cotton.)

(*on the cover*) In this photo, Mrs. George (Dorothy) Thomas walks along the sea wall with baby Bill in 1952. "I must have walked up and down there a thousand times," she recalled. (Courtesy Mr. and Mrs. George Thomas.)

IMAGES
of America

THE COVE

PANAMA CITY'S NEIGHBORHOOD

Jeannie Weller Cooper

ARCADIA
PUBLISHING

ISBN 978-0-7385-1474-1

Published by Arcadia Publishing
Charleston, South Carolina

Printed in the United States of America

Library of Congress Catalog Card Number: 2002109580

For all general information contact Arcadia Publishing at:
Telephone 843-853-2070
Fax 843-853-0044
E-Mail sales@arcadiapublishing.com
For customer service and orders:
Toll-Free 1-888-313-2665

Visit us on the Internet at www.arcadiapublishing.com

To my husband.

Without his enthusiasm and support I would not have attempted this project. Without his knowledge, patience, and eye, I would not have succeeded.

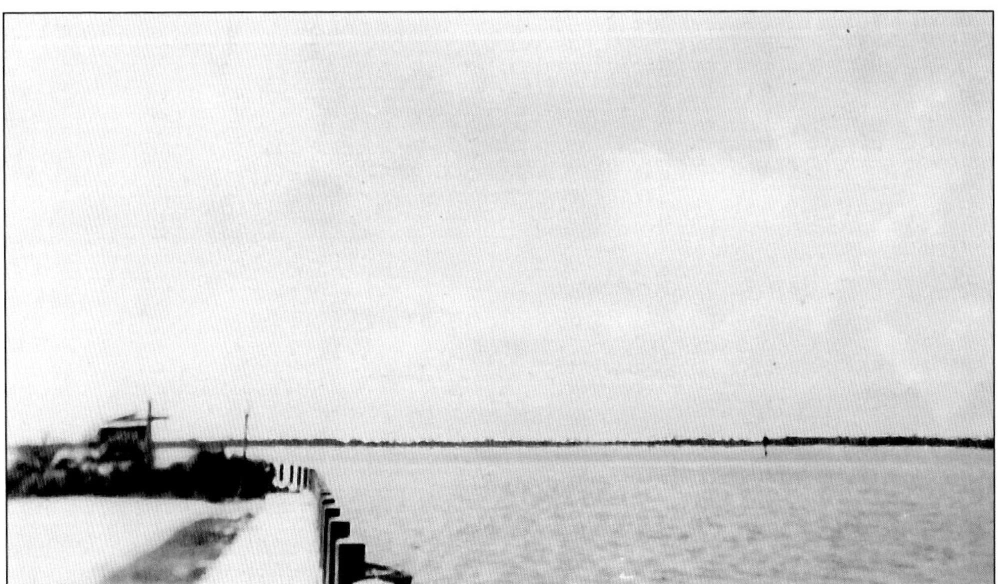

In this photo, the sea wall is shown as it appeared in the early 1940s. Note the Cove Hotel sign at the left of the photo. (Courtesy Bette Williams Butler.)

CONTENTS

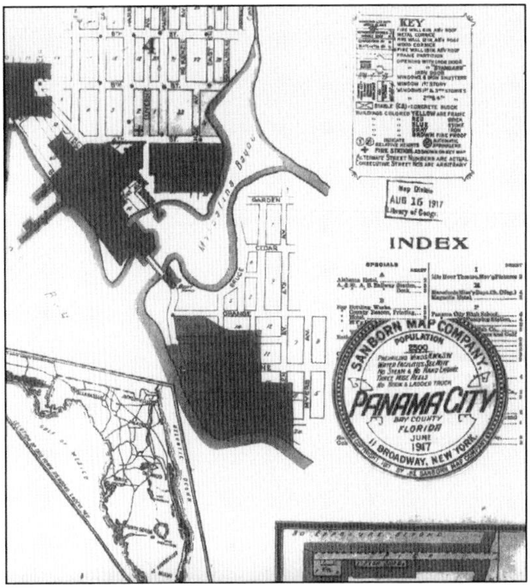

This Sanborn Map Co. fire insurance map dates from 1917. The shaded areas were the only parts of town sufficiently populated to warrant inclusion. (Courtesy BCPL.)

ACKNOWLEDGMENTS

This book has been a Cove-wide effort. As a relative newcomer, I have had to rely upon the expertise and generosity of established members of the community, which include the following: Carl Bennett, Bette Williams Butler, Mr. and Mrs. Raymond Cannon, Roslyn Chandler, Salie Browne Cotton, Clarice Davis, Beverly Nixon Dessault, Elyse Fishel, Janice FitzSimons, Hellen Freeman, Doris Gipson, Lillie Harden, Dr. and Mrs. Jerry Harrison, Ruth Howell Hauser, Bob Hurst, Reba Johnson, Jane Keller, Hank Lawrence, Sealy Harris Ledman, Anita Lucas, Ann Daughtry Lytle, Mr. and Mrs. Lee Mattern, Robert and Floy Ann McKenzie, Merial Melquist, John Robert and Kendall Middlemas, Mr. and Mrs. Buell Murfee, Genear Murfee, M.G. "Bubba" Nelson, Karen O'Keefe, Ann Kruse Percival, Dr. Hugh Pyle, John Charles Raffield, Rebecca Saunders, Elliott Smith, Mandeville and Eleanor Ann Smith, Gay Sudduth, George and Dorothy Thomas, Sarah Grace Thomas, Jane Powell Tweedy, and Dorothy Wright. Much thanks to our helpful neighbors Mr. and Mrs. Ken Bick, Ashley Eaton, Mr. and Mrs. Dan Guerry, Candis Harbison, Carolyn Harris, Rex and Cathy Harrison, William and Susan Harrison, Mr. and Mrs. Greg Hunsicker, and Mr. and Mrs. Mike Neiman. This book would not have come been completed if not for my mother, Mr. and Mrs. W.R. Clifton, Mavis DeWees, Carol, Anna, and Pam. Last but not least, thanks to Robert Cooper Sr. for the inspiration.

KEY TO PHOTOGRAPH COURTESY ABBREVIATIONS

BCPL: Bay County Public Library
BCPLLHC: Bay County Public Library Local History Collection
BWB: Bette Williams Butler
SBC: Salie Brown Cotton
CD: Clarice Davis
BND: Beverly Nixon Dessault
RHH: Ruth Howell Hauser
SHL: Sealy Harris Ledman
STABYC: St. Andrews Bay Yacht Club

Introduction

"Within walking distance of the courthouse" was one of the features touted by far-sighted developer H.L. Sudduth in 1925. Bunker's Cove has been appreciated for far more and for far longer, however.

The Cove is a jut of land bordered on the northeast by Massalina Bayou, surrounded by St. Andrews Bay to the west and south, with Watson Bayou forming its eastern border. Native Americans frequented the area and left huge mounds of oyster shells and broken pottery, which were still being picked at almost indifferently by residents and sightseers as late as the 1910s. In the 1700s, Spanish missionaries and explorers (maybe pirates!) came to the well protected natural harbor. Nineteenth-century merchants are thought to have settled in the coves, so peaceful except during the War Between the States when maurauders and patriots skirmished along the shores.Watson had a mill on the bayou that bears his name, and a Mr. Bunker is said to have established a business or a homestead on the bay, but actual evidence is sketchy.

By the early 1900s, men such as T.H. Harmon, A.J. Gay, and L.H. Howell were developing the wild, palmetto-choked peninsula, mostly concentrating on the land around Massalina Bayou, branching southward only along St. Andrews Bay. Various small settlements were distilled into the optimistically christened Panama (as in Panama Canal) City in 1909, and Bay County was created, like Eve, from the rib of Washington County in 1913.

The 1920s saw the Florida land boom and no one wanted to miss out. Homer L. Sudduth and his brother came from Birmingham, Alabama, approving what they found. H.L. moved his family here and began what would become a tradition—boosting Sudduth Real Estate, Panama City, and his special discovery, Bunkers Cove. Sudduth's vision led him to create a neighborhood with sidewalks and a broad central avenue, Cove Boulevard, landscaped with the flowers and palms motorists enjoy today. He built homes of brick, as well as stucco homes in the popular Spanish mission revival style. More of his predecessor's heart pine frame houses remain than the stucco houses, however; the stucco allegedly suffered from the poorer quality cement available here at the time. Sudduth laid out a golf course and a tourist camp, both of which were gone by the 1930s. He was also responsible for the luxurious Hotel Cove. Built in 1926, the hotel became nationally known (as the Cove Hotel) when the Sealy family (of the mattress company) purchased it. Bob Sealy brought his experience as a plantation hunter and game master, while sister Ruth Sealy Harris offered elegant Southern hospitality. She approved the guest list for every function held there, even as she allowed every kid in the area free run of the dock and beach. The bay offered blinding sunsets and abundant sea life. This combination supported locals and drew tourists, including Clark Gable, who attended gunnery school at Tyndall Field in 1942. Mr. Gable always took advantage of good hunting and fishing, as well as good company, all of which could be found at the Cove Hotel. Regrettably for The King, one local lady found his pants to be cut too short for her taste, so he missed out on one good dance partner during his stay here. Today, some residents mull over the concept of "The New Urbanism" and some are concerned about Bay County's appeal as a site for large scale residential resort development, but a look back shows that none of these are new to the Cove.

The Cove, like the rest of the country, grew after World War II as homecoming service men and women reunited with or began families. The area, like the rest of Florida, grew because of the Armed Forces Bases here, in this case, Tyndall Field. Service personnel who had been stationed at Tyndall remembered the bay's sunny charm and returned with their families to stay. In the early 1950s Lester Jinks built a modern shopping center for their convenience at The Cove's new geographic center at what had been the end of any paved roadway. H.L.Sudduth and his son Rowe were building new homes where there had shortly before (and were occasionally still) bears. The only post-Native American human inhabitants were squatters who lived in Holy

Hammock (now Tyndall Drive) in houses made of kraft paper from the paper mill that had opened across the bayou in 1932.

Cove School had served for 20 years by this time; in 1953 an additional new elementary school was completed near the commercial district on the extended Cherry Street. This business district featured gas stations (still properly called service stations), dry cleaners, barbers, pie shops, and more. Churches moved "out" from downtown to The Cove. A church of Christ came from Springfield in 1946, the Methodists built a modern facility in 1950, and Cove Baptist was built in the heart of The Cove in 1953. In 1955 services were held in the parish hall of Holy Nativity Episcopal Church. They began their educational ministry with the kindergarten in 1959.

In contrast to the phenomenal residential growth, the 1950s found tourists following Captain Anderson's excursion boats from their old launch at Tarpon Dock to the Gulf beaches. The Cove Hotel, still led by the indomitable Mrs. Harris, continued to draw discerning guests and local youngsters to the bay beach until Mrs. Harris sold the property to Hamilton Kennar in 1975. Mrs. Harris moved to the Seaside Inn and resumed her fare for the benefit of a few fortunate guests.

In 1976, the unthinkable happened when the Cove Hotel burned. Mr. Kennar then built the Cove condominiums and Bay Oaks condominiums on the property.

When The Cove was (most recently) settled in the early 1900s, it was settled by close-knit families like the Harmons, the Howells, and later the Raffields. As The Cove continued into the 1970s, as through the present, family feeling was and is what keeps the neighborhood strong. Merriam Cherry Street Elementary School educates the children and grandchildren of alumnus, and Holy Nativity Episcopal School has done a graceful, detailed, and authentic restoration of the old Cove School for use as their upper-school campus. They serve the community by allowing homeschooling groups use of the facilities, and the Historical Society of Bay County has just begun holding their monthly programs in the auditorium.

Longtime residents are beginning to restore old family homes. Newcomers and natives are banding together to seek ways to preserve the bountiful natural resources placed in their care. In a few years The Cove will be able to celebrate the Centennial of the building of the Harmon homes and the Howell homes, which have all been in continuous use as residences. If Cove citizens continue to work together there will truly be something to celebrate.

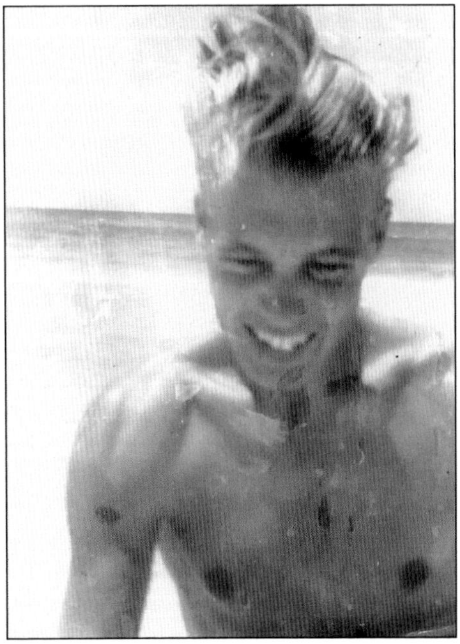

Buell (Bill) Murfee is pictured enjoying the sun and the bay at the Cove Hotel in the early 1940s. (Courtesy Bette Williams Butler.)

One

BEGINNINGS

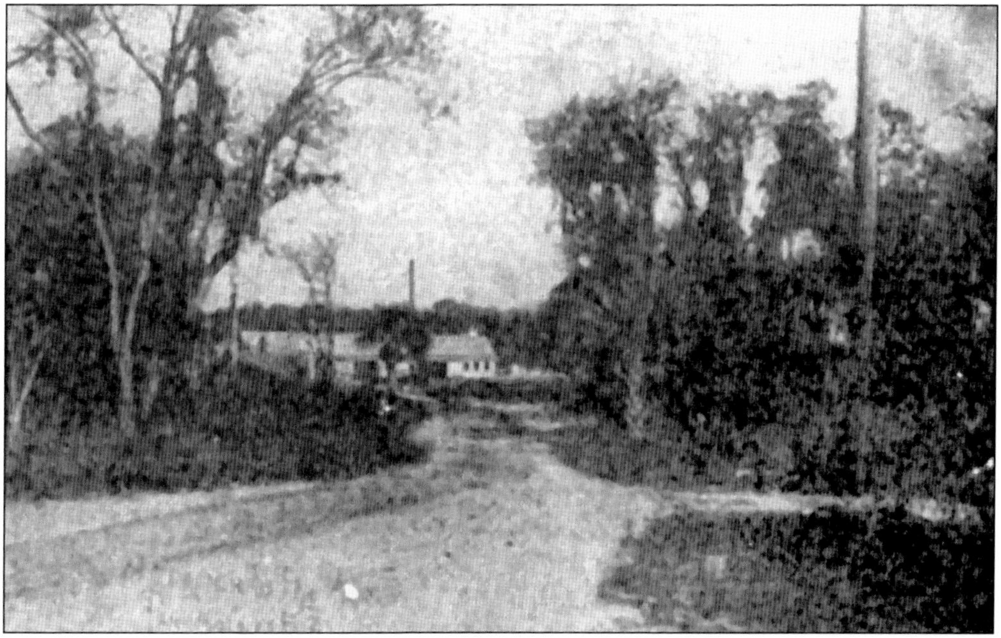

This c. 1910 view looks westward over the Tarpon Dock area toward Panama City. Brown Howell remembered moving to The Cove about this time in a horse and wagon, crossing at low tide. (Author's collection.)

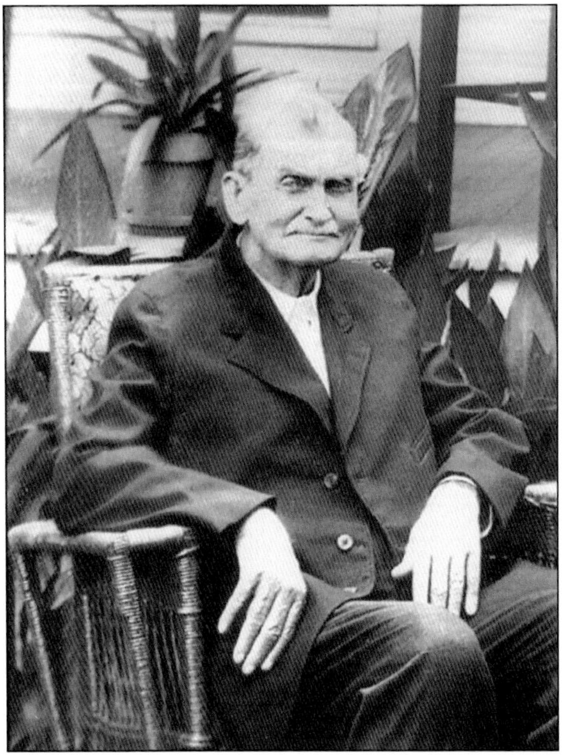

In the late 1800s, A.J. (Andrew Jackson) Gay moved from Georgia to the North Bay for his health. Here he established the town of Gay, Florida. During this same period, a Cincinnati group was conducting one of the first mail order sales of Florida real estate. When some of the projected amenities (like the rail line) failed to appear in the new development, many buyers left. Mr. Gay purchased large tracts, including land in The Cove area. Mr. Gay was on Panama City's first city commission in 1909. He also founded the area's first telephone system. A.J. Gay died here in 1918, but left a legacy of service through his son L.C., on through to his great-grandchildren, the McKenzies, who live here today. (Courtesy BCPLLHC.)

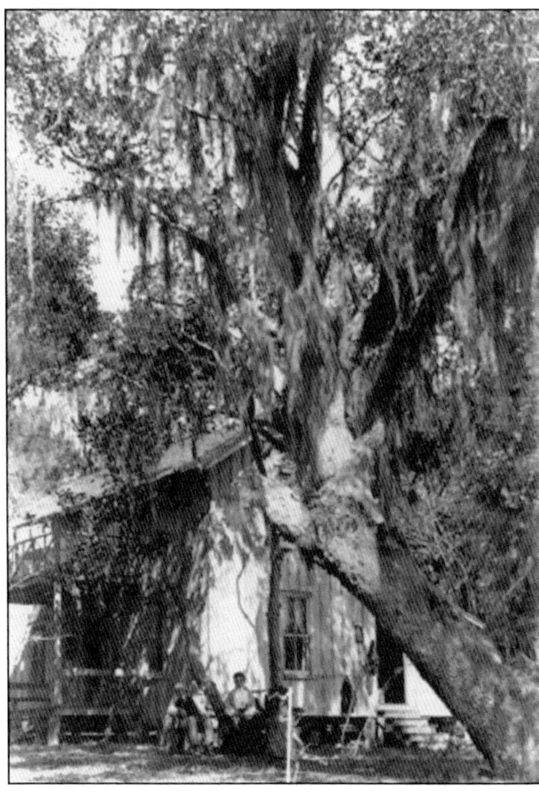

Members of the Seldon family were early 1900s settlers of the Massalina Bayou area. This area has also been referred to as Slade Lake. (Courtesy BCPLLHC.)

Minor Keith was a lumber and railroad magnate as well as a founder of the United Fruit Co. According to Marlene Womack in *Along the Bay*, "In 1919, Brooklyn-born Minor C. Keith, the largest banana grower in Central America, sought a shipping terminal for his bananas when he became attracted to financial opportunities in St. Andrew's Bay." According to the *Panama City Pilot*, Mr. Keith was a relative by marriage of Mr. Lynn, the founder of Lynn Haven, and it was he who induced Mr. Keith to visit the area. He did invest heavily and began to shape the new city, including beginning a fashionable home on St. Andrew's Bay. Tradition has it that his wife refused to live here. Minor Keith died in 1929. (Courtesy BCPLLHC.)

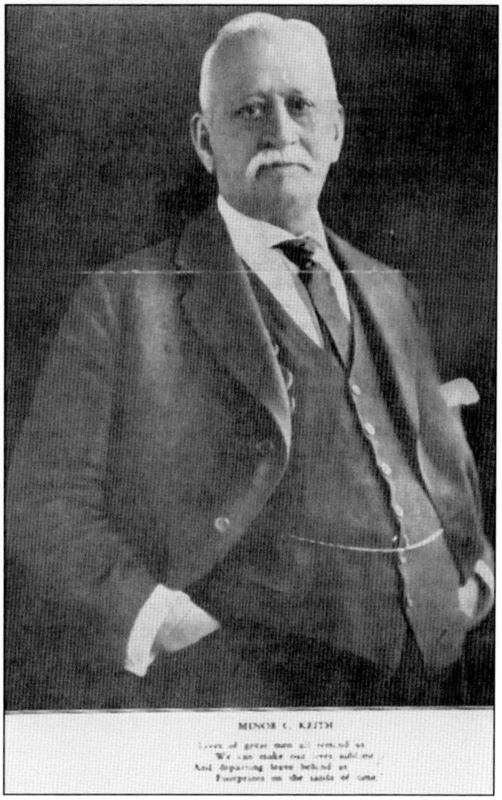

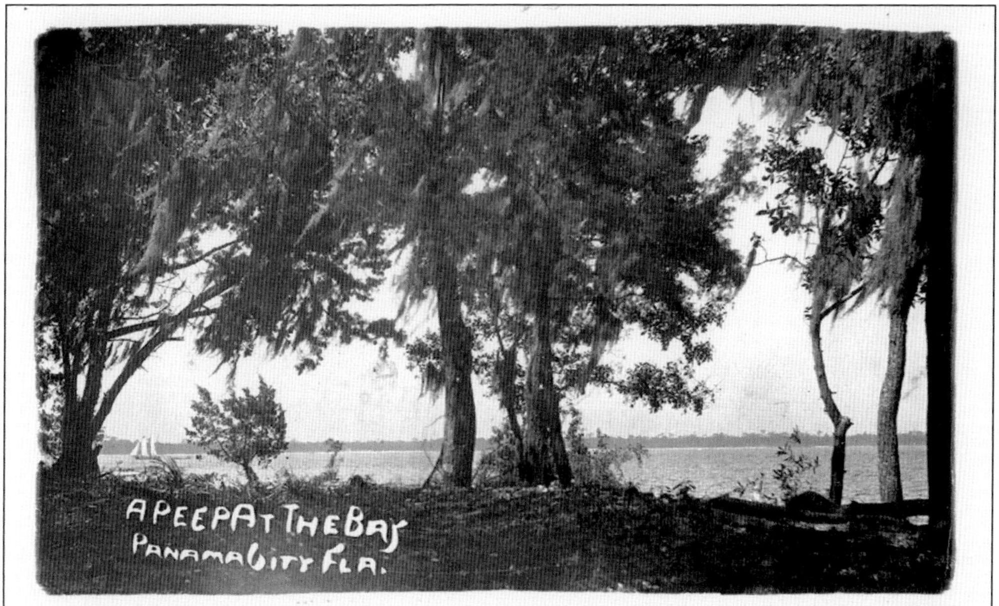

This is a 1912 view of St. Andrews Bay at the future site of St. Andrews Bay Yacht Club. (Courtesy Dewey Smith, BCPLLHC.)

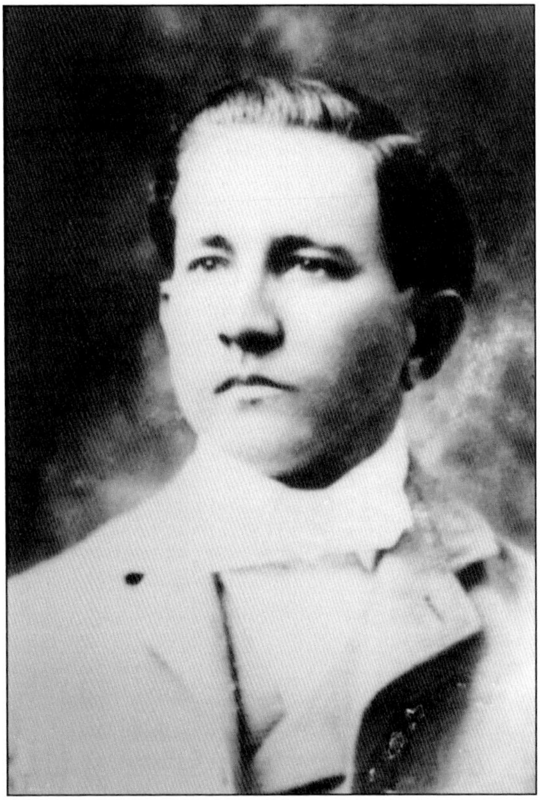

The L.H. Howells moved to The Cove area in 1909. Howell was in the turpentine business as well as being an automobile dealer. He also served the area as the Washington County representative (there being no Bay County until 1913), was Panama City's second mayor from 1912 through 1916, and served in the state Senate for Bay County. Howell died in 1935. The Florida House passed a resolution in his memory in 1937. (Courtesy RHH.)

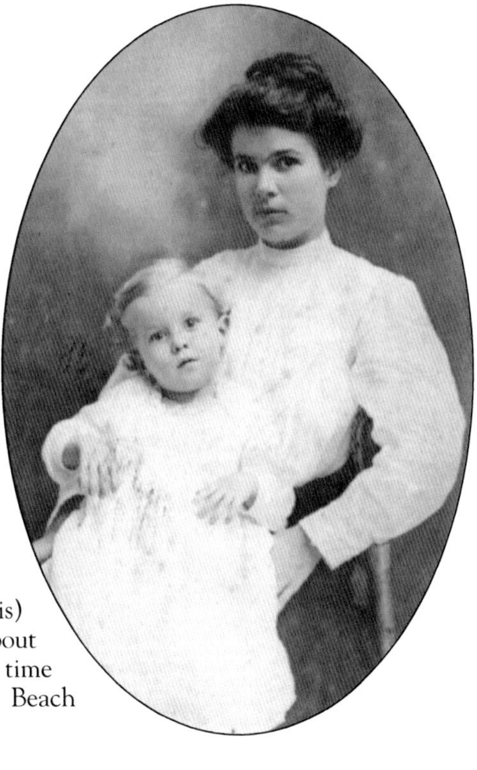

Eula Lassiter Howell, the wife of L.H. (Lewis) Howell, is pictured here with baby Brown about 1909. This photograph was taken close to the time the Howells moved to First Street (now East Beach Drive). (Courtesy RHH.)

Brown Howell is shown wearing a pin set with diamonds denoting a Rotary Club president. He was a local banker and realtor, and served as secretary of the school board during a time when the schoolteachers' checks were still handwritten. His daughter remembers him sitting at a card table at home, signing check after check. He and his wife, Estelle, raised a handsome family in The Cove. (Courtesy RHH.)

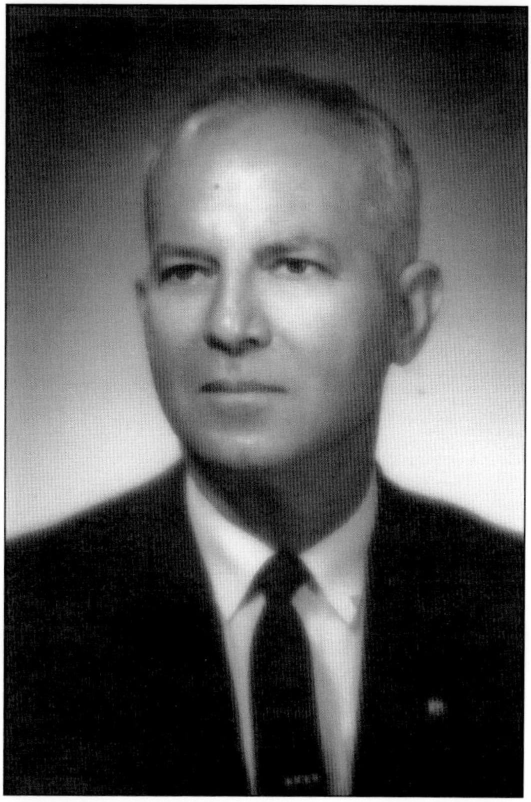

This house, standing at the corner of First and Olive Streets (now East Beach Drive and Second Place), was built by Lewis Howell in 1909 for his family. He soon built two more along Olive Street. Descendants of Lewis Howell, the Vandergrifts live here now. (Courtesy BCPLLHC.)

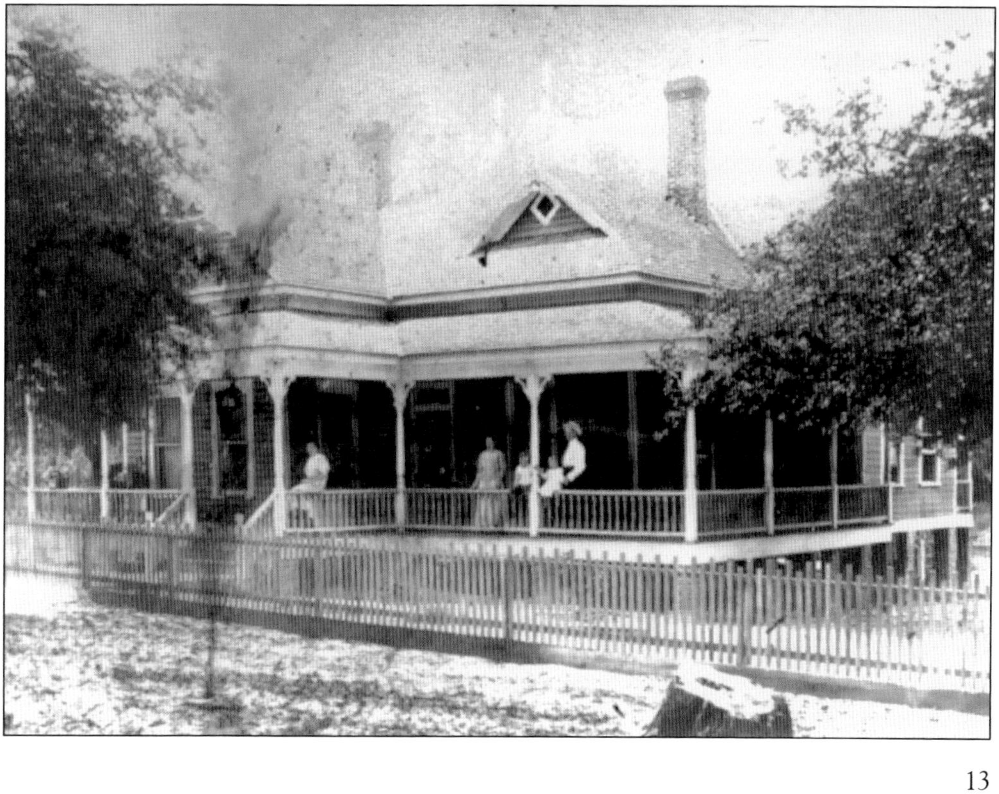

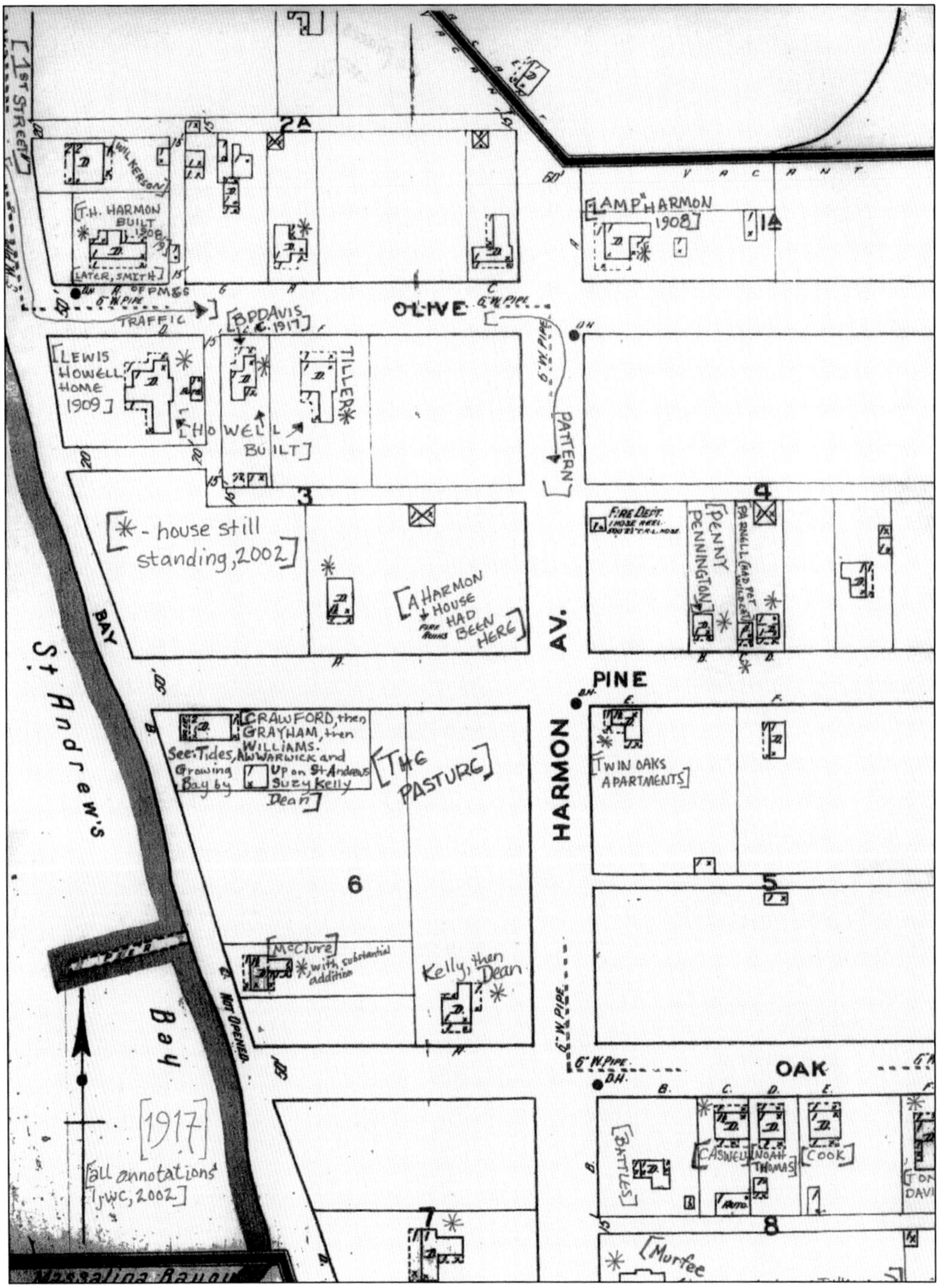

This Sanford Map Company fire insurance map was created in 1917. The author has annotations in brackets. (Courtesy BCPL.)

Jessie Lassiter Brown Davis holds Clarice, c. 1917, at their home on what is now Second Place. This is the second house Lewis Howell built of three. Mrs. Davis was the half sister of Eula Howell. The Davis family still owns this home. (Courtesy CD.)

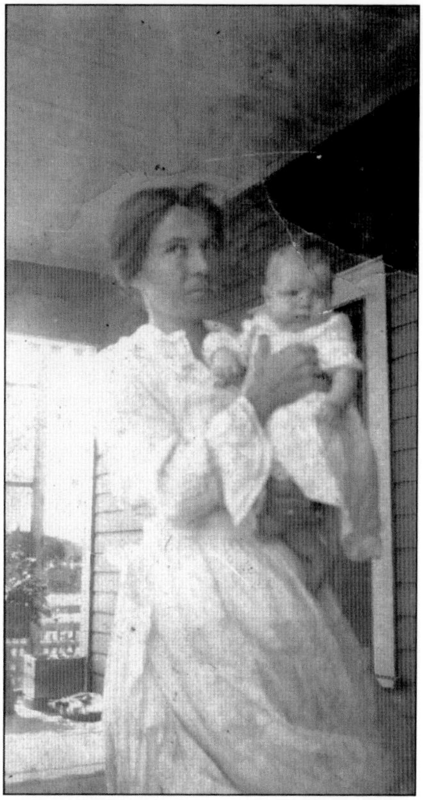

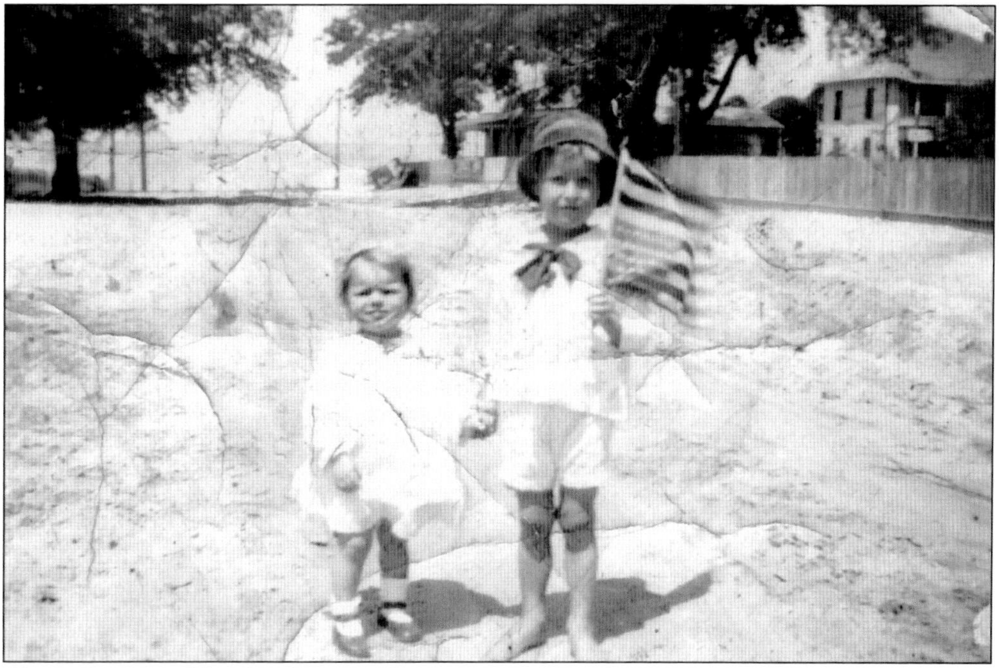

Clarice Davis and her brother Harold are pictured standing in front of their house, c. 1919. (Courtesy CD.)

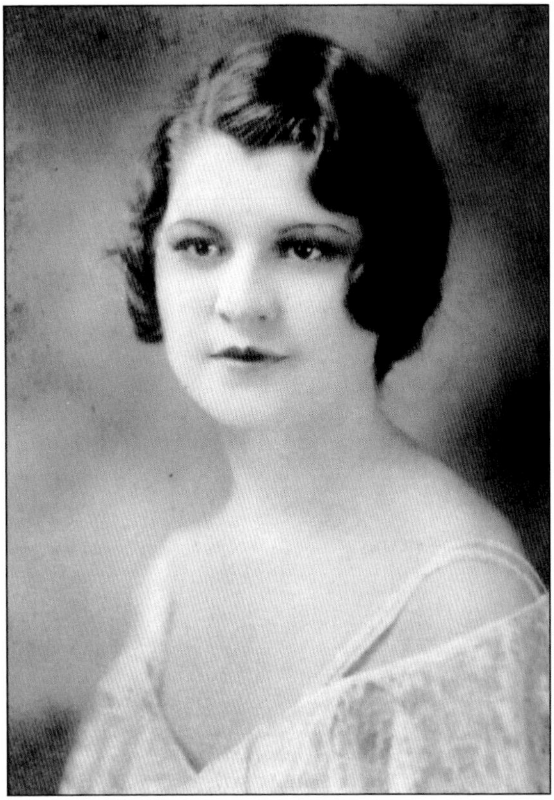

Beautiful and beloved, Floie was the older of Lewis and Eula Howell's two surviving daughters. Floie married a talented painter, Ken Bergman. They made their home in Pennsylvania. (Courtesy RHH.)

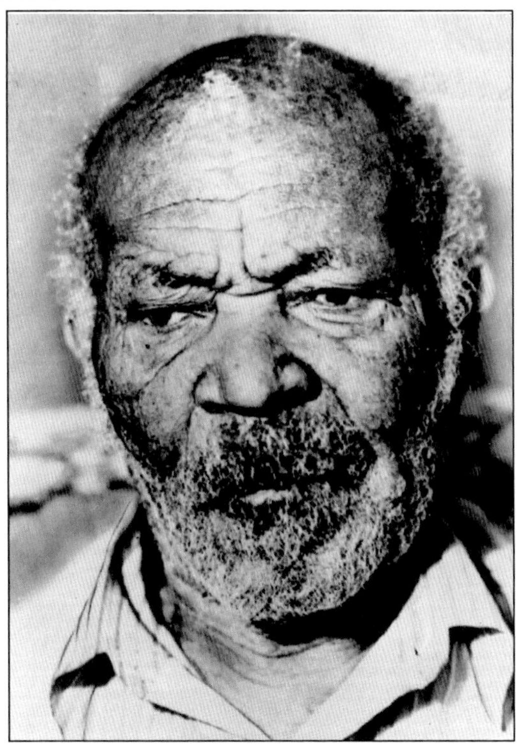

Hawk Massalina, for whom Massalina Bayou is named, is shown here. His father was a free man of both Spanish and African descent and came to the area in about 1832. Narcisco (Hawk) was born here in 1840, dying here 108 years later in 1948. The Massalina clan was the nucleus of an independent-minded community at Redfish Point, where they earned their livelihood in various pursuits such as fishing and guiding tourists. This community was lost, as were others, including Auburn and Cromanton, when the government built Tyndall Air Base in 1941 at the advent of World War II. (Courtesy BCPLLHC.)

Two

Tarpon Dock

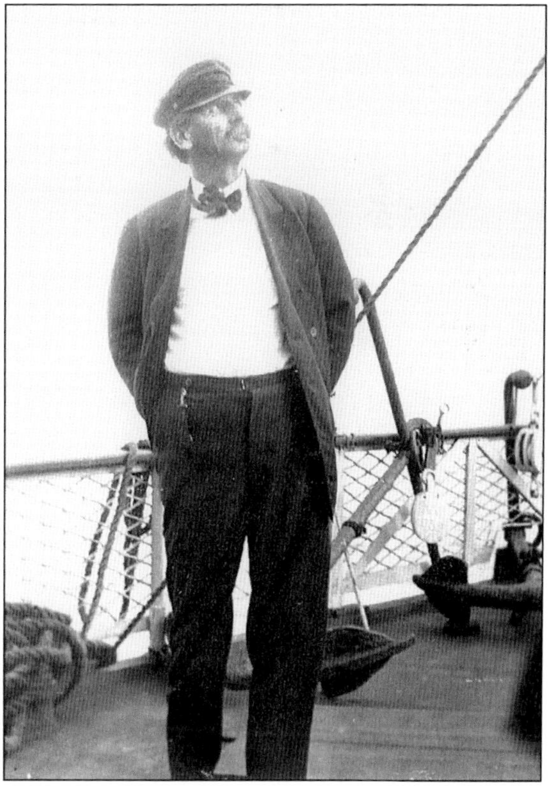

Captain Barrow of the *Tarpon*, the steadfast steamship from which Tarpon Dock got its name, is shown in this photograph. From 1906, the *Tarpon* brought supplies, mail, and people before rail or automobiles were reliably used. In 1937, Captain Barrow went down with his ship as she sank in a storm. This photo is from the 1920s. (Courtesy BCPLLHC.)

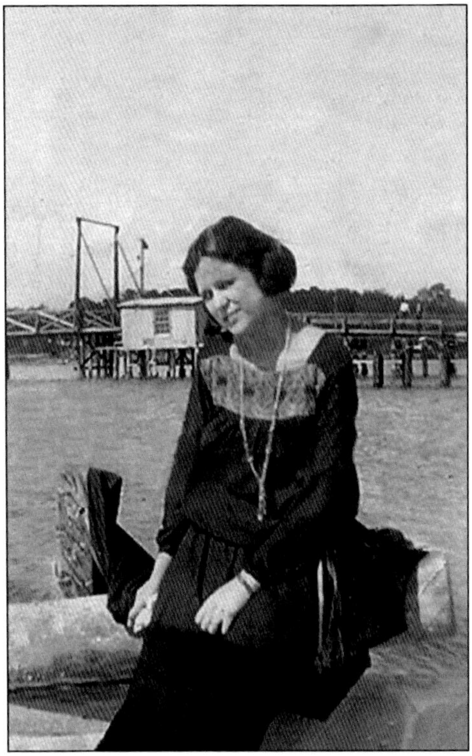

Helen Atkinson was born in 1904 and is pictured here at Tarpon Dock in about 1922. She married Horace Cook and they lived on Oak Street (now First Court) next to the Thomas family. By the time they had their third child, Floy Ann, they had moved to Magnolia Avenue. (Courtesy Robert and Floy Ann McKenzie, BCPLLHC.)

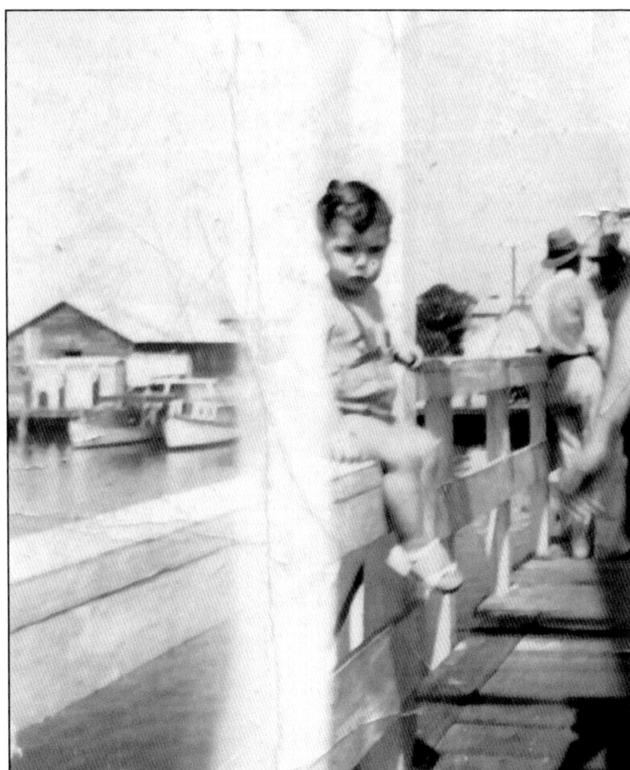

Little Jim Murfee, born in 1939, is shown at Tarpon Dock in 1940. In the right of the photo is perhaps an arm held out, ready to grab him if he should fall. Could it belong to mom Genear or dad Glenn? (Courtesy Genear Murfee.)

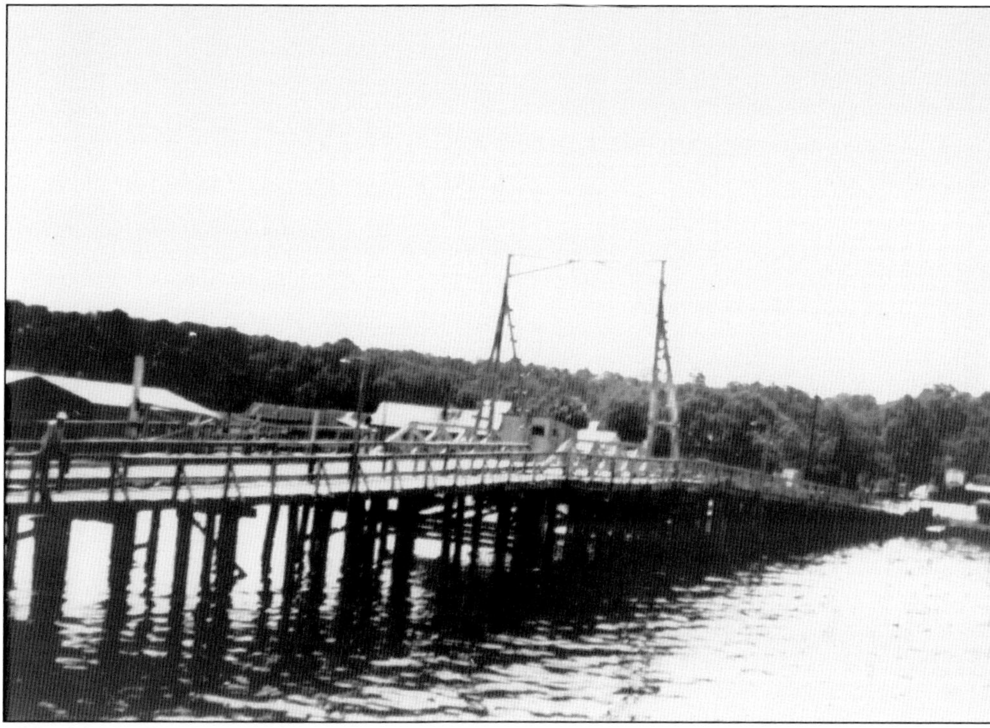

The old wooden Tarpon Dock Bridge, with a view toward the Cove, is pictured around the 1940s. (Courtesy Mr. and Mrs. Raymond Cannon.)

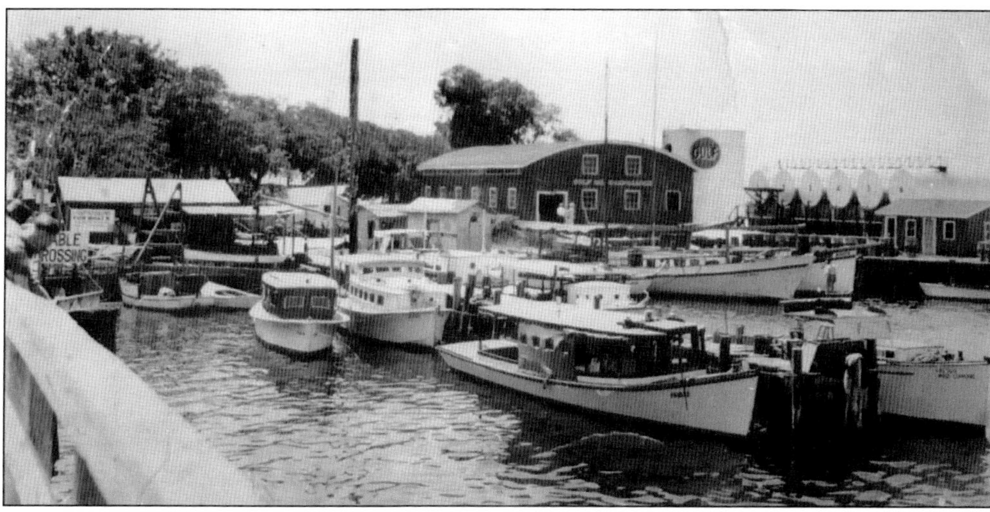

This view is from about the same direction, looking toward the Gulf Oil Refinery. (Courtesy BCPLLHC.)

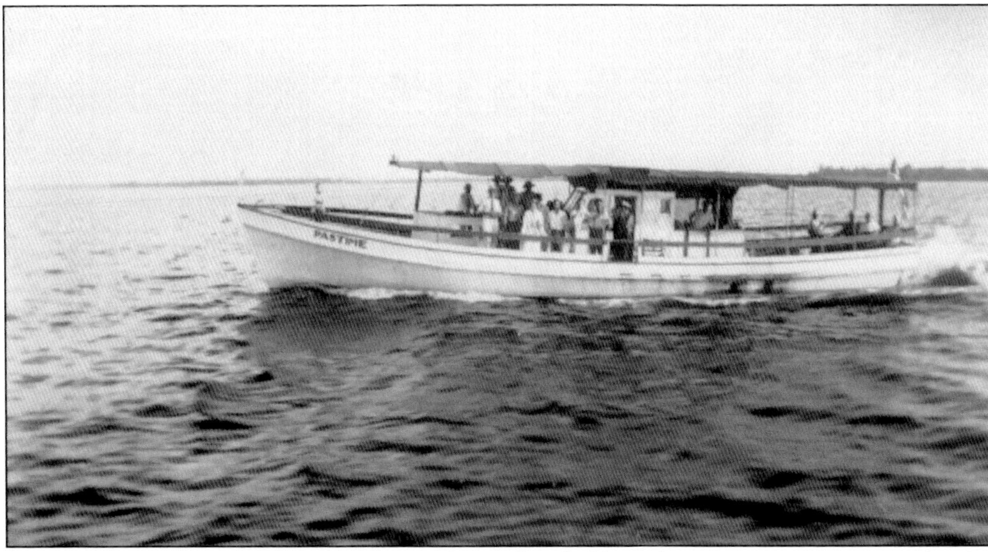

The *Pastimes* were excursion boats operated out of Raffield's Fish House. By 1950, it was decided that the old wooden bridge should be replaced. The State Road Board hired the *Pastime II* to ferry passengers from one side of Massalina Bayou to the other during construction of the new concrete bridge. (Collection of John C. Raffield, Courtesy BCPLLHC.)

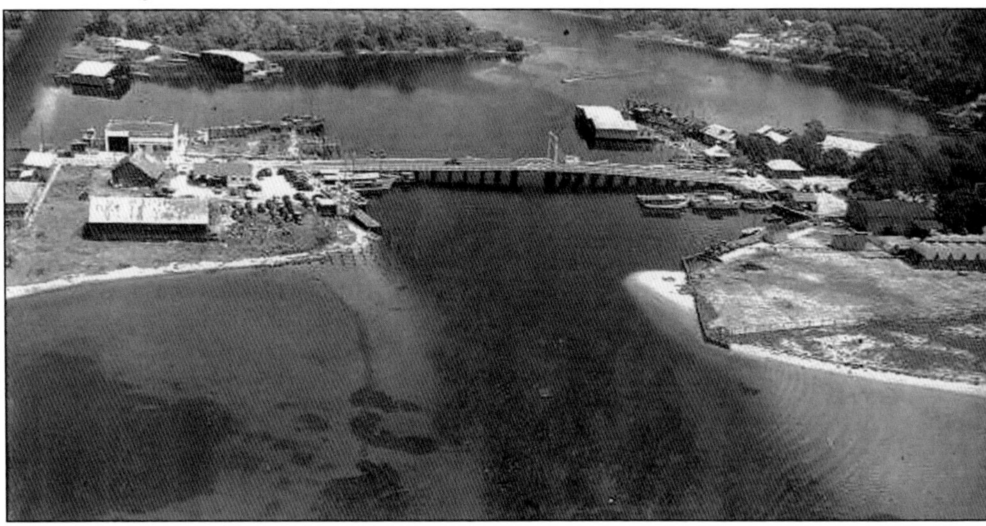

This aerial shot of Massalina Bayou comes from John Charles Raffield, whose uncle, Charles F., owned Raffield's Fish House. Raffield identified some of the concerns around the bayou. Starting at the lower left, there was a boarding house with a bad reputation. The long building was a cooperage. Up the photo across First (Beach Drive) there is pictured the (Charles F.) Raffield's Fish House. This was the only floating fish house in the southeast, according to John Charles Raffield, who incidentally lived in a boat moored at that northeast corner jutting into the bayou. Back across First/Beach Drive, there was Exxon gas for autos and boats. The *Pastime* and other party and sport fishing boats were here, and here one boarded the *Pastime II* when she ferried across to a point at about Rayford Jones's fish market, which was located on the southwest corner of the Tarpon Bridge. Almost straight up in the photo and across the street was the boat ways. Straight up and across appears what may have been old apartments. (Collection of John Charles Raffield, Courtesy BCPL.)

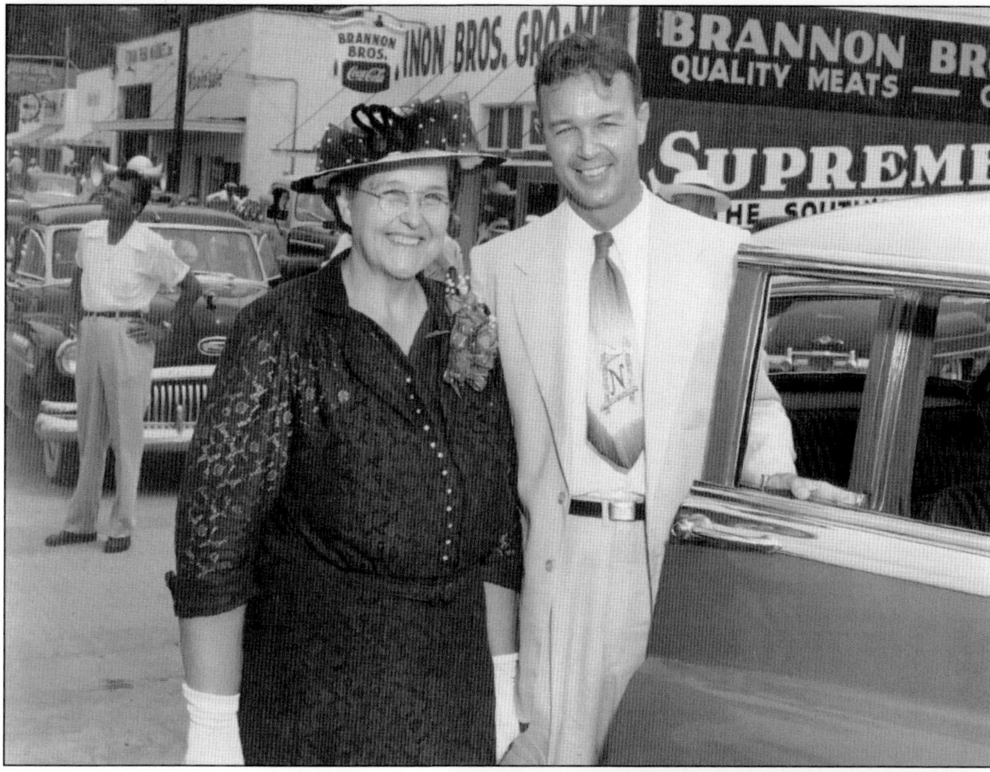

Mrs. Frank Nelson Sr. is pictured with her son, M.G. "Bubba" Nelson, at the dedication of the Frank Nelson Bridge in 1951. Frank Nelson Sr. and Jr. were both Panama City mayors. The bridge, however, is still commonly referred to as the Tarpon Dock. It is the only operating drawbridge in Northwest Florida. (Courtesy Sarah Grace Thomas.)

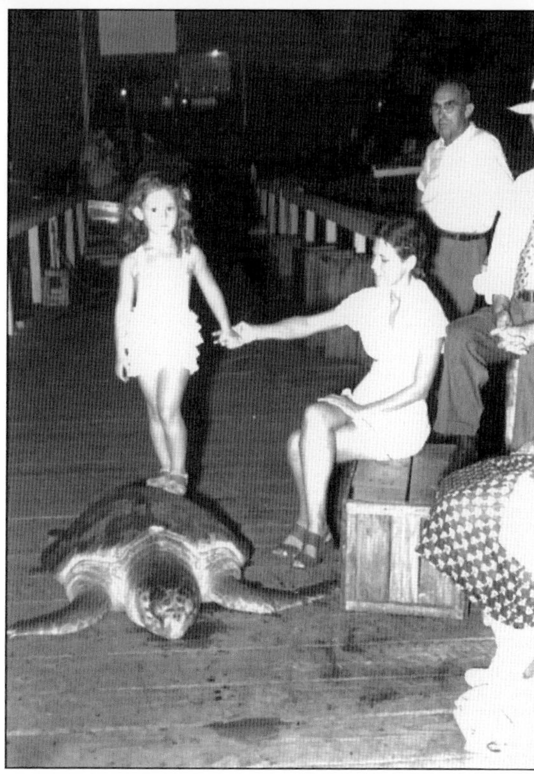

J.L. "Jimmie" Jones was a well-known local photographer who loved his work. In this fun image taken in the 1950s his daughter Susan stands on a sea turtle, steadied by her mother Josie Lee. (Courtesy BCPLLHC.)

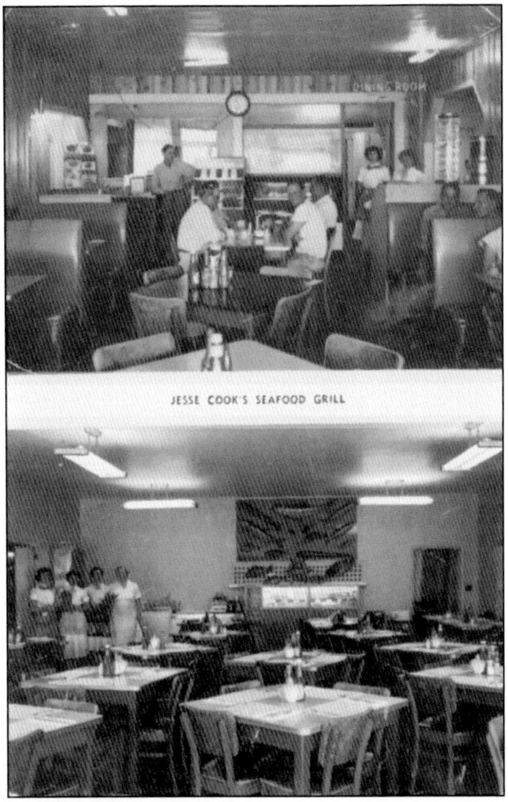

This 1950 postcard features Jesse Cook's Seafood, located in the old Raffield's fish building. The restaurant was owned and operated by Jesse and Louise Hobbs Cook and specialized in fried seafood. (Courtesy Mr. and Mrs. George Thomas.)

This painting of Rayford Jones's fish market was created by Jim Murfee as a gift to his mother, Genear, for Mother's Day in 1975. He penned the following verse to accompany it:

A small spot where he used to live;
Didn't change much, like a neighbor grown old.
With the same trappings, nothing new to give,
It kept what it had and refused to grow.
He's not saddened to see this building stagnate: Nor
would he change the bridge's span.
If the place's status quo, he appreciates.
Why did he change, on becoming a man? Watching
the draw, now's for those half his size.
And lazing around the dock?
His time's too valuable!
But he does allow, when occasions arise
To back his feet under Mamma's table.

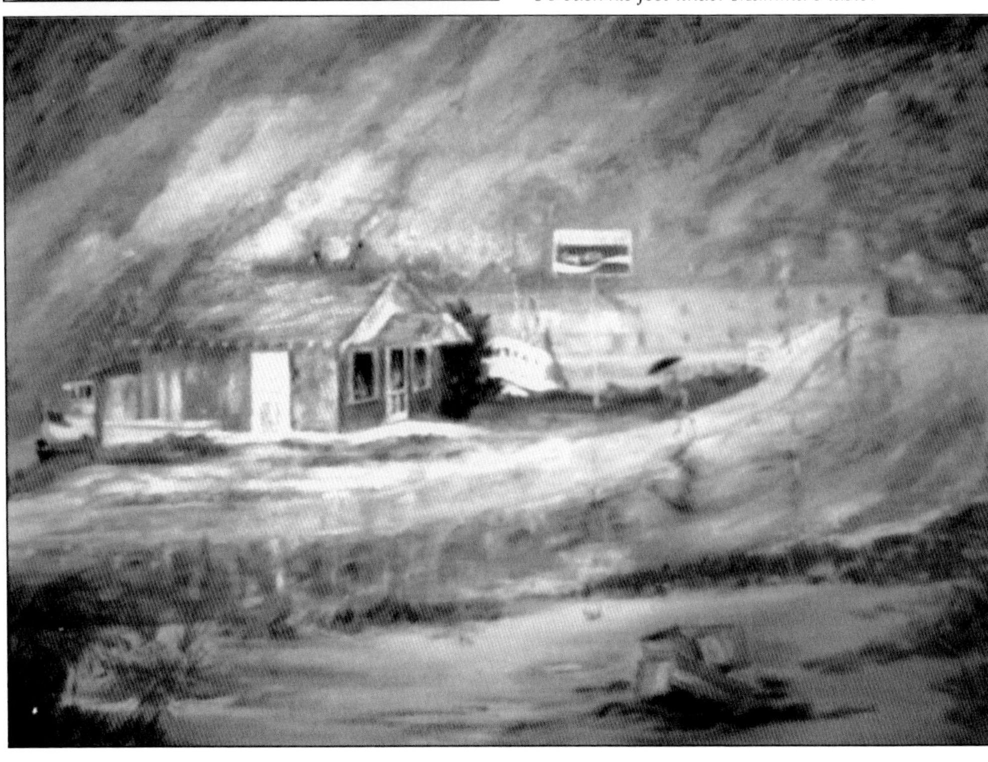

Three

Boomtown

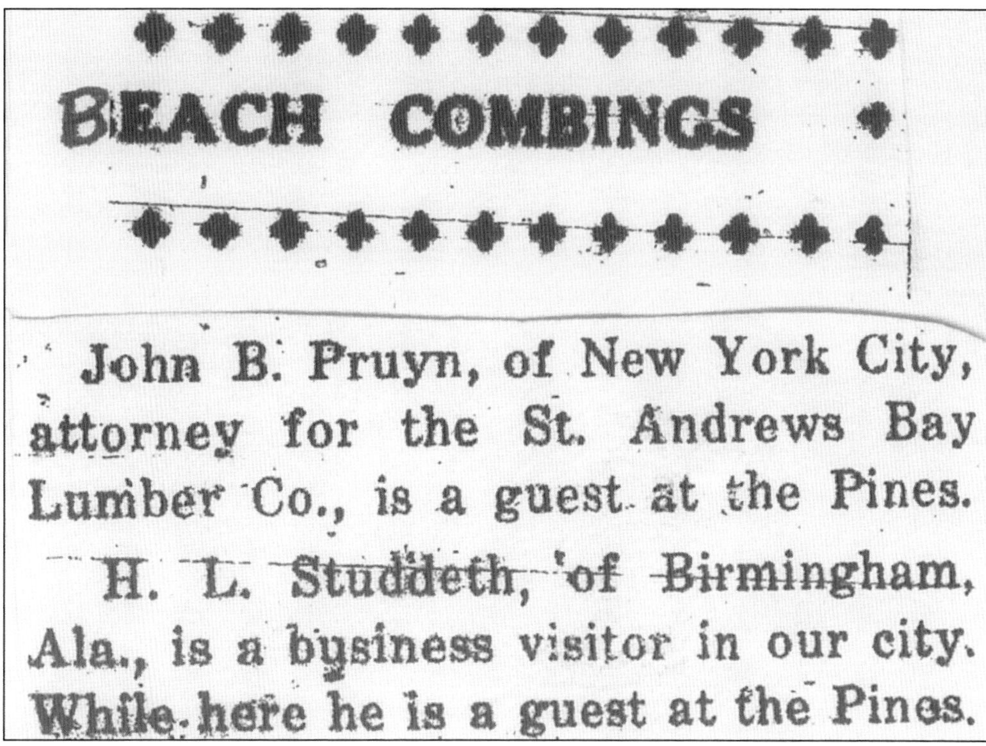

BEACH COMBINGS

John B. Pruyn, of New York City, attorney for the St. Andrews Bay Lumber Co., is a guest at the Pines.

H. L. Studdeth, of Birmingham, Ala., is a business visitor in our city. While here he is a guest at the Pines.

This was probably the last time H.L. Sudduth's name was misspelled in a Panama City newspaper. This is from the June 19, 1925 issue of the *Panama City Pilot*, which served Washington, then Bay County from 1906 to 1941. (Courtesy Bay County Public Library.)

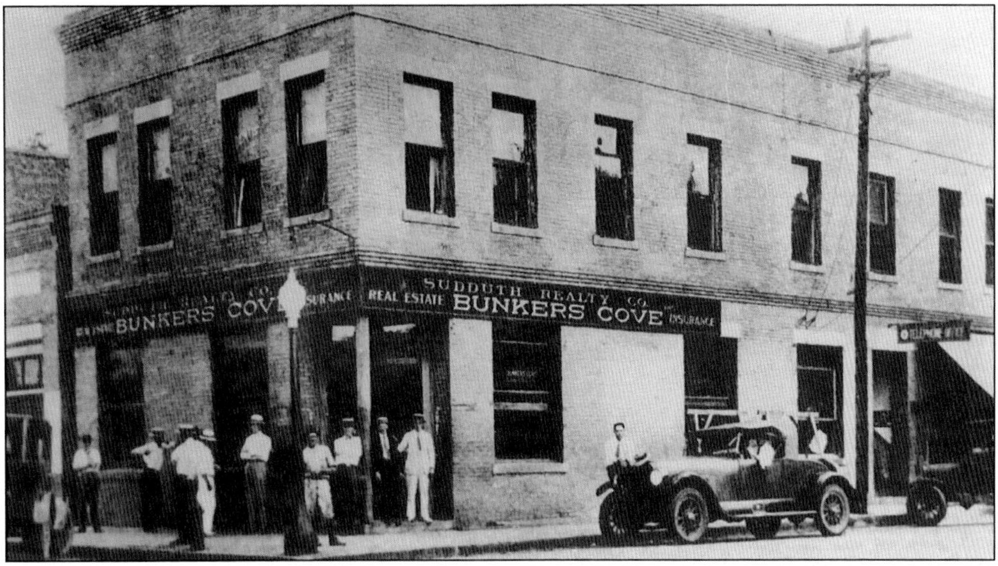

Sudduth Real Estate was located in the mislabeled Bank of Panama City Building on Harrison Avenue. H.L. Sudduth brought with him a bold vision for the area when he came to Panama City from Birmingham, Alabama. He held a huge picnic on July 4, 1925, and gave away a lot (number 11, to Mrs. S.B. Jones of Carrabelle) out of his new Bunker's Cove development. According to an article appearing in the *Panama City Pilot* that day, "as this is such an unusual sale, catering to high class homes, there is no doubt that this property will in the course of time come to be the choicest residential property of this city." Many still thought The Cove was too far out of town to be convenient. (Courtesy BCPLLHC.)

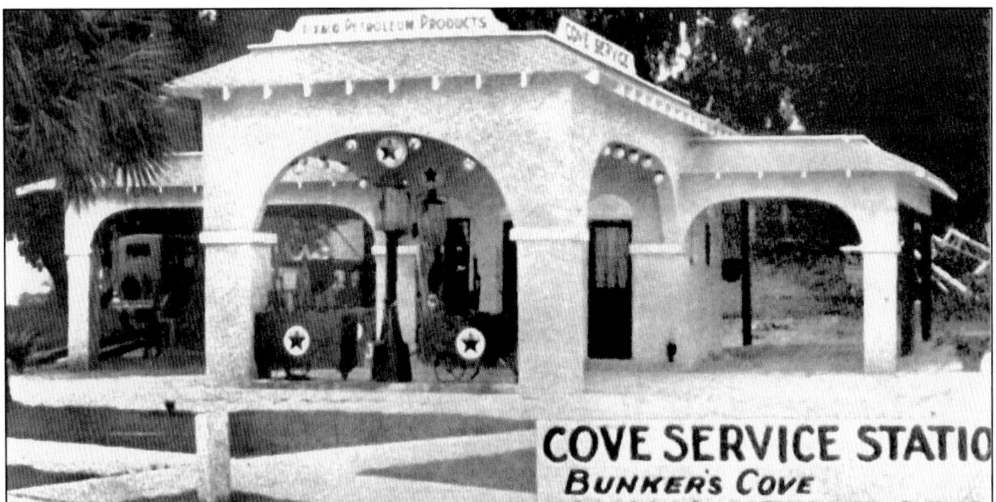

Cove Service Station on 105 Cherry Street is shown in this image dating from the 1930s. According to Buell Murfee, a big magnolia tree once stood on this corner. At the time of this photo, E.L. (Elmo) Barrett was the manager and he continued until the mid-1940s when Mr. and Mrs. Robert E. (Mabel) Adams bought the business. During this time a man named Mr. Kaiser gave children Hershey bars when their parents bought gasoline. The Adams operated The Cove Service Station and Grocery until 1965. This family lived on Bunker's Cove Road at Adams' Alley, which is now Adams' Street. (Courtesy BBCPLLHC.)

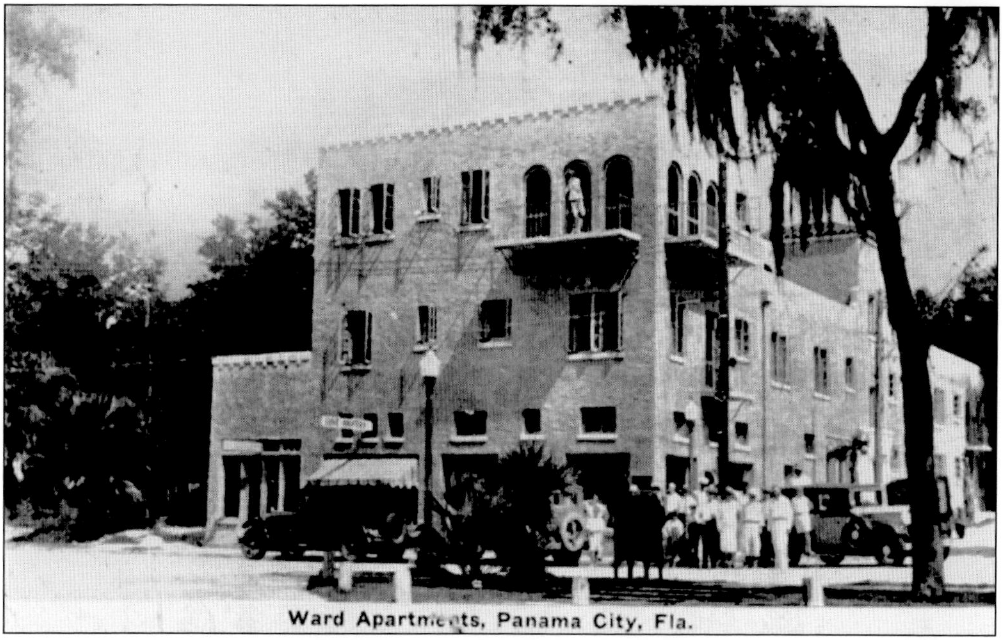

This postcard from the late 1920s or early 1930s shows Ward Apartments across the street from the Cove Hotel. Bay Anchor Apartments stands here now, minus the grocery. (Courtesy BBCPLLHC.)

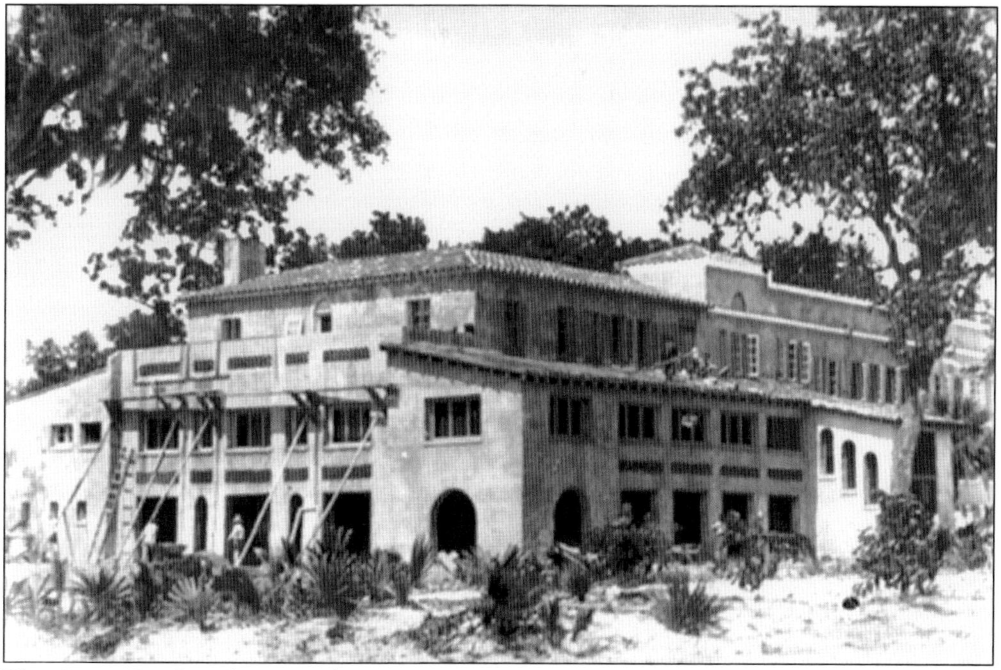

The Cove Hotel is shown under construction, *c.* 1926. A *Panama City Pilot* headline from November 12, 1925, reads, "SPACIOUS HOTEL NOW UNDER CONSTRUTION" with the subheading, "MANY NEW BEAUTIFUL BUNGALOWS NEARING COMPLETION." The text below, however, ends with, "much of the material is now on the ground, more is on the way and construction will be begun at once." (Courtesy BBCPLLHC.)

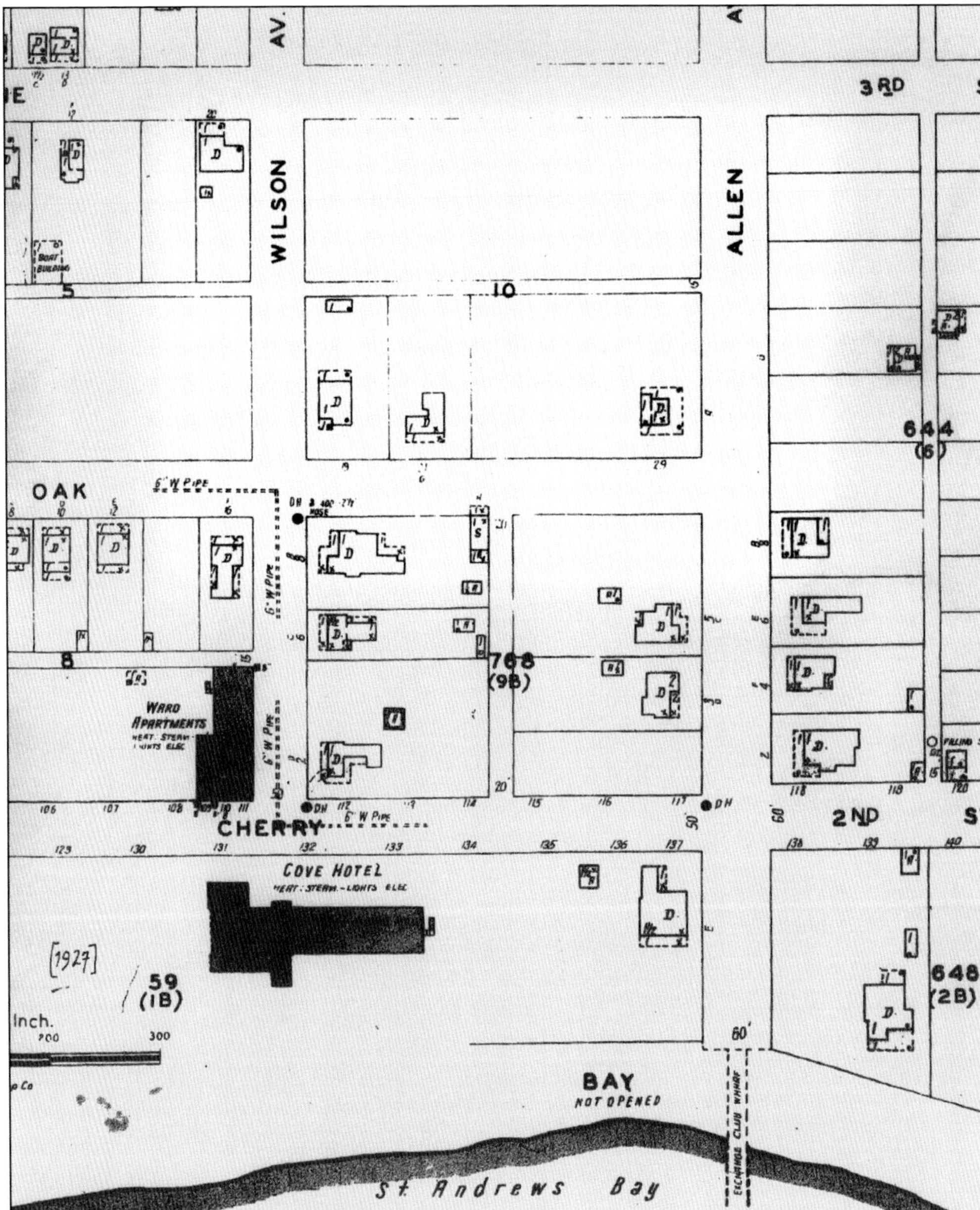

This Sanborn Map Company fire insurance map was made in 1927. Note the Exchange Club (or city) Wharf at the end of Allen Avenue. Also note the word "BAY" denoting that the beach was considered a right of way, even if it was not "opened." (Courtesy BCPL.)

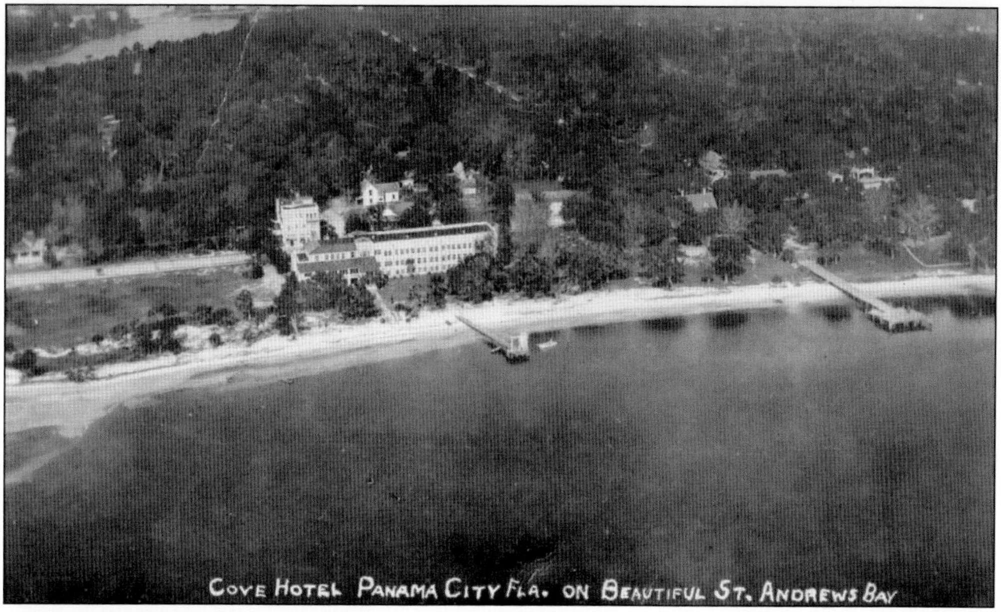

This aerial photo postcard highlights the Cove Hotel. The time is roughly the same as the map on page 26. (Courtesy Mr. and Mrs. George Thomas.)

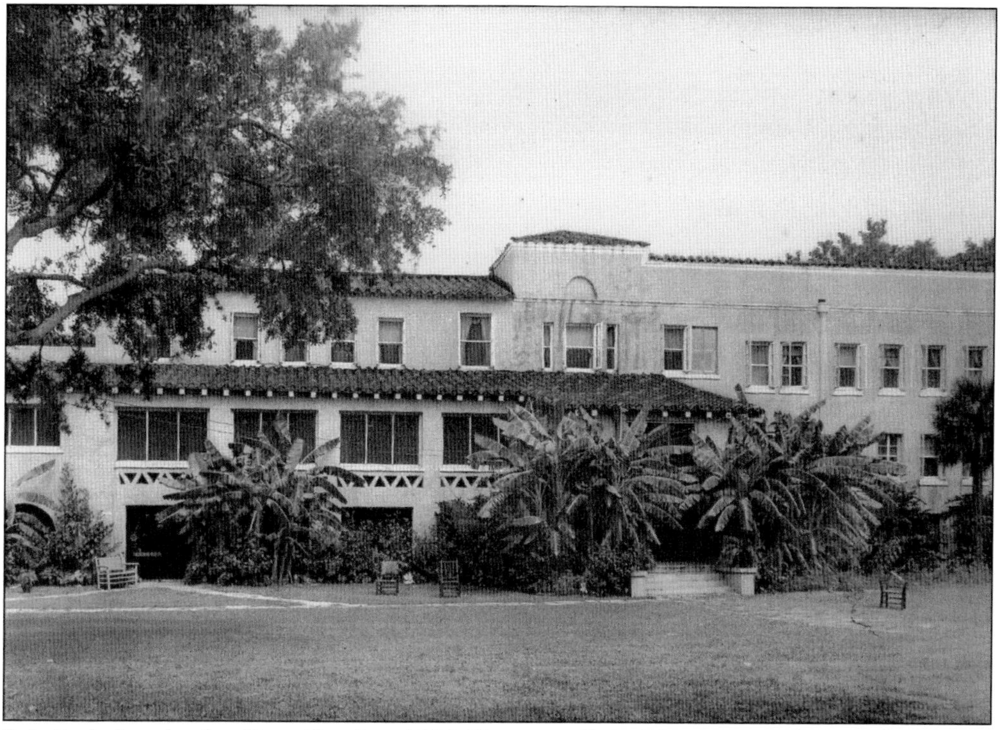

Bob Sealy bought the Cove Hotel in 1926. His sister, Ruby Harris, came down and ran it for years and is missed to this day. Both George Thomas, who often consented to guide guests in their hunting and fishing pursuits, and Sealy Harris Ledman, Ruby Harris's granddaughter, had this image.

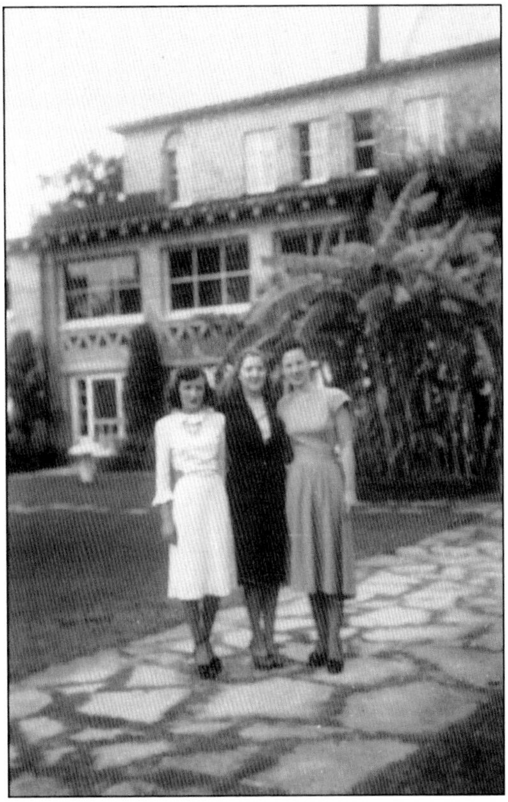

Bette Williams (Butler) is shown (far right) with unidentified friends, standing before the famed dining room at the rear of the Cove Hotel in the early 1940s. (Courtesy BWB.)

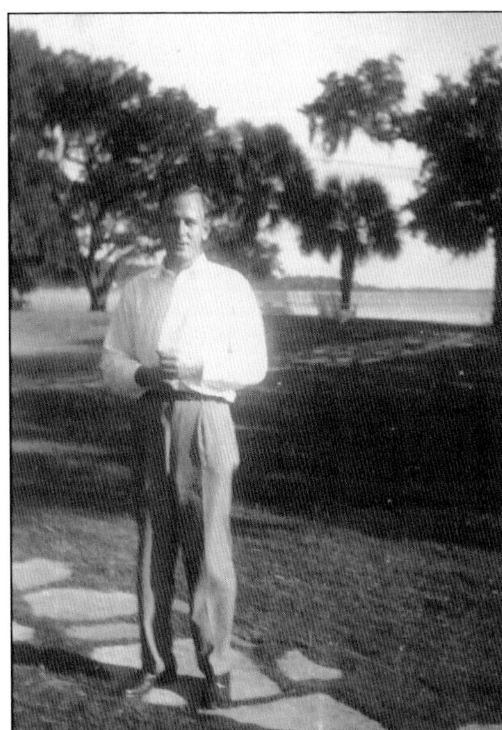

Ruby Harris's son Jase is shown on the lawn of the hotel in the early 1940s. (Courtesy BWB.)

This photo shows Bob and Marge McClenathen. During the early part of World War II (1941–1945), Bob served in the Coast Guard at the time the Coast Guard used the Seaside Inn for barracks. The couple rented from Bashe Davis at 116 Olive Street. By the end of the war, Olive Street would be renamed Second Place. (Courtesy CD.)

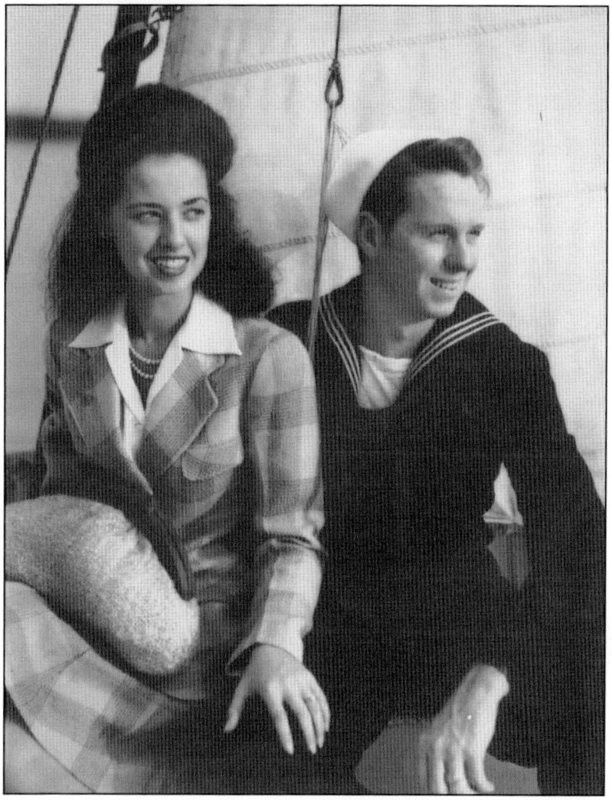

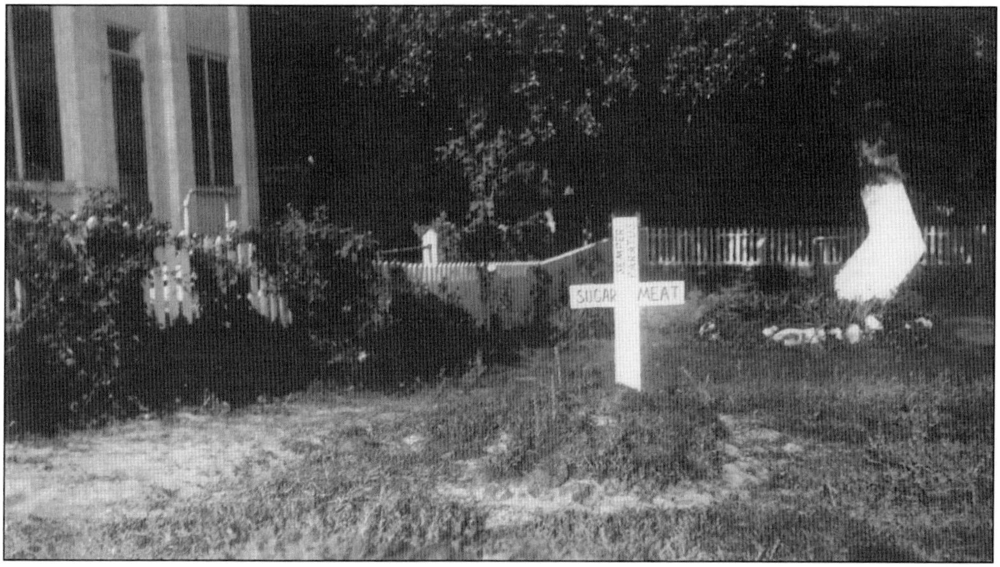

When their mascot, a bulldog named Sugar Meat, died, loyal members of the Coast Guard stationed at the Seaside Inn buried him with full honors in the front yard. The marker reads, "Sugar Meat Semper Paratus." There is a deck over the site now. (Courtesy BWB.)

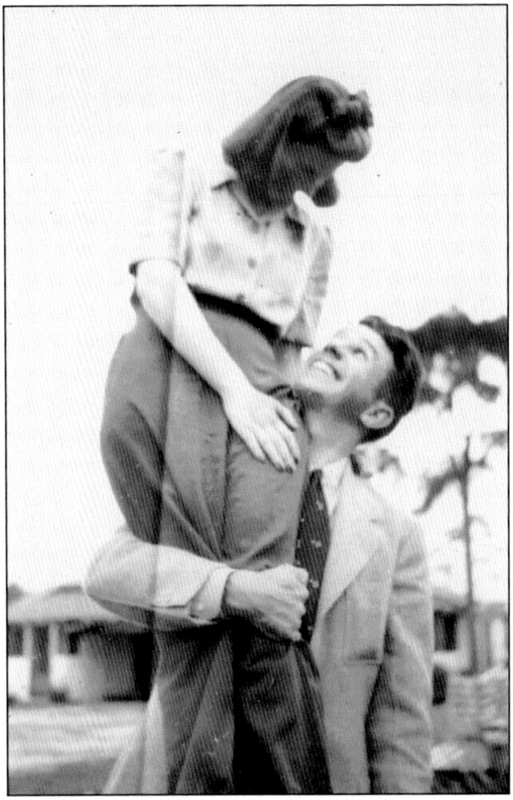

This unidentified couple exemplifies the spirit of the times in this early 1940s shot by Clarice Davis. Clarice Davis was a talented and enthusiastic amateur photographer who worked at Bryan's Photo Shop for years.

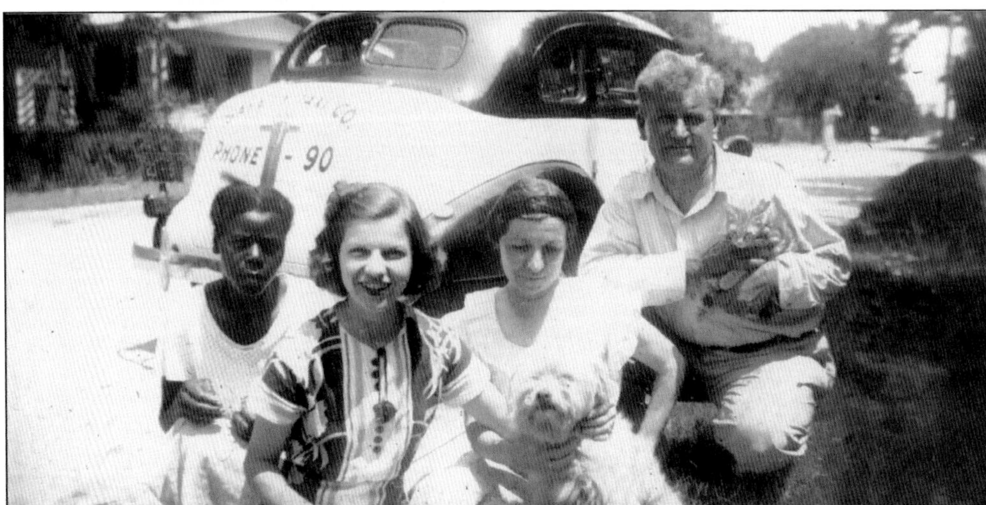

From left to right are Beulah Lee of Redfish Point (baker of delicious fig muffins), Clarice Davis, and her parents Jessie and B.P. "Bashe" Davis. The group is in front of Mr. Davis's taxi parked in front of their home at 106 Olive Street. Also in the picture are the family dog and cat and an unidentified woman appearing to point a camera in the direction of a duplex two houses east. Clark Gable attended Tyndall Flexible Gunnery School for six weeks beginning in October 1942. Persistent local legend insists that Gable attended parties at this duplex. He was a guest at the Cove Hotel during his stay here. This photo is from the early 1940s. (Courtesy CD.)

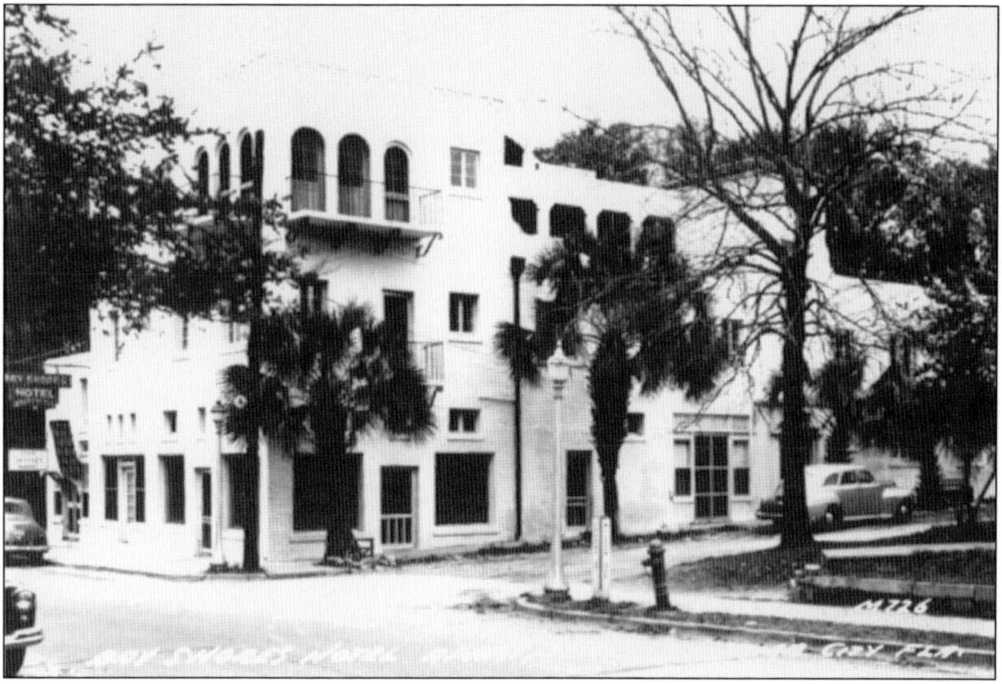

By the 1940s Ward Apartments had become Bay Shores Hotel. This image was taken from a postcard. (Courtesy BCPLLHC.)

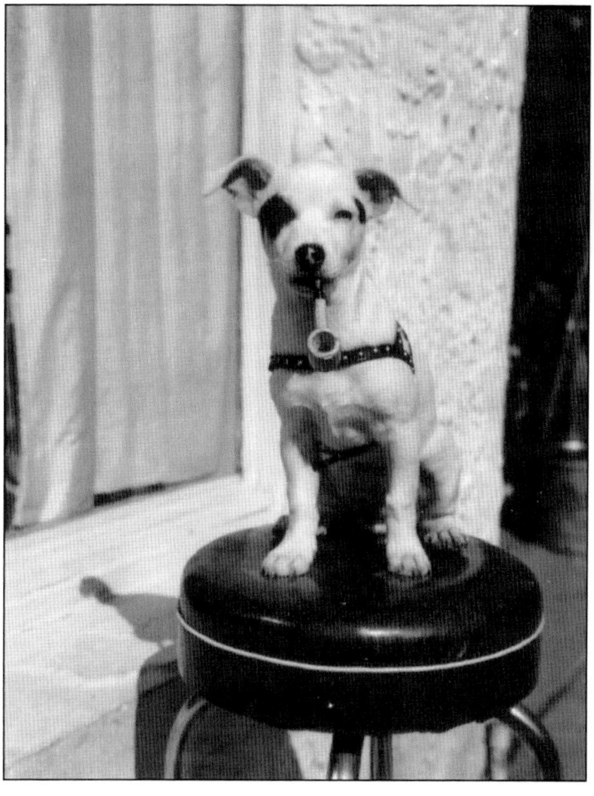

Mr. Eve made appearances on local television in the 1950s based on his celebrity as a "talking dog." He made his home with the proprietors of the Bay Shores Hotel. (Courtesy Ann Daughtry Lytle.)

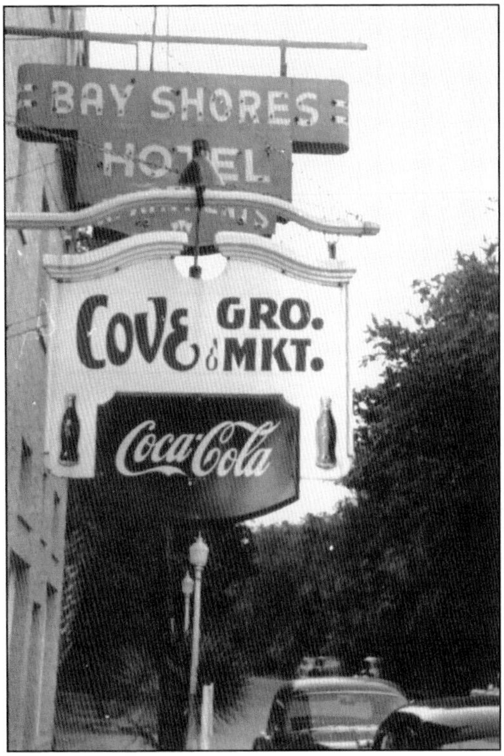

Mr. and Mrs. Edwin Daughtry (Myrle) came from Cordele, Georgia in 1947 and bought the Cove Grocery from the Allens. (Courtesy Ann Daughtry Lytle.)

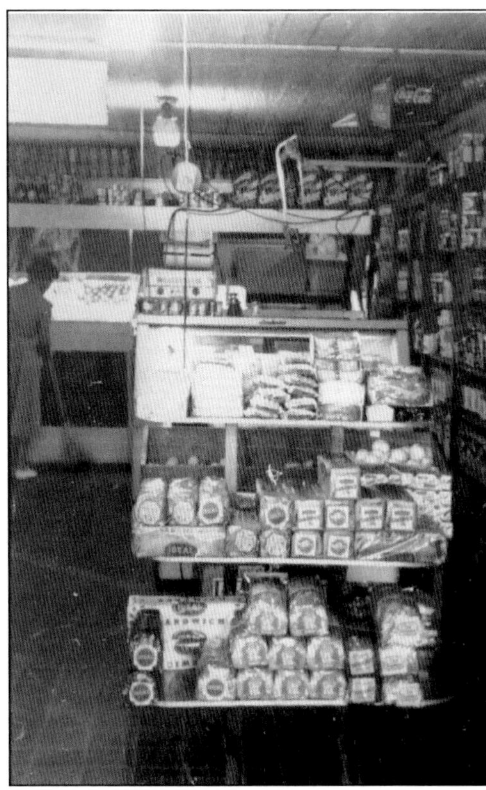

Mrs. Daughtry is pictured in the Cove Grocery. The Daughtrys owned the store until 1954. (Courtesy Ann Daughtry Lytle.)

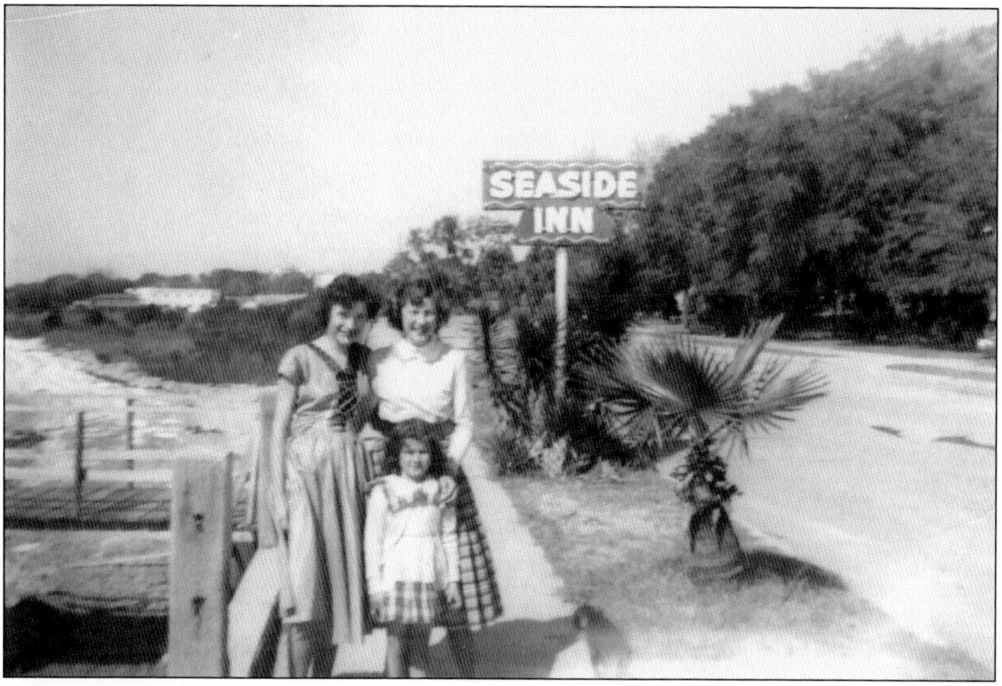

Barbara Murfee, Wanda Harmon, and an unidentified friend pose for a photo on the sea wall across from the Seaside Inn in the 1950s. (Courtesy Genear Murfee.)

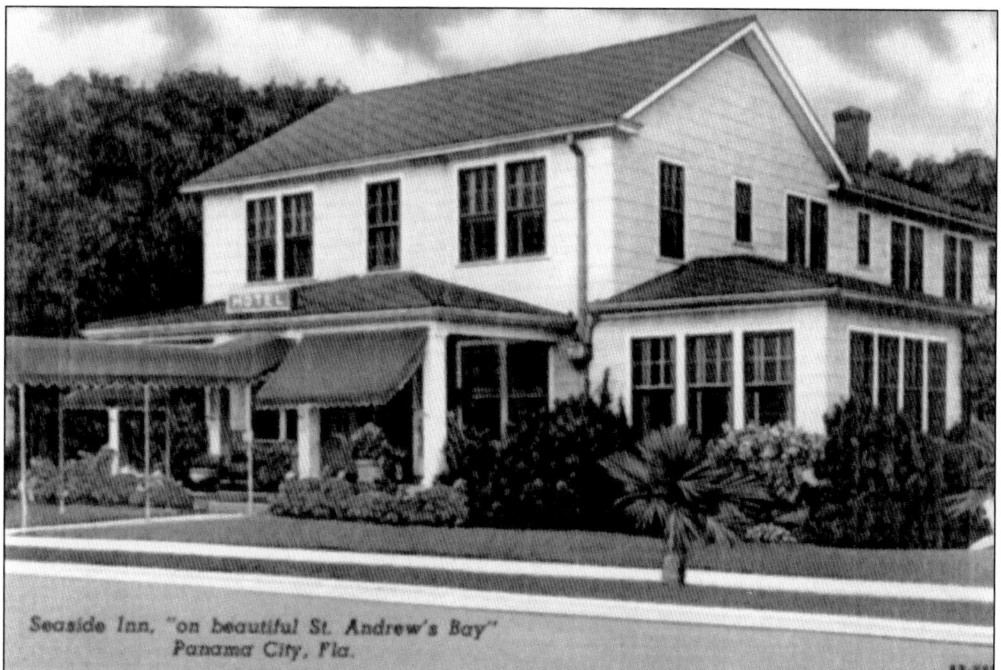

The Seaside Inn is an older, frame hotel facing the bay and looking out to the gulf. Charles Raffield bought the inn in 1945 and lived there with his family. Tressie Hartfield managed the home and the hotel. (Courtesy BCPLLHC.)

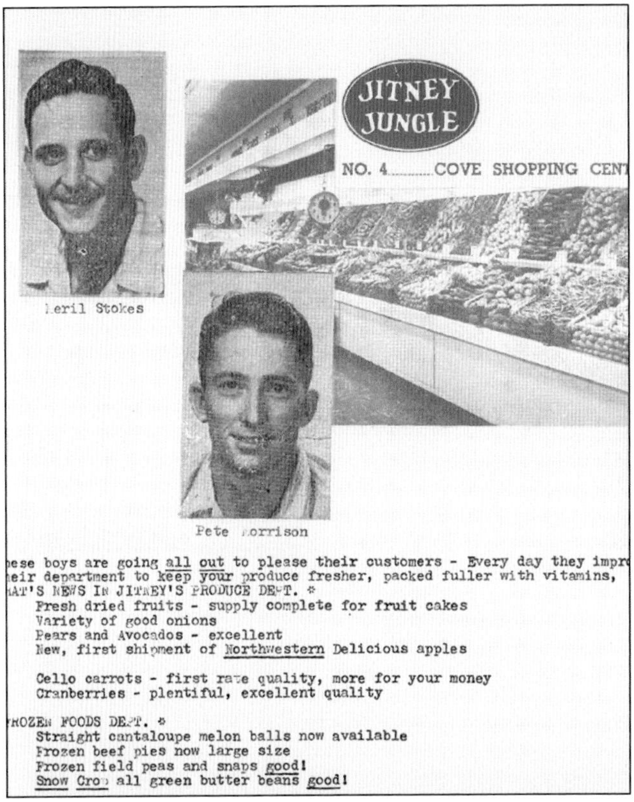

The 1950s saw the future—a shopping center in the Cove. Jitney Jungle was the supermarket that anchored the Cove Shopping Center. *The Cove Shopper*, from which this ad is taken, touted the center's value and convenience.

Humphries was located next to Jitney Jungle in the 1950s. The caption that accompanied this image read, "SEEING is BELIEVING. This is a view of the lovely interior of Dr. Humphries Pharmacy. In later issues of the *Cove Shopper* we will tell you more about this magnificent store with its dependable departments." Humphries offered free ice cream to lucky young shoppers who found their names in an issue. Cooper's Drugs opened a store in this location in 1962. (Courtesy BCPLLHC.)

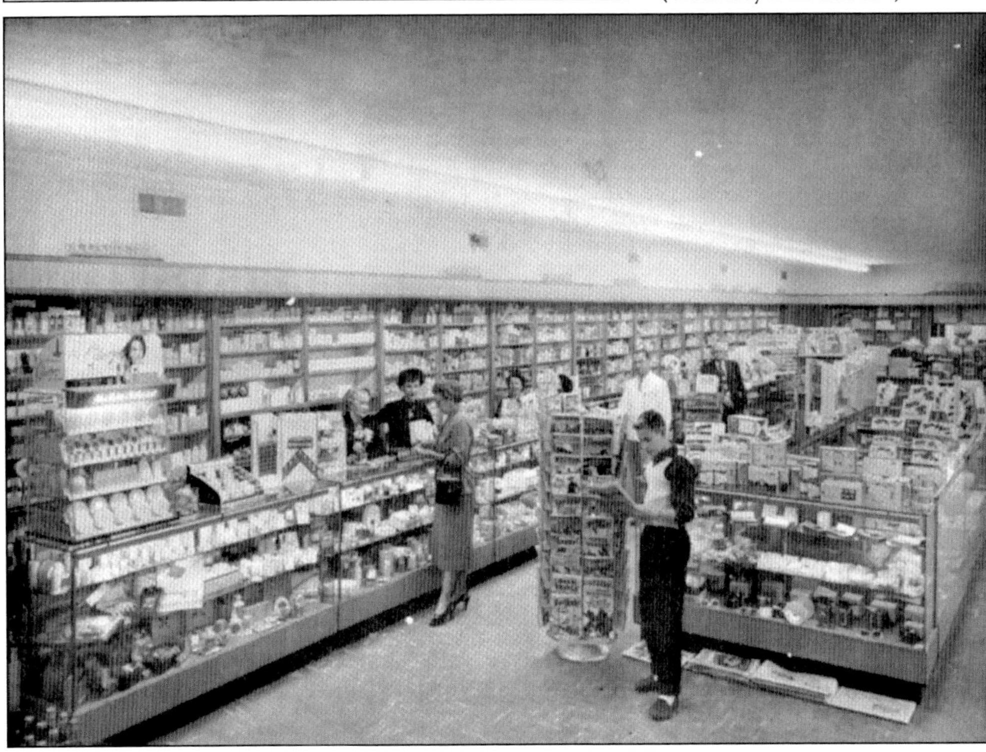

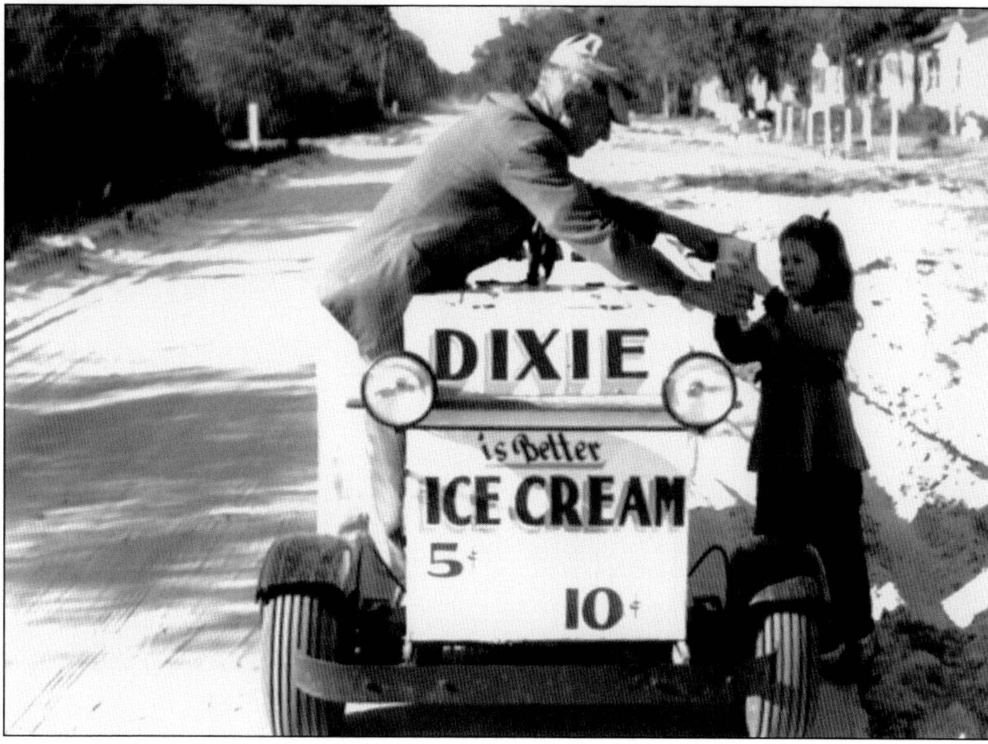

Here is another wonderful Jimmie Jones shot with daughter Susan, taken on Allen Avenue in the early 1950s. (Courtesy BCPLLHC.)

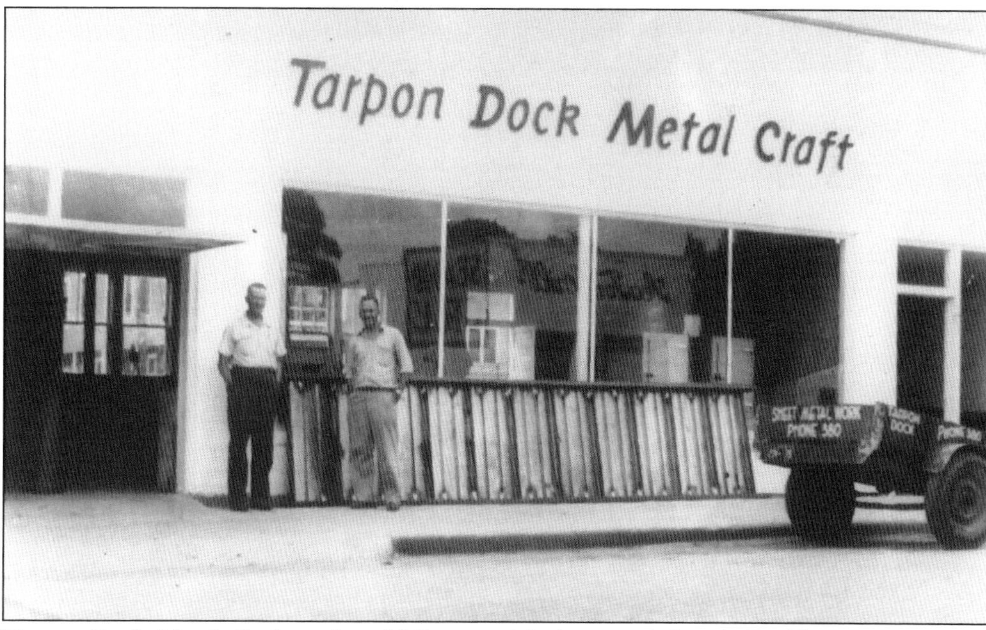

Tarpon Dock Metal Craft at the old Panama Machine and Supply Building is pictured in the mid-1940s. Olie Peterson and Charles Coonrandt from the North founded this early air-conditioning concern. Later the FitzSimons and the Busbys owned the business. (Courtesy Janice FitzSimons.)

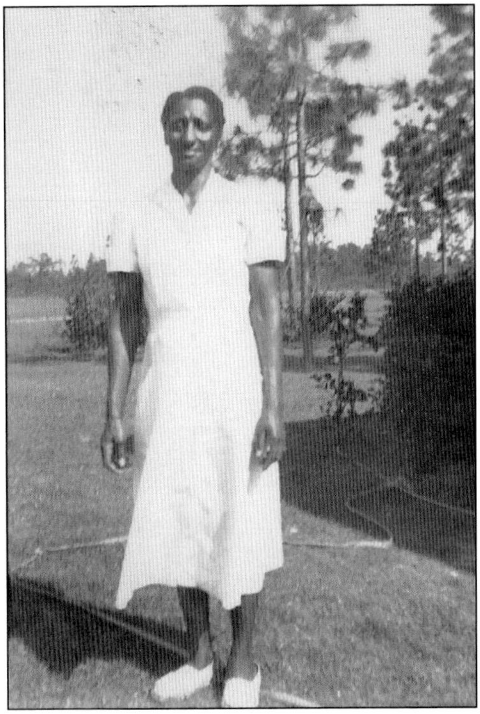

Bessie Stephens worked at the Cove Hotel with Ruby Harris for many years. This photo of Bessie was probably taken in the 1940s or 1950s. (Courtesy SHL.)

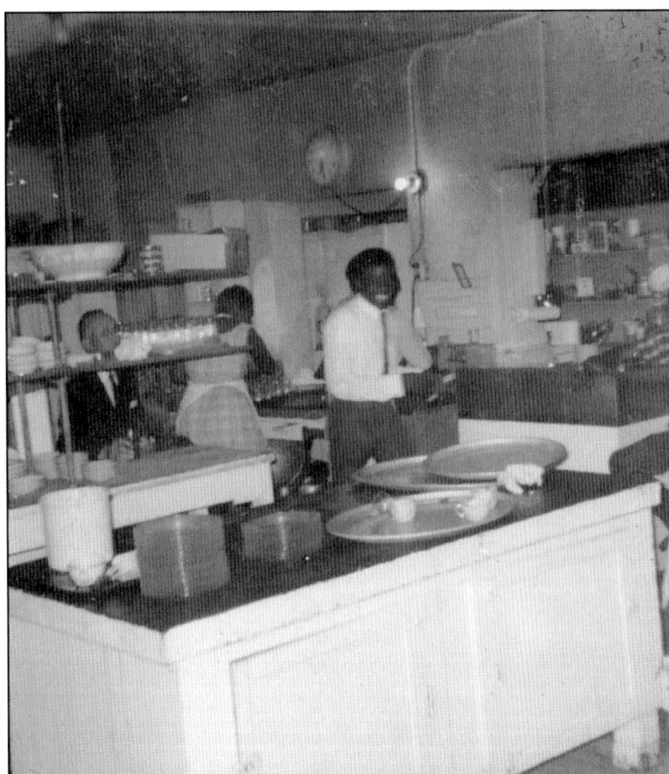

This is a familiar kitchen scene at the Cove Hotel in the early 1960s. From left to right are Gene Ellis, Mary Lee Baker, and Robert Philyaw. Robert Philyaw, described as Mrs. Harris's right-hand man, coordinated elegant decoration and executed memorable fetes at the hotel. Mrs. Ledman remembers that he was able to use place settings and accessories from her grandmother's collection. Mrs. Ledman and her cousin Andrea would ride with Philyaw down to the Safari, where he would assemble lovely parties for his guests there. (Courtesy SHL.)

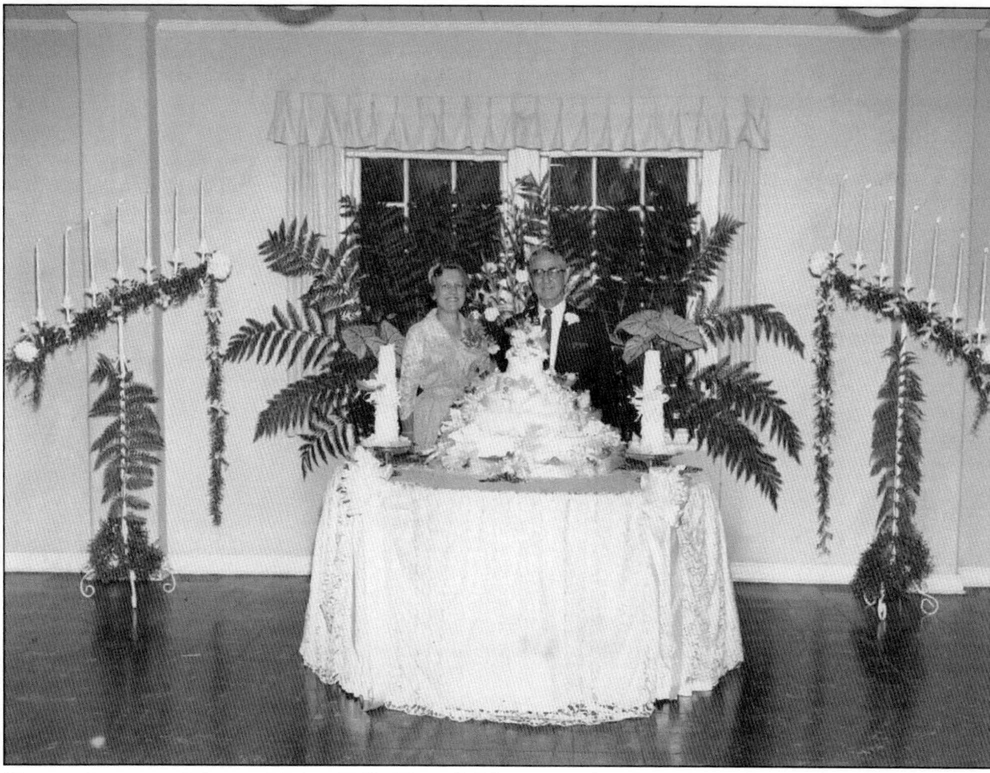

Shown here are Mr. and Mrs. Bill (Sigrit) Morar at the Cove Hotel in July 1959, at their daughter's wedding. Their son was married one week later. The Morars provided flowers for many occasions at the hotel. Their daughter Sibil Donalson is currently the florist with Hallmark at Cooper's Drugs on Business 98. (Courtesy SHL.)

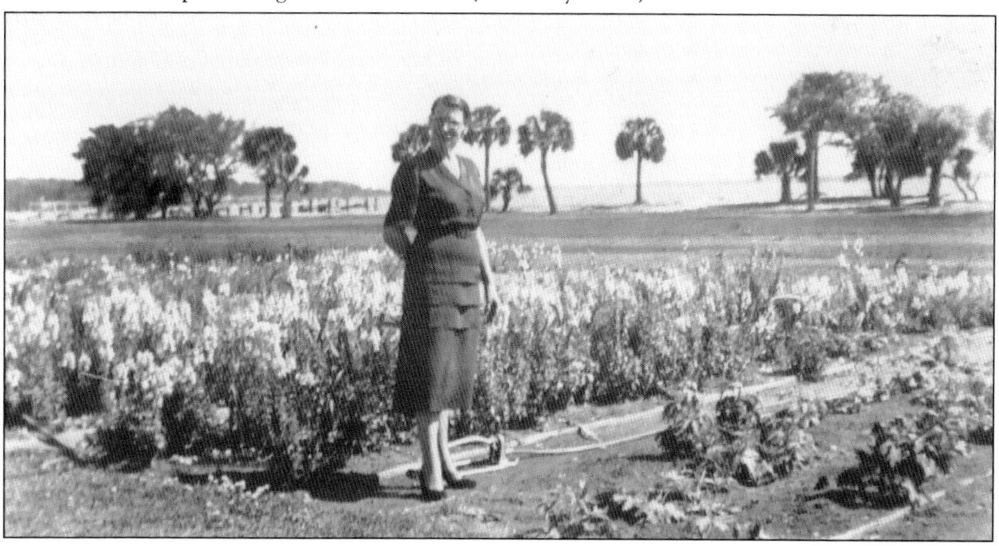

Dorothy Miller Thomas's mother, Mrs. Lee Miller, stands at the side garden of the Cove Hotel. Not only did Mrs. Harris have colorful flowers for indoors and out, there was also a small petting zoo. Plenty of boys played football here. Mrs. Miller taught school for years at Parker and Callaway. (Courtesy Dorothy Thomas.)

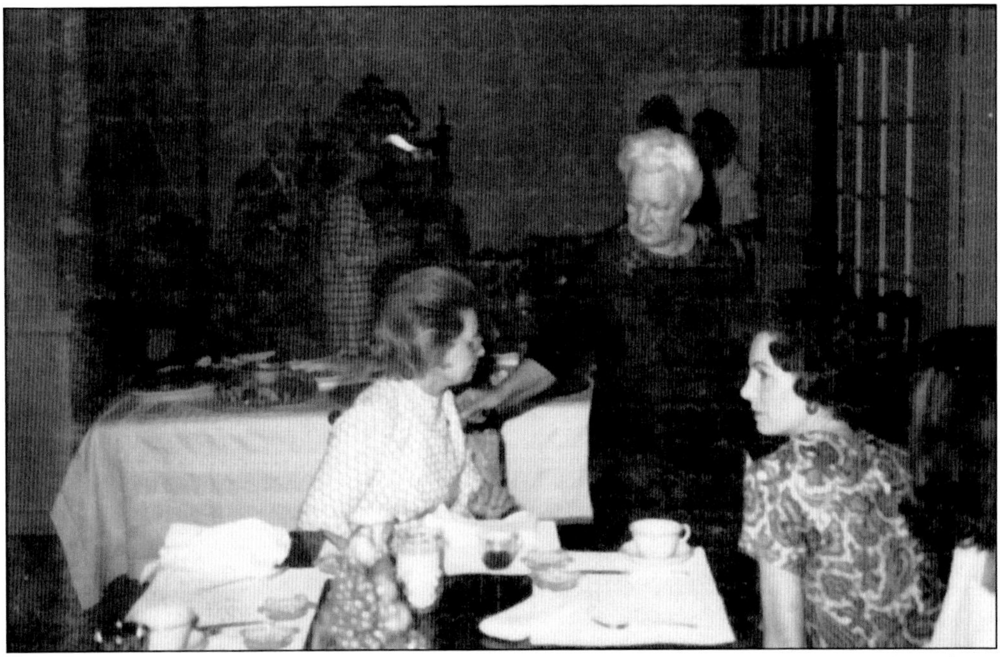

Ruby Harris, pictured here, always made sure her guests were comfortable. The photo reads, "Ivy, Mrs. Harris and Phyllis. 1968." The hotel was featured in a May 5, 1968 *New York Times* article under the headline "Cove Hotel Returning the Splendor to the Old South."(Courtesy SHL.)

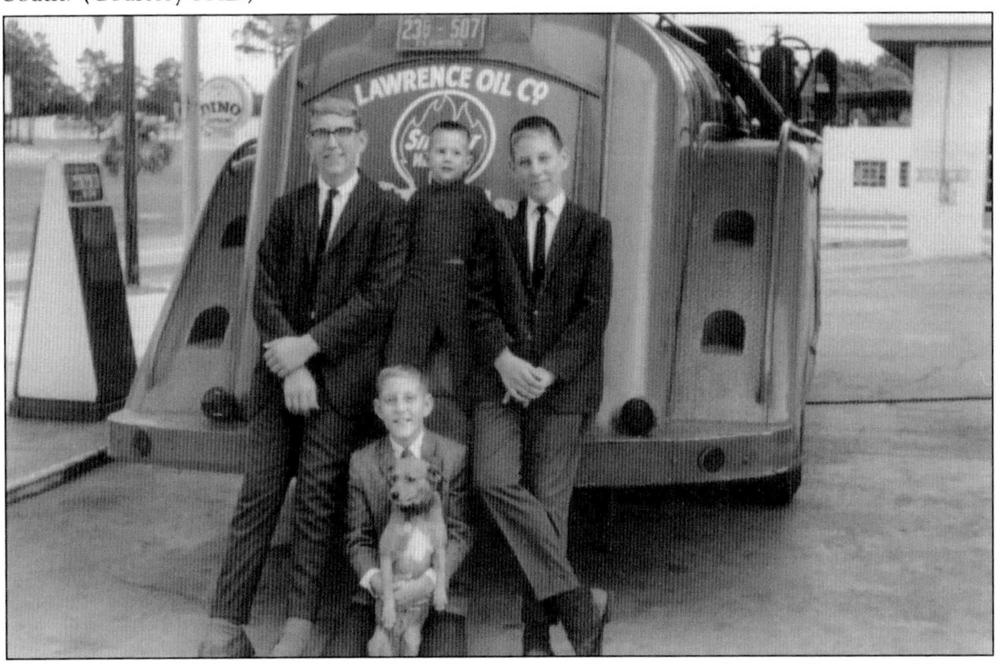

Henry, Tommy, Jimmy, and Bobby Lawrence play with a puppy during Christmas 1965 at Cove Sinclair, Palo Alto, and Cherry Street. Hank Lawrence and his wife, Margaret Huckabee, moved to Panama City in 1965. Mr. Lawrence operated the Lawrence Oil Co. until the early 1980s.

Four

AT HOME

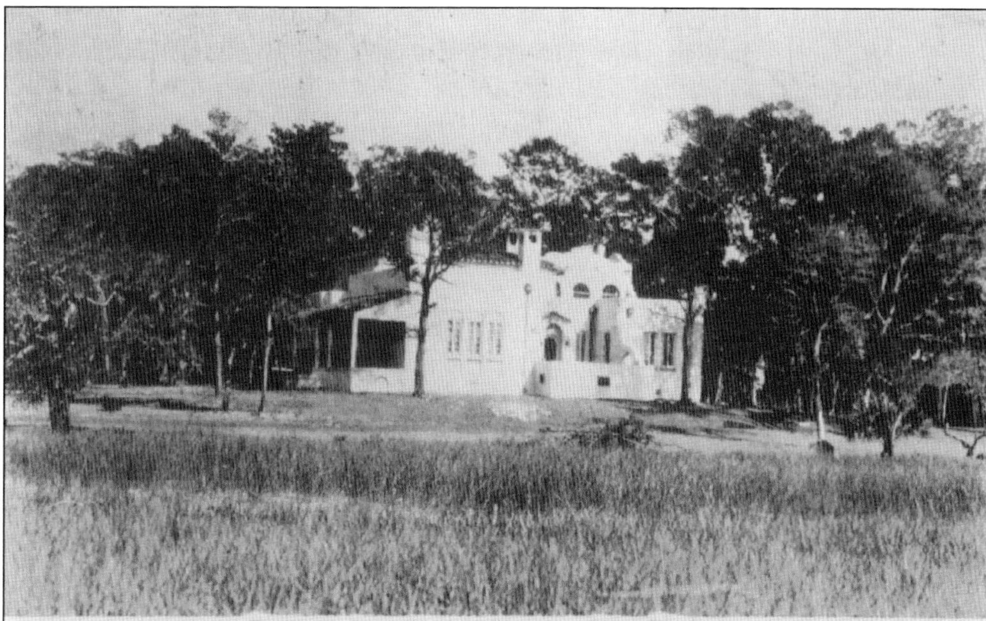

Bunkers Cove Home, Panama City, Fla.

This postcard comes from the collection of Janice FitzSimons. A reproduction of this shot is found in a scrapbook assembled by Gay Sudduth for her husband Rowe. The scrapbook notation reads, "First home we [Sudduth family] built in Panama City , Fl (across from the 2nd home we built)."

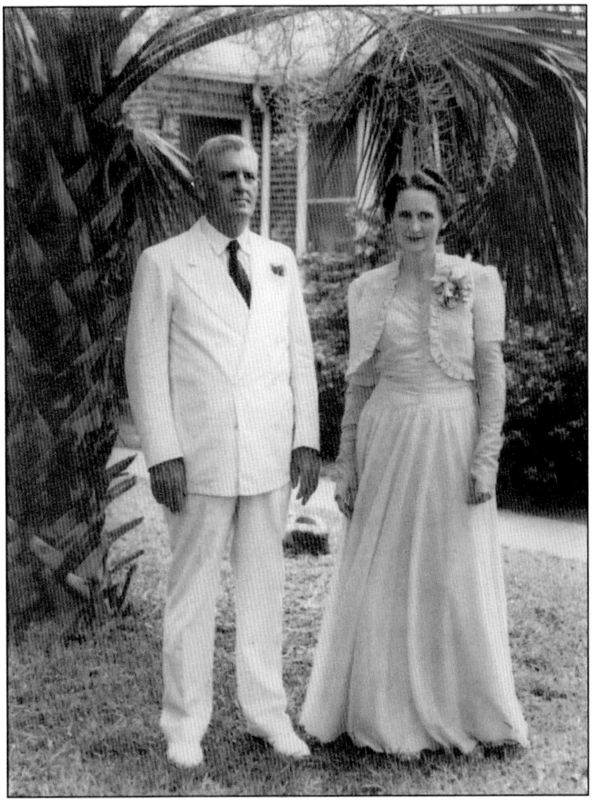

Mr. and Mrs. H.L (Lannie Rowe) Sudduth are pictured on the day of their daughter's wedding. This photograph was taken in front of their second home on Bunker's Cove Road. (Courtesy Gay Sudduth.)

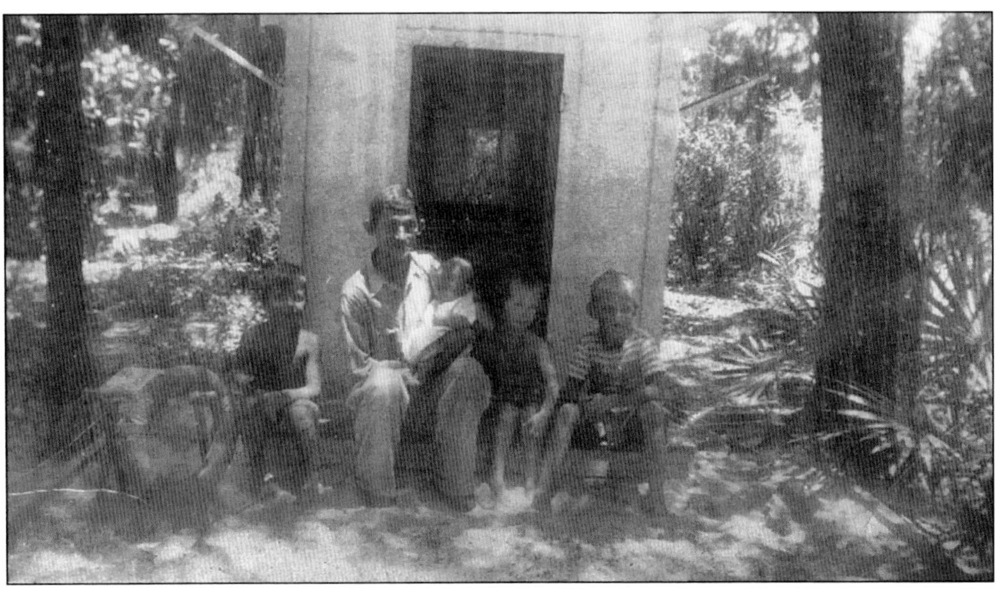

Henry Bennett, Carl Browne (holding Bucky), Salie Allen Browne, and Carl Bennett sit on the front step of the playhouse in the early 1940s. The playhouse stood beside this home, which was across Bunker's Cove Road from Sudduth Avenue. (Courtesy SBC.)

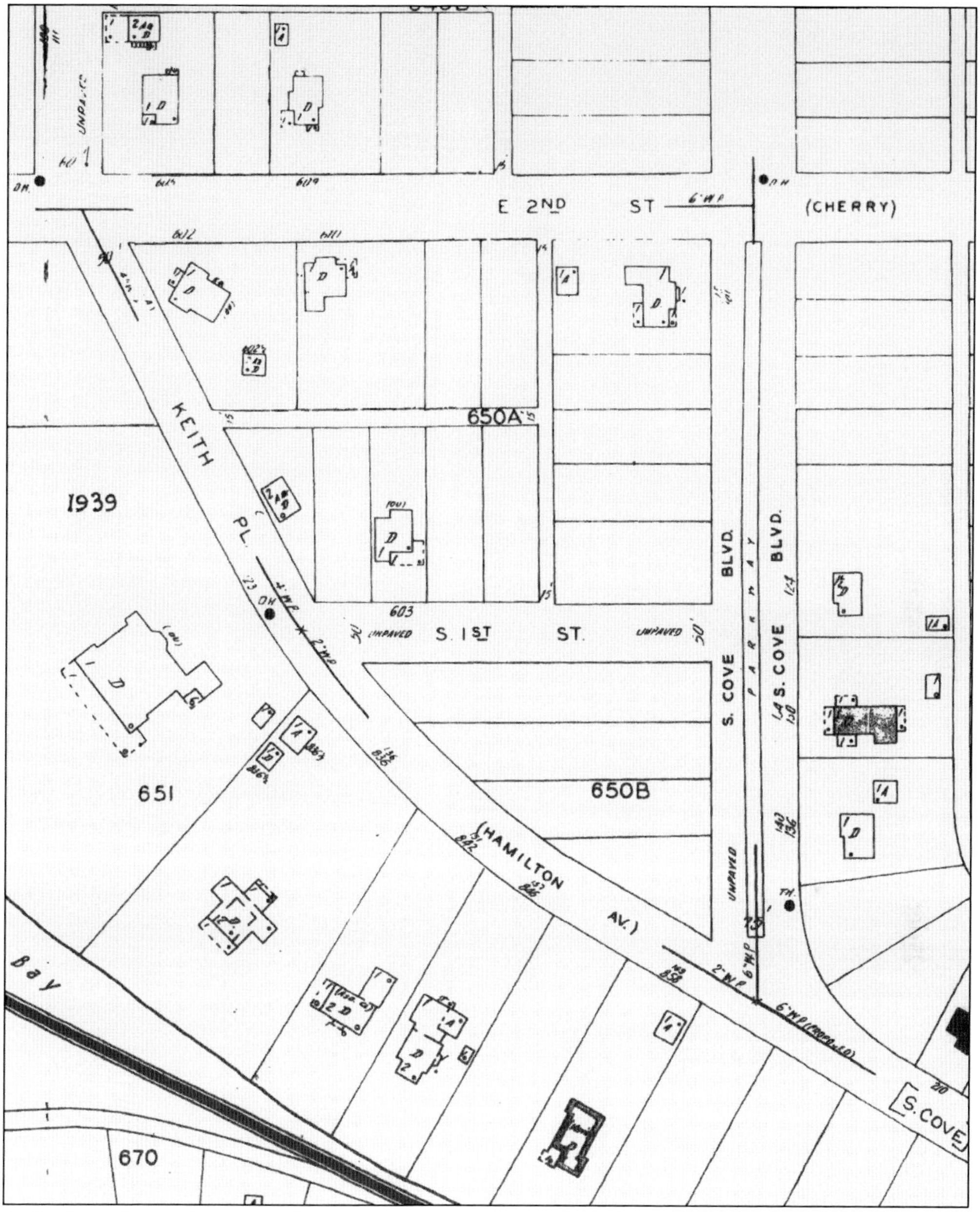

A Sanborn Map Company fire insurance map from 1939 shows that street names have long presented a challenge in The Cove. The author's notation is bracketed. (Courtesy BCPL.)

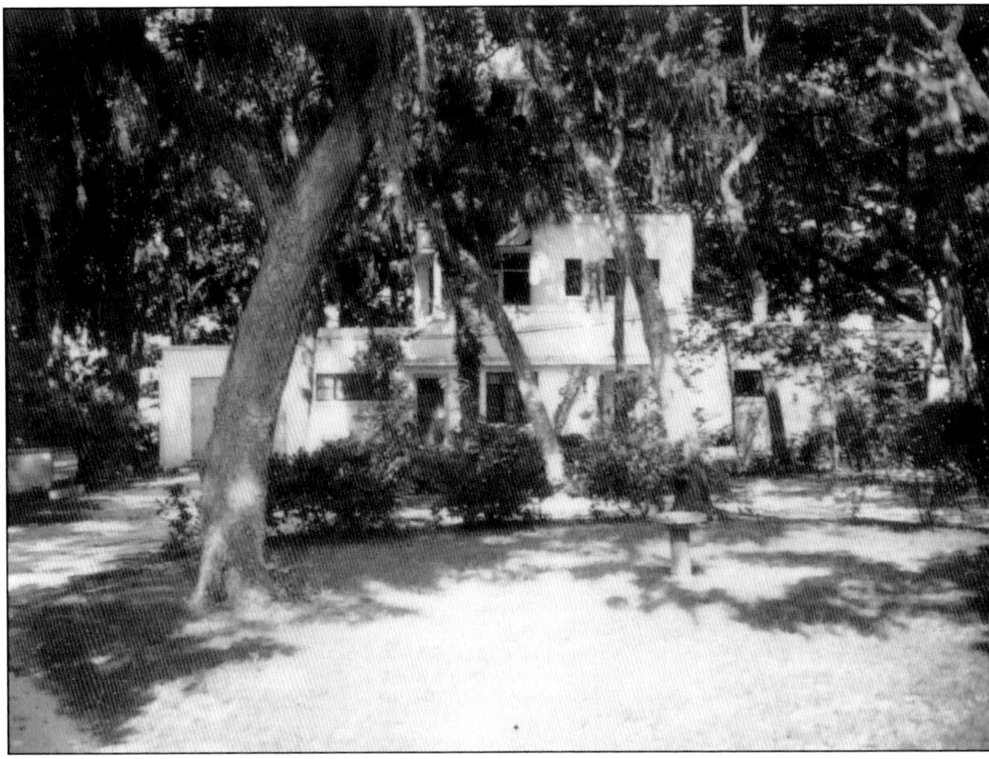

This is the Skipper Laughlin home built in 1938 at 336 Bunker's Cove Road. The bayfront house featured a concrete circular stairway. Laughlin had a green light and a red light on each side of his top-story bedroom, but was asked to take them down because they confused those on the water. (Courtesy Dr. and Mrs. Jerry Harrison.)

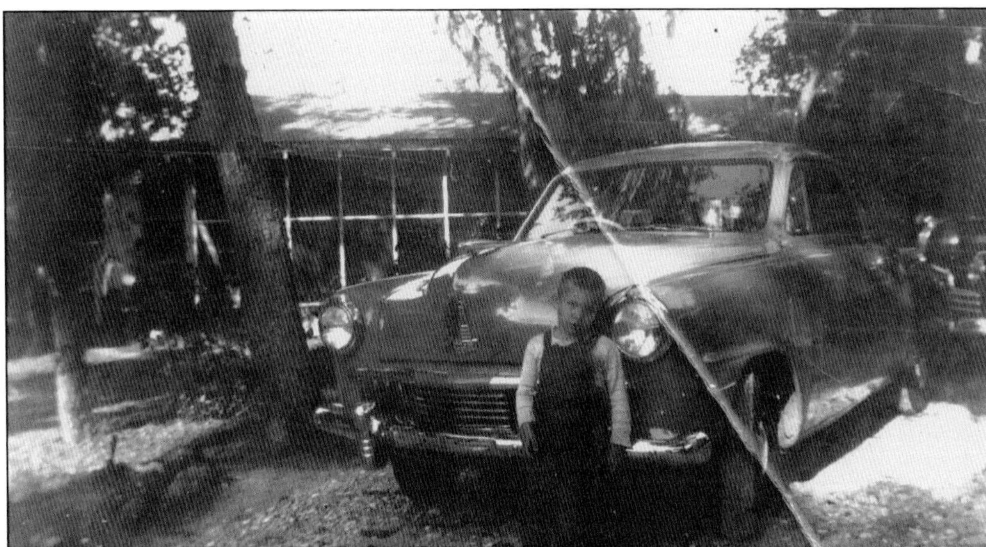

Bucky Browne stands in front of a car at the Browne home on Bunker's Cove Road in the mid-1940s. (Courtesy SBC.)

Little Ruthie Howell, daughter of Brown and Estelle, is consoled by her doll in front of their house at the corner of Harmon Avenue and Olive Street (now Second Place). Ruth had injured her foot in a bicycle accident. Mr. and Mrs. Walter Seymour lived here until the late 1940s and Mr. and Mrs. George (Stella) Hill bought the house in the 1950s. Their yard is always green and trim.

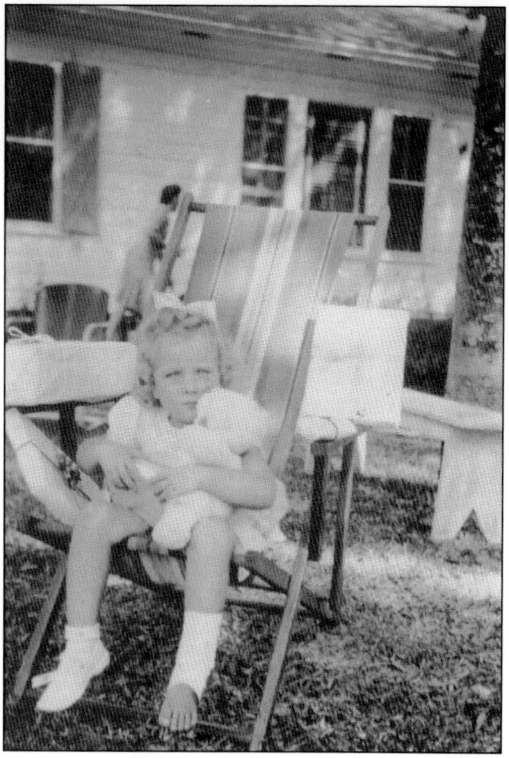

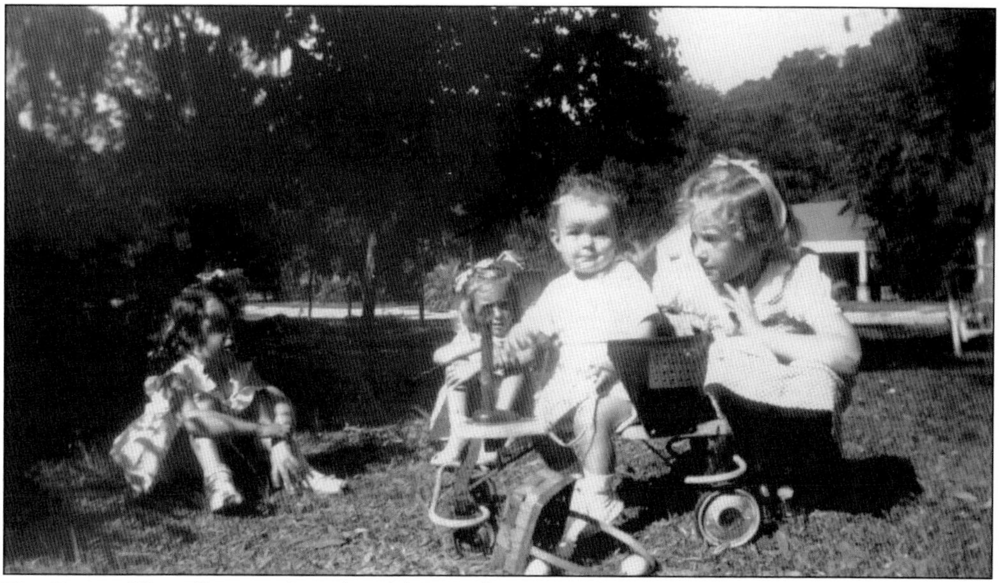

The Brown Howells moved to the old Dean house on the corner of Harmon and First Court (formerly Oak Street) in 1945. The children enjoy the shady side—later front—yard, evidently having an Easter egg hunt about 1945. Pictured from left to right are (possibly) Mary Nell Hobbs (Stone), Francis Mathis, Marie Howell, and Ruth Howell (Hauser). (Courtesy RHH.)

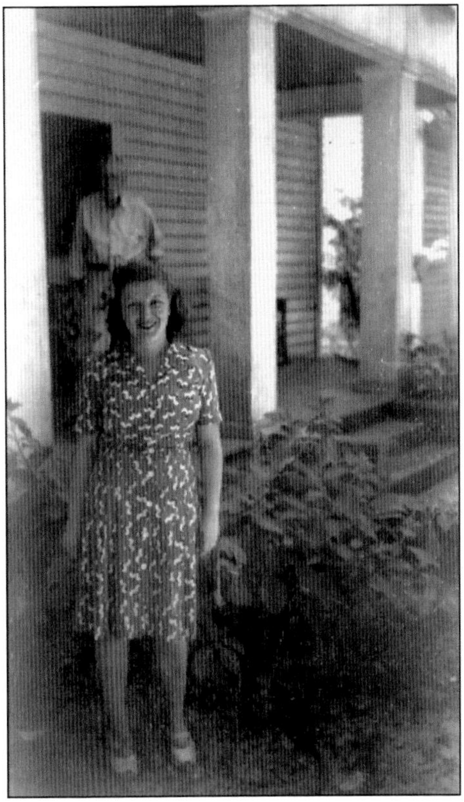

The back of this snapshot reads, "Evelyn and Pa." This photo was sent by his sister Beth to George Thomas when he served in the Pacific with the Seabees during World War II. He says he never did meet the girl. Mr. Noah Thomas stands on the porch of their home on First Court. (Courtesy Mr. and Mrs. George Thomas.)

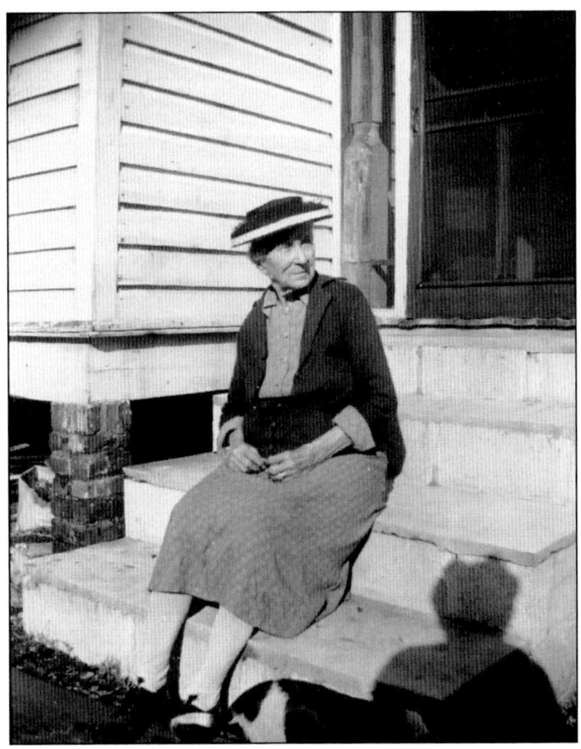

"Aunt" Belle Tiller is pictured at her home. This home, one of the original three built by her brother Lewis Howell in 1909, still stands at 120 East Second Place. Others who lived here were her daughter, Lizzie, her grandson, Henry, and her granddaughters, Anna Bell and Beanie Tiller. This photo was taken by Clarice Davis in the 1940s.

Clarice Davis is sitting pretty on the front lawn on Olive Street. In the background, a garage apartment behind the house built by T.H. Harmon is visible. At that time, that home was inhabited by the Smith family and the Flemings. (Courtesy CD.)

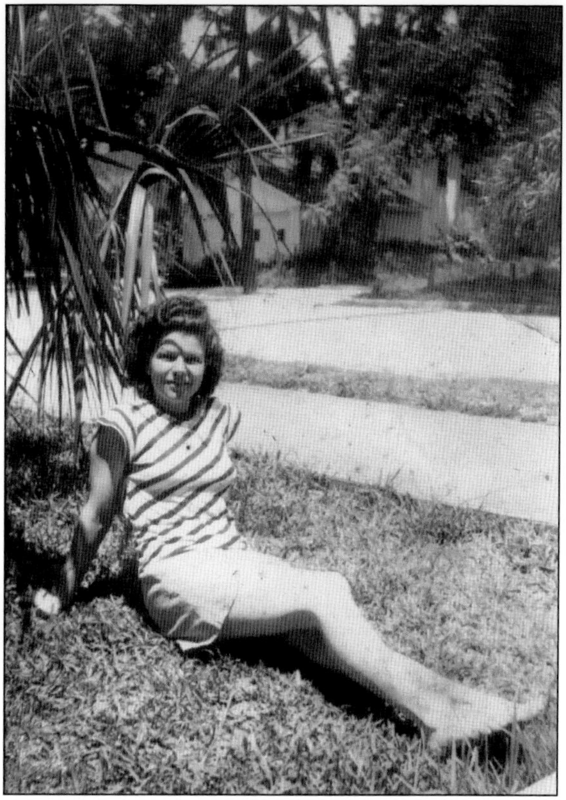

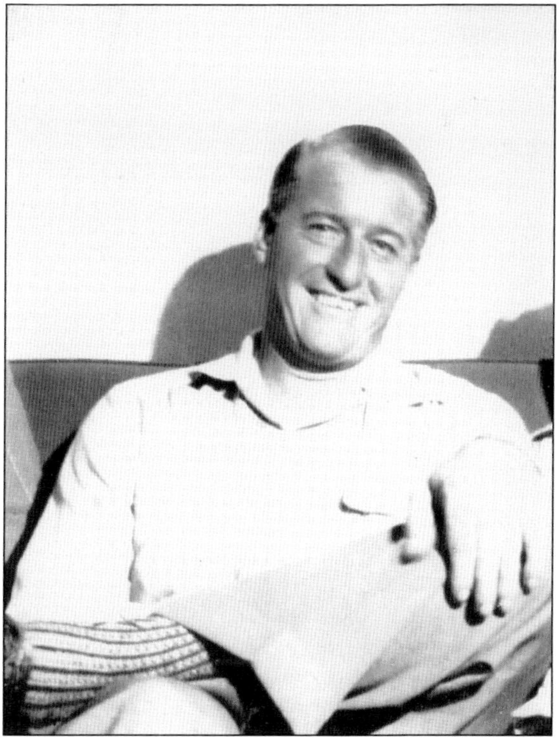

Harold Davis sits on the sofa in the living room of the family home on Second Place. This photo was taken after he returned from his service with the Navy in World War II. (Courtesy CD.)

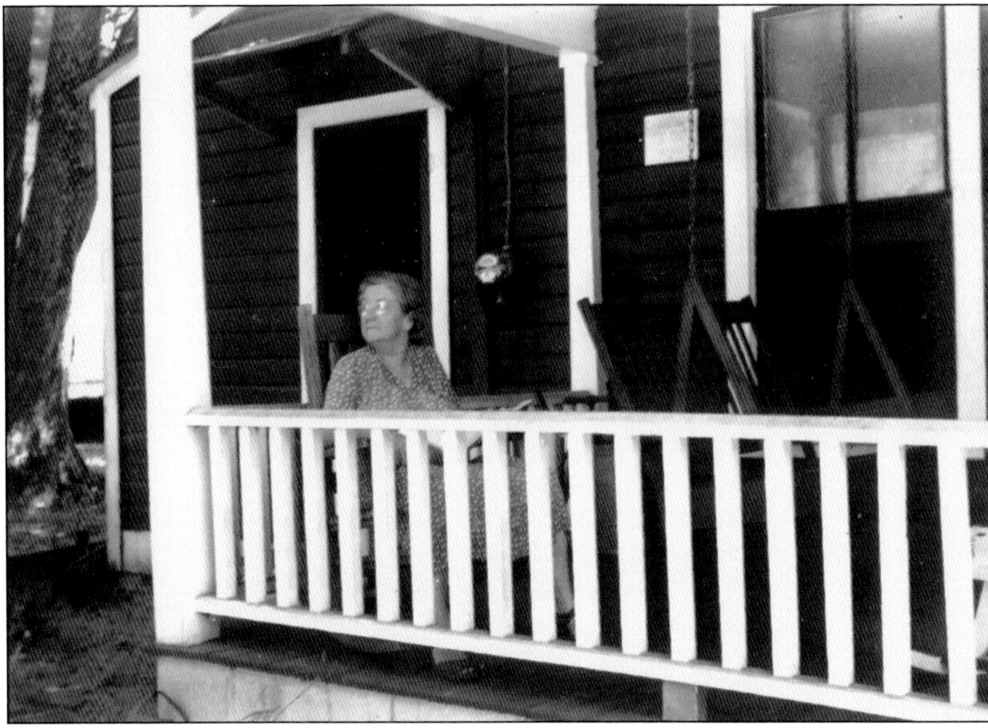

Mrs. B.P. Davis prefers the rocker. Balos Pierson Davis moved his family to this Olive/Second Place home around 1917 and added on to accommodate the influx of first shipyard workers and then World War II servicemen and their families. This picture was taken in the 1940s with the porch not yet extended across the front of the house.

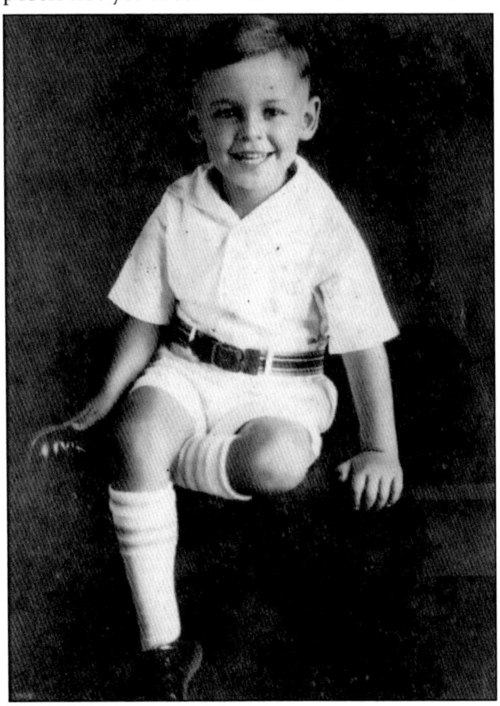

Harry Smith lived with his family at the corner of First Street and Olive Street (East Beach and Second Place.) Harry liked Mrs. Davis's cornbread and came across the street often to ask for it. His parents were Mr. and Mrs. J.A. Smith of Panama Machinery and Supply. (Courtesy CD.)

Bobby Davis is shown sitting on the retaining wall as it still stands on the corner of East Beach Drive and Second Place around 1947. (Courtesy CD.)

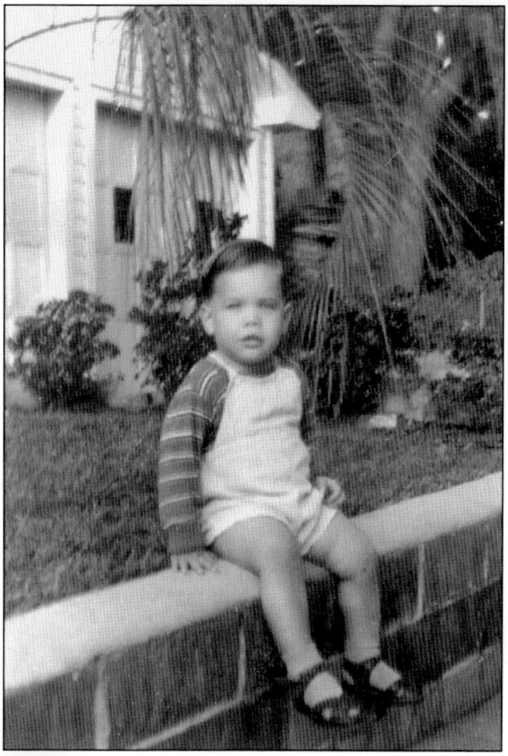

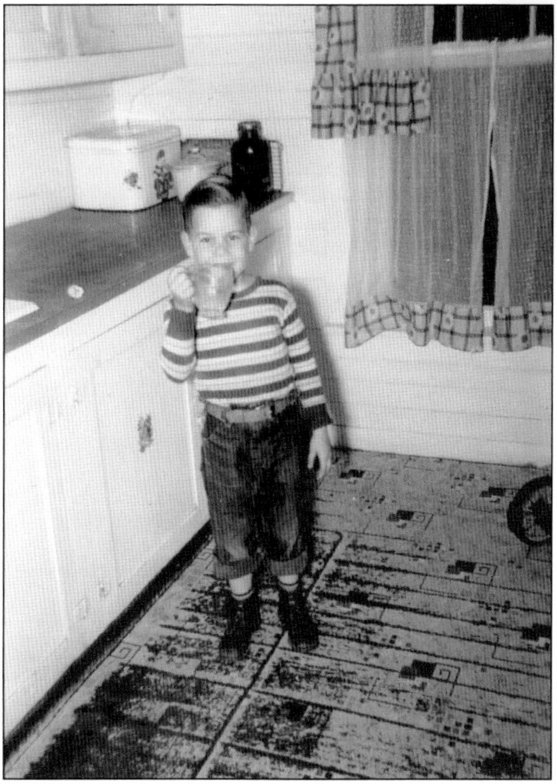

Bobby Davis is pictured in the kitchen at 114 Second Place around 1949. (Courtesy CD.)

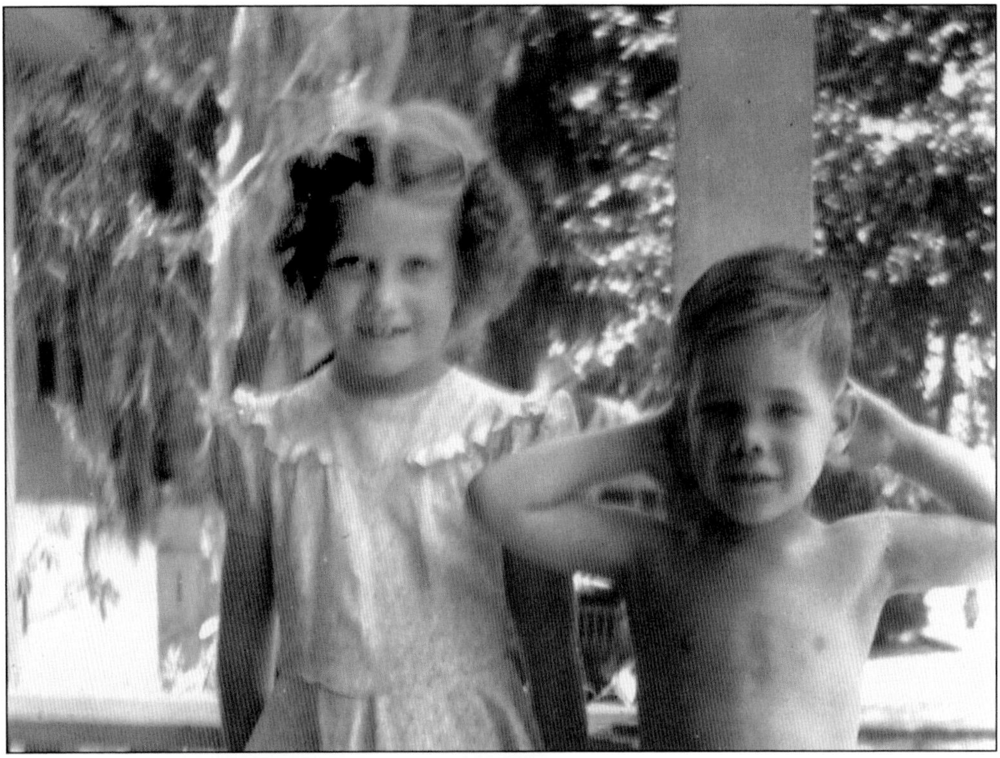

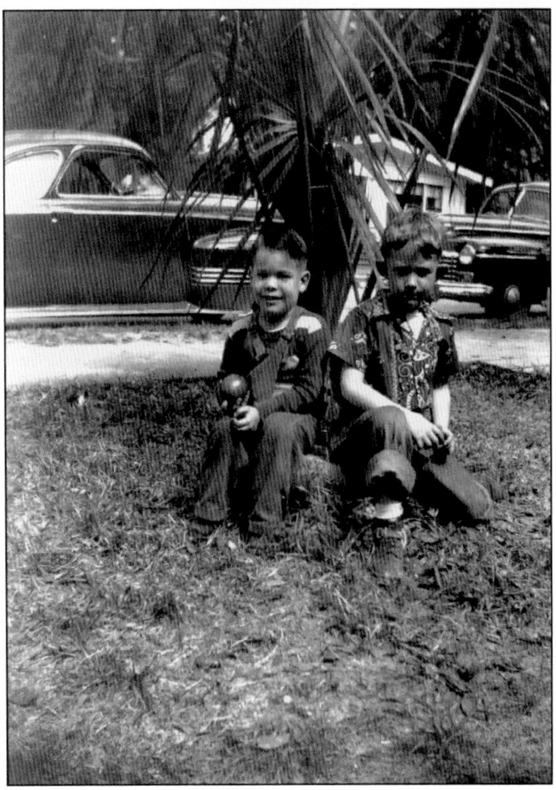

Joyce Zelm and Bobby Davis are pictured on a front porch. The Zelm family lived on Pine (now Second) Street, in the pink stucco "Spanish villa." H.L. Sudduth built several bungalows of the type in The Cove, including a house still standing on Cove Boulevard, pictured on page 65. (Courtesy CD.)

Bill Cook, right (the son of Jesse and Louise Hobbs Cook, the owners of Jesse Cook Seafood) and Bobby Davis, left, are shown in the front yard in 1949. (Courtesy CD.)

Bashe Davis is practicing his old trade on Bobby Davis on July 4, 1949. Mr. Davis had trained and practiced barbering until he was severely injured in an auto accident. The doctors gave up on him but he did recover and sustained his family by various successful enterprises, including operating a taxi service and tending the bridge over Massalina Bayou. (Courtesy CD.)

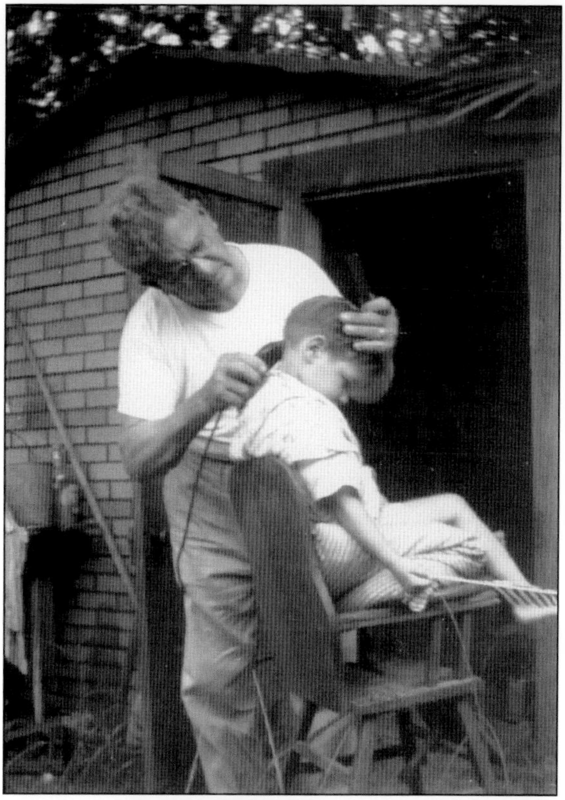

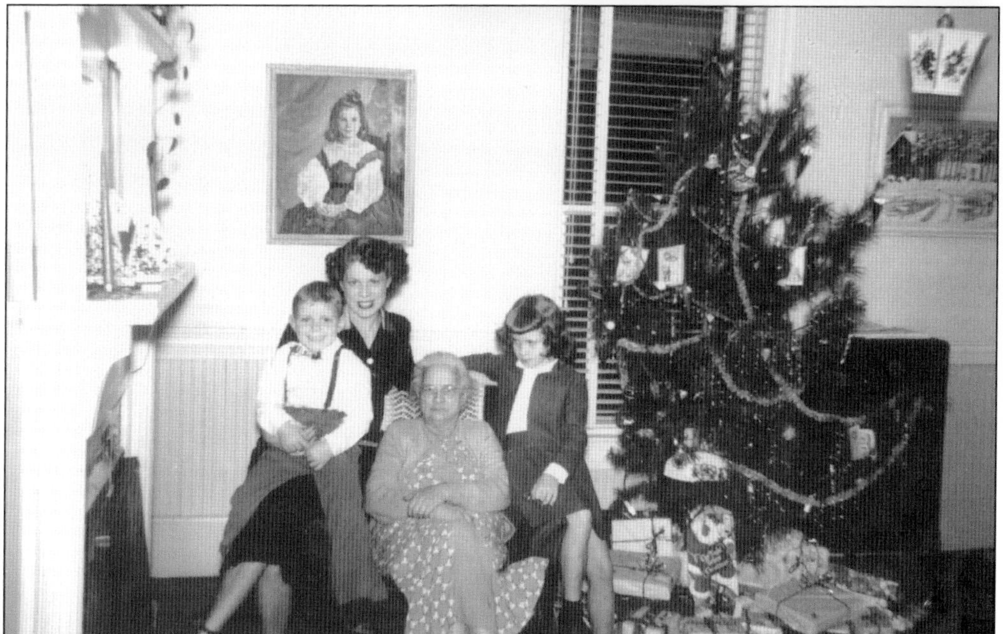

Here is a Christmas scene at the Howell/Hobbs house. From left to right are Michael Hobbs, Nellie Hobbs, Mrs. Lewis (Eula) Howell, and Mary Nell Hobbs. The portrait on the wall was created by Ken Bergman, Floie Howell Bergman's husband. (Courtesy CD.)

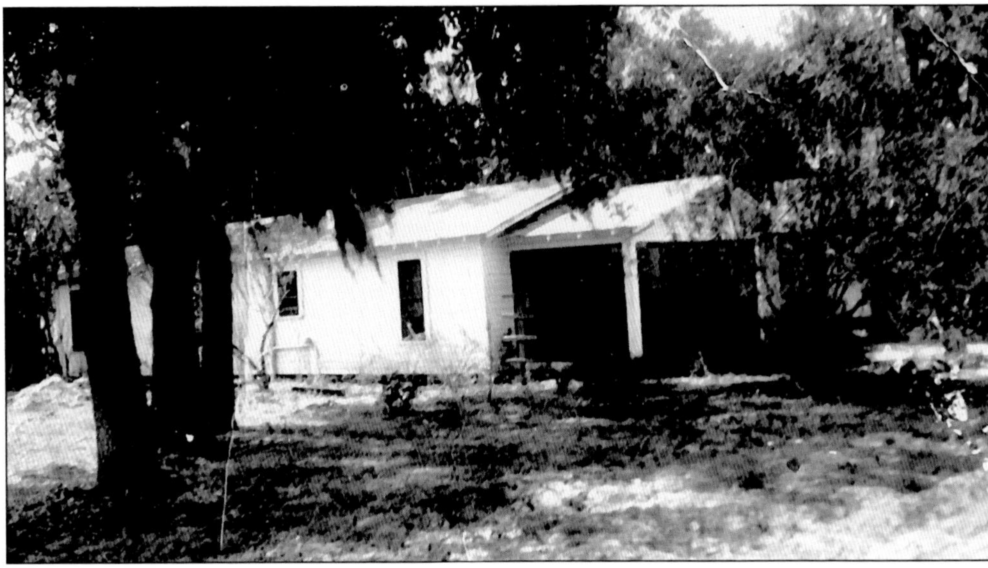

This home at 226 Olive/Second Place belonged to Wiley and Dorothy Williams, and is seen here in the 1930s. Note that Olive was not paved as seen in the lower right corner of the picture. (Courtesy BWB.)

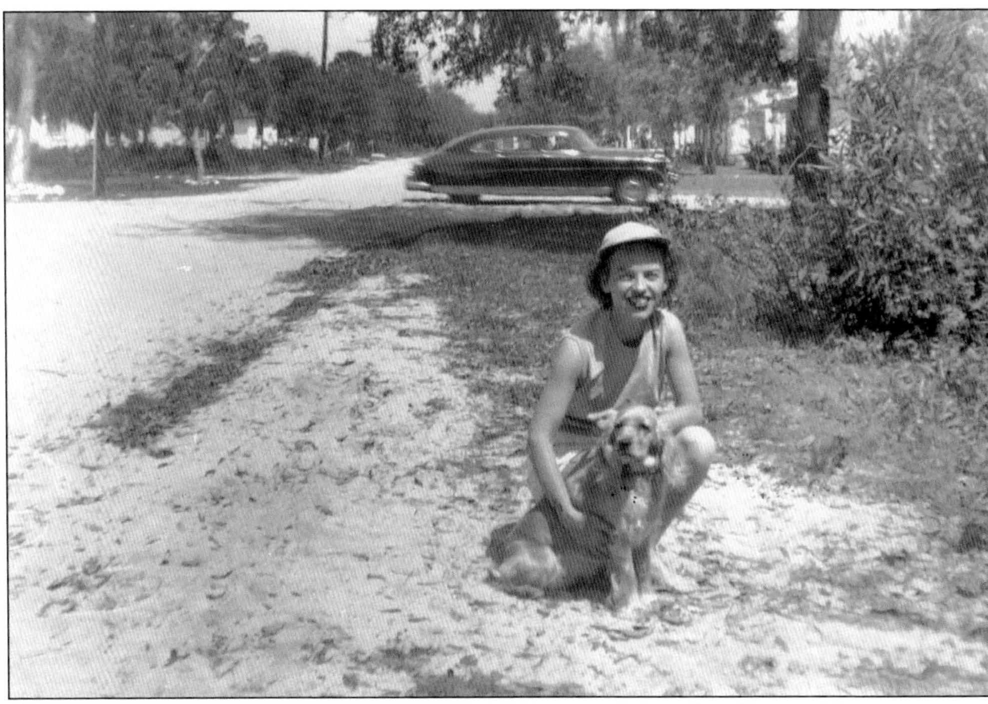

Bette Williams (Butler) is shown at her parents' home with her dog, Honey. The intersection is Second Place and Wilson. This photo was taken in the mid-1940s after her hair was cut by order of the nuns who trained her in New Orleans for the Nurse Cadets. (Courtesy BWB.)

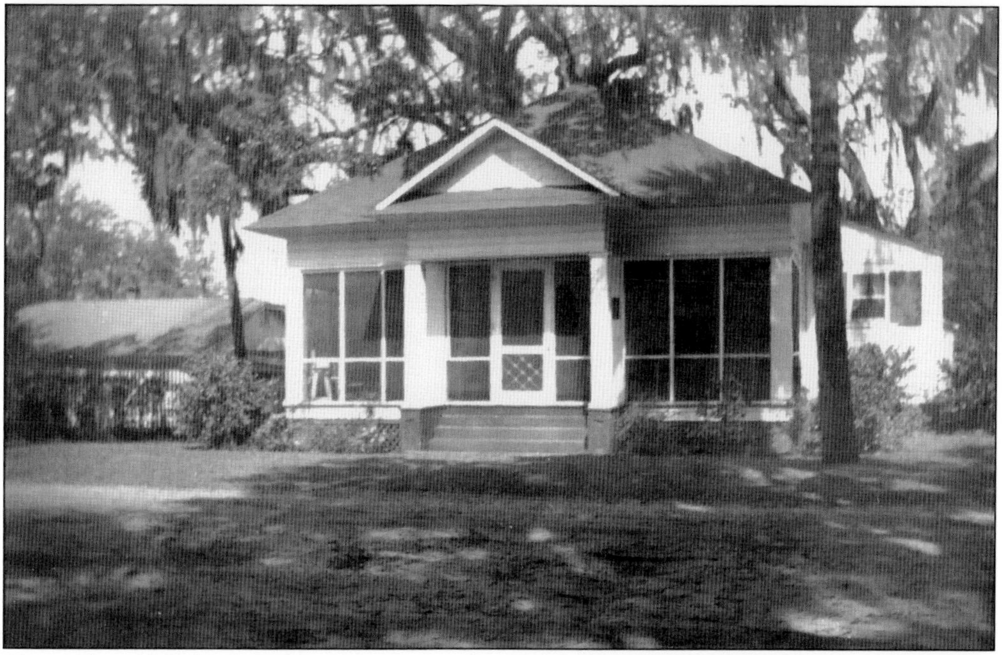

This is the old Kelly, later Dean, house on the corner lot of First Court and Harmon Avenue, still facing First Court and the Bay. There is a beautiful photo of this house in the informative book by Susy Kelly Dean titled *Growing Up on St. Andrews Bay*. The same architect who worked on the new First Methodist Church building in 1950 redesigned this home to add room and face Harmon Avenue. The Howell family moved here in 1945. (Courtesy RHH.)

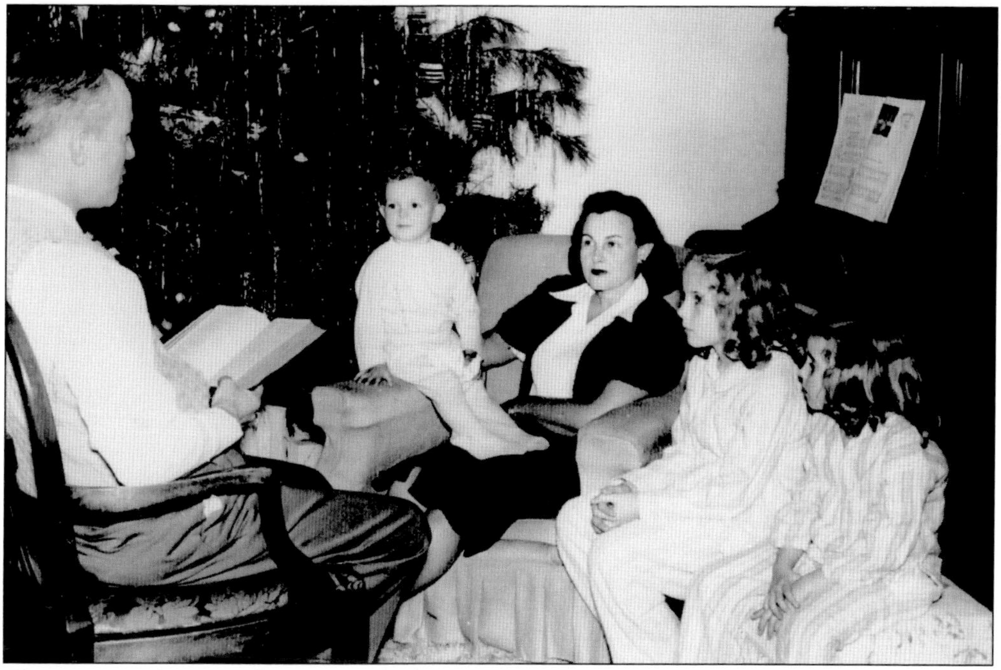

Christmas at the Howells in 1946 finds Brown Howell reading from the Bible to his family. From left to right are Lewis, Estelle, Ruth, and Marie. (Courtesy RHH.)

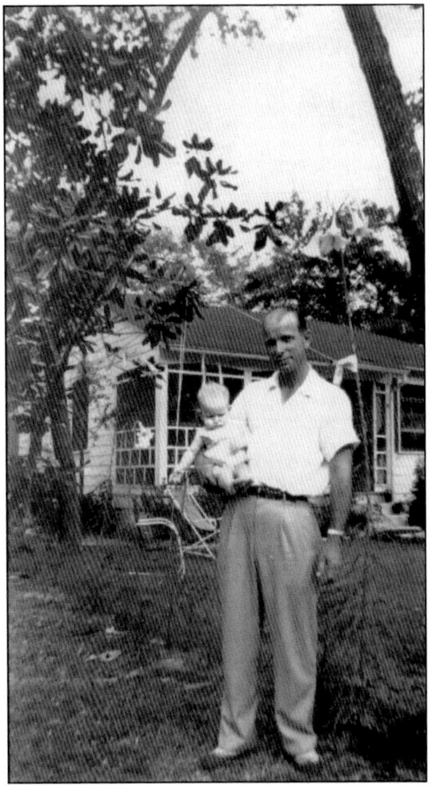

Robert Odum and baby Roslyn are pictured in 1948 at their home at 234 Wilson Avenue. (Courtesy Roslyn Chandler.)

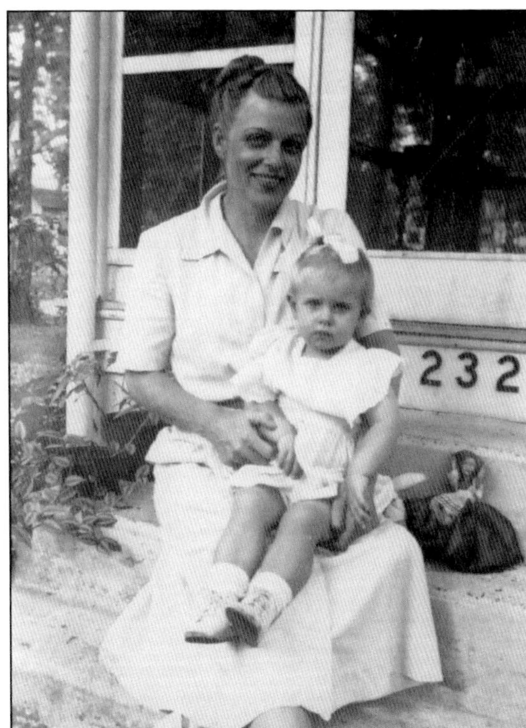

Frances Stone Odum is holding baby Ros about 1949 on the porch at 232 Wilson Avenue. (Courtesy RC.)

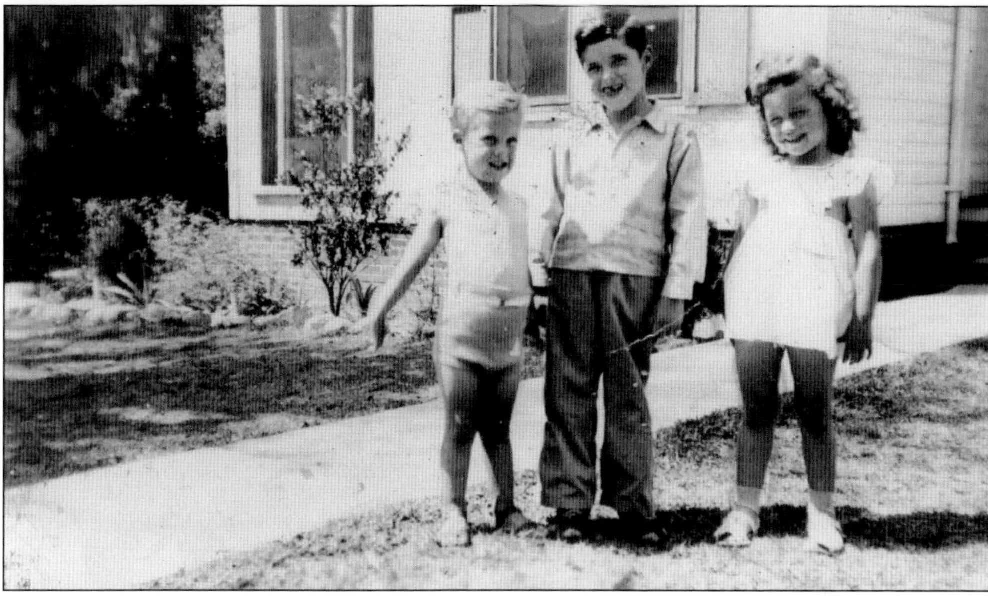

Michael, Jim, and Barbara Murfee are shown in front of their home on East Second Street. Glenn and Genear Murfee bought this house in the early 1930s and raised a lively family here. Mrs. Murfee still lives here and is beloved by her neighbors. (Courtesy Genear Murfee.)

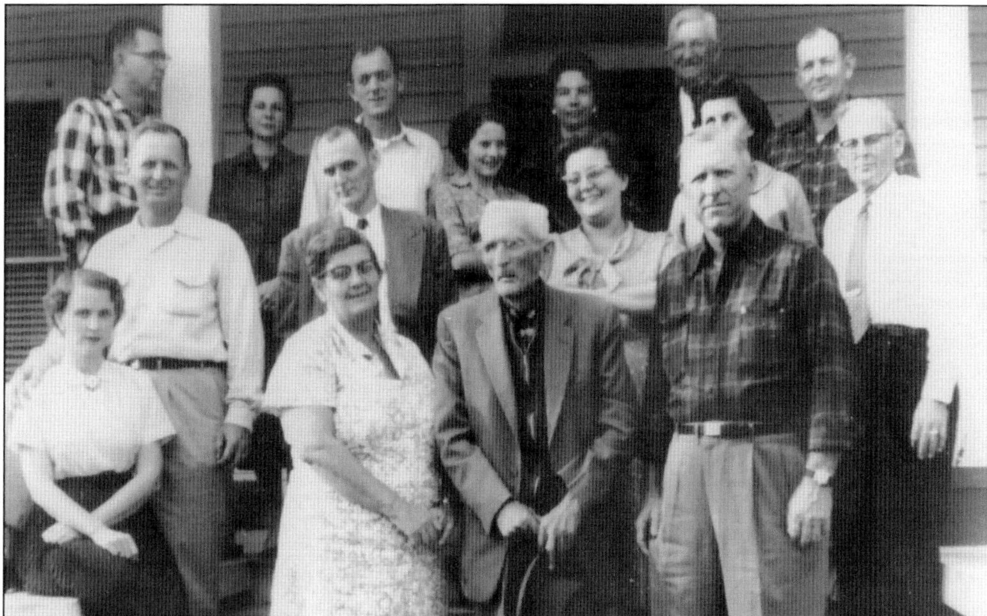

The Thomas family gathers on the front porch of their home on Oak (First Court.) Mr. and Mrs. Noah Thomas came here in 1917 and raised seven boys and two girls. This photo was taken in 1956 after Mrs. Thomas died. From left to right are (front row) Dorothy M. Thomas, Ruth Oates, father Noah E. Thomas, and Mark Thomas; (middle row) George Thomas, Lawrence Thomas, Elizabeth Thomas, Mary Thomas, and Hugh Thomas; (top row) Earl Thomas, Virginia S. Thomas, Hoyt Thomas, Bernice Thomas, Sarah Grace Thomas, John Oates, and Kermit Thomas. (Courtesy Mr. and Mrs. George Thomas.)

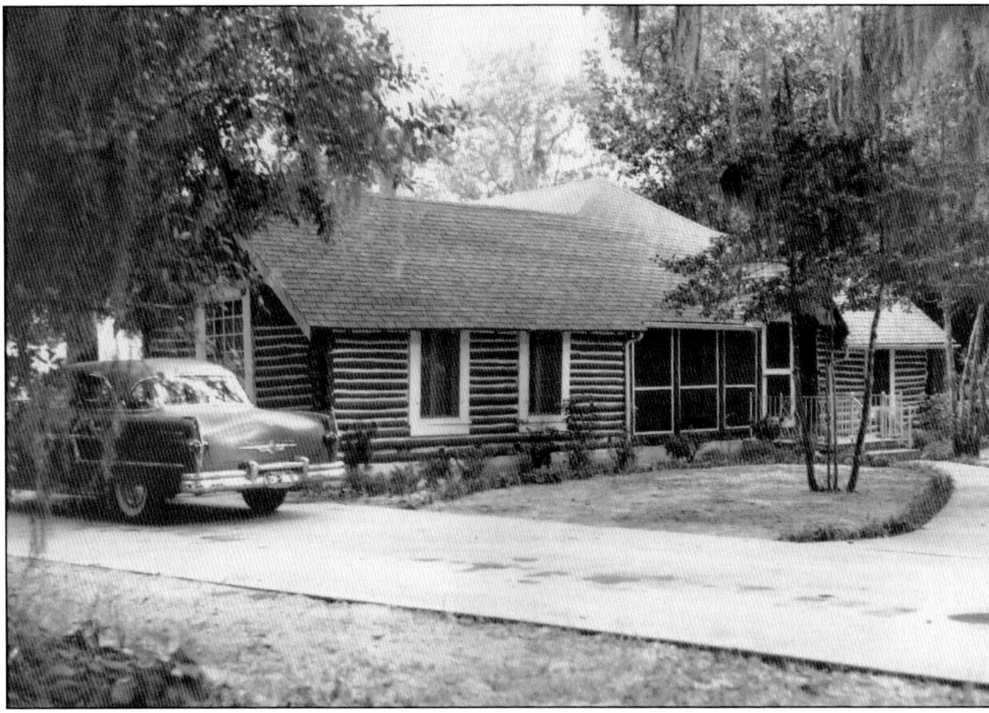

This little log cabin is actually two cabins combined. Log cabins were a popular tourist motif; the raw materials were plentiful and cheap at the time that most of these were put together. The younger Kruse family, Foster and Helen, lived here from about 1940 until they sold and moved across the street in about 1956. (Courtesy Ann Kruse Percival.)

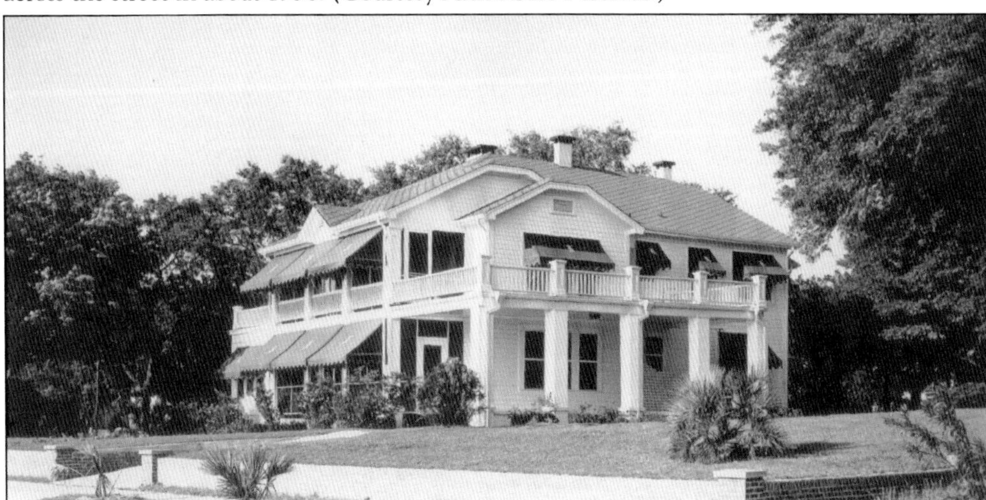

In 1938, Mr. and Mrs. Herbert (Grete) Kruse, Foster's parents, sold their bank in Ohio and moved to Panama City on the advice of Mr. Kruse's doctor, who evidently wasn't aware of the heat. The Kruses invested in awnings, and later, some of the first home air conditioning in the area. Mr. Kruse died in 1947 and Mrs. Kruse in 1950. The family sold the house to the Grant Goodrich family, of tire fame, in the early 1950s. The Smoaks, local attorneys, later purchased the home and large side lot. The side lot is the site of the old Grayham place recalled by Anne Williams Warwick in her excellent Cove memoir, *Tides*. (Courtesy AKP.)

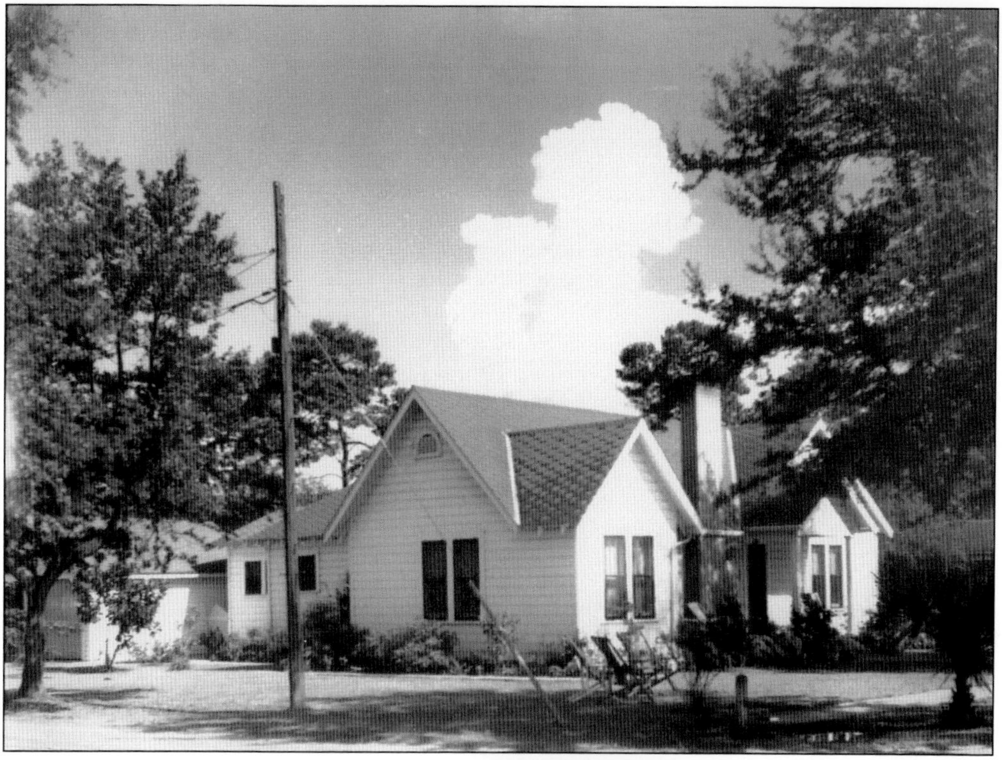

J.W. Powell built this home at 122 Hamilton Avenue around 1937. The Powells raised their family here and Mrs. Powell (Bettie) lived here until 1975, when she moved across the street to one of four rental houses Mr. Powell had built in the late 1940s. These houses go along Second Street toward the bay, the last one facing Linda Avenue. This family preserves the wonderful tradition of sitting on the front porch and waving to neighbors.

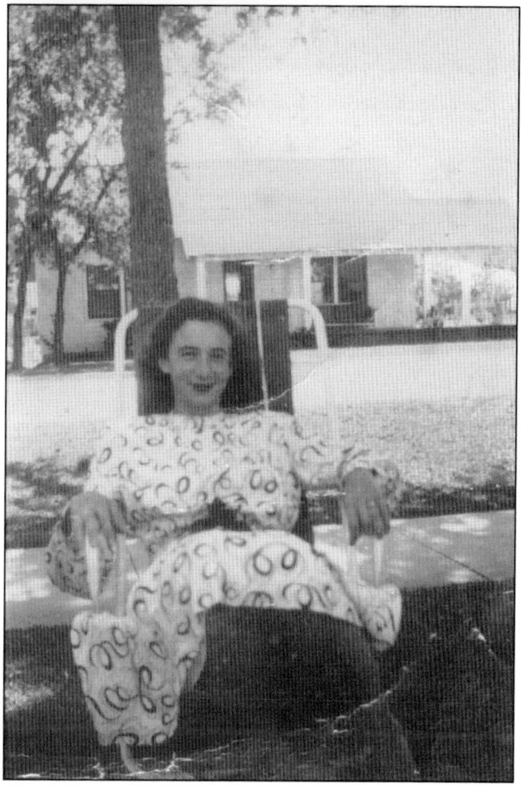

This is the first of the rental houses Mr. Powell built. Mr. and Mrs. Nathan (Sara) Revel were the first to live here. Mrs. Revel is pictured in the shade in the mid-1940s.

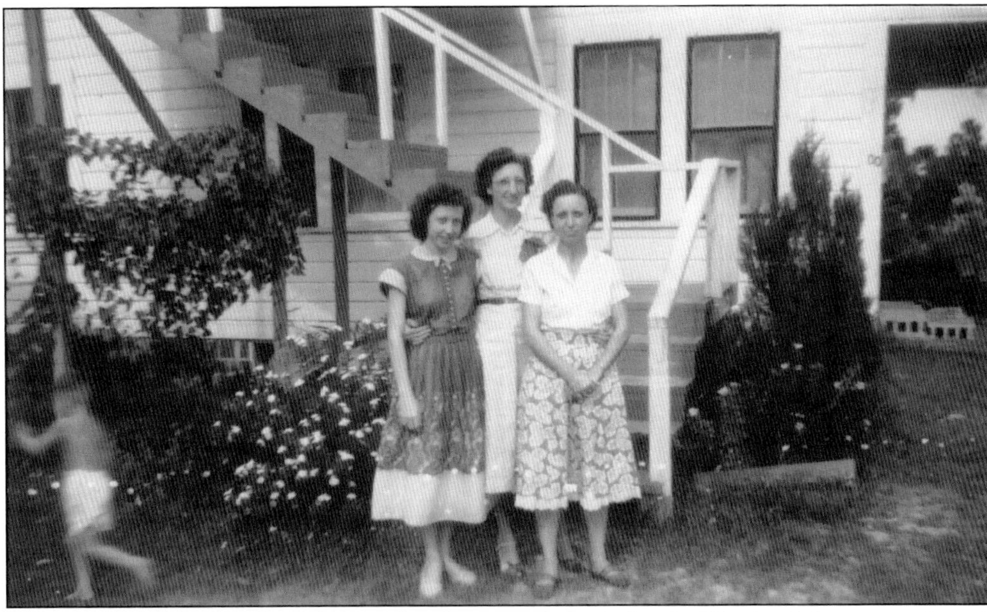

Dorothy Wright, Hellen Wright Hendrix (Freeman), and Maselle Wright Coker are at the side of their house on Palo Alto, about 1949. Wayne Hendrix dashes by to the left of the picture.

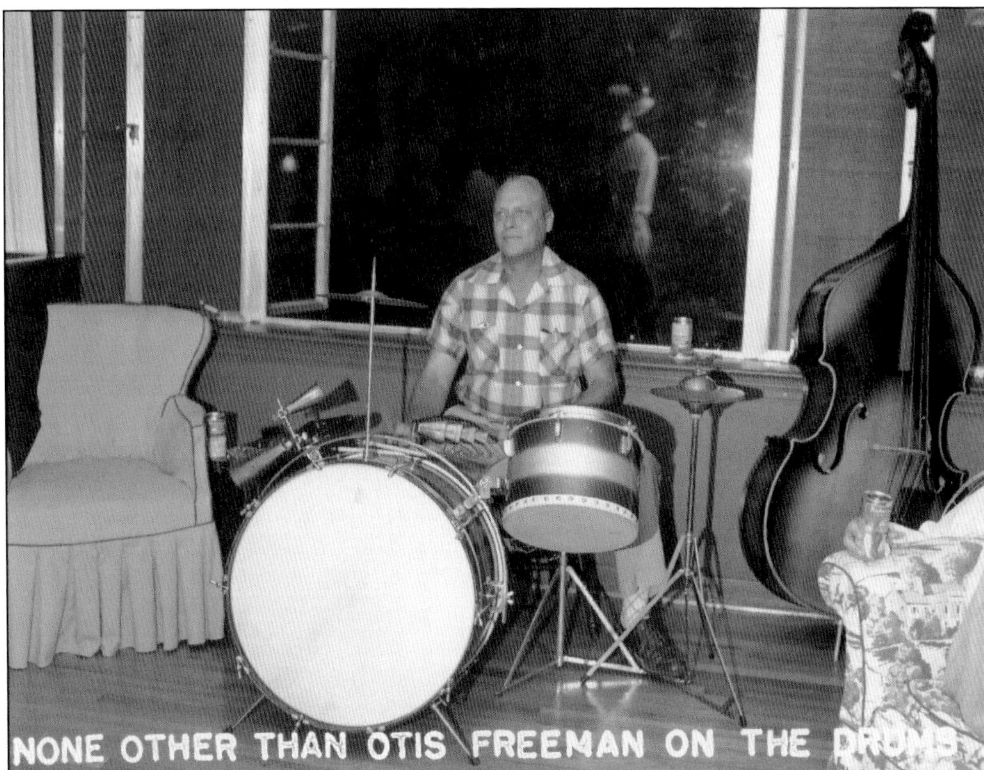

Otis Freeman, in addition to being a musician, started Freeman Electric and served in World War II. He lived close to his parents on Massalina Bayou. In their later years they had a bell on their door so he would know when his mother left the house. (Courtesy Hellen Freeman.)

Mrs. Ivrial McMillian Wright stands beside the unique cypress posts on the front porch of their home on Palo Alto. She and husband Charles Britton Wright raised three daughters here and housed and fed countless renters and guests. This photo is from the1950s. (Courtesy Dorothy Wright.)

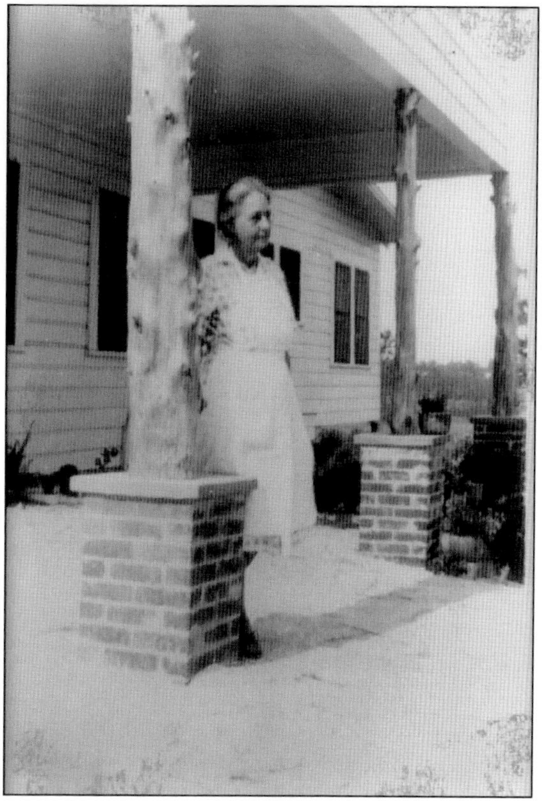

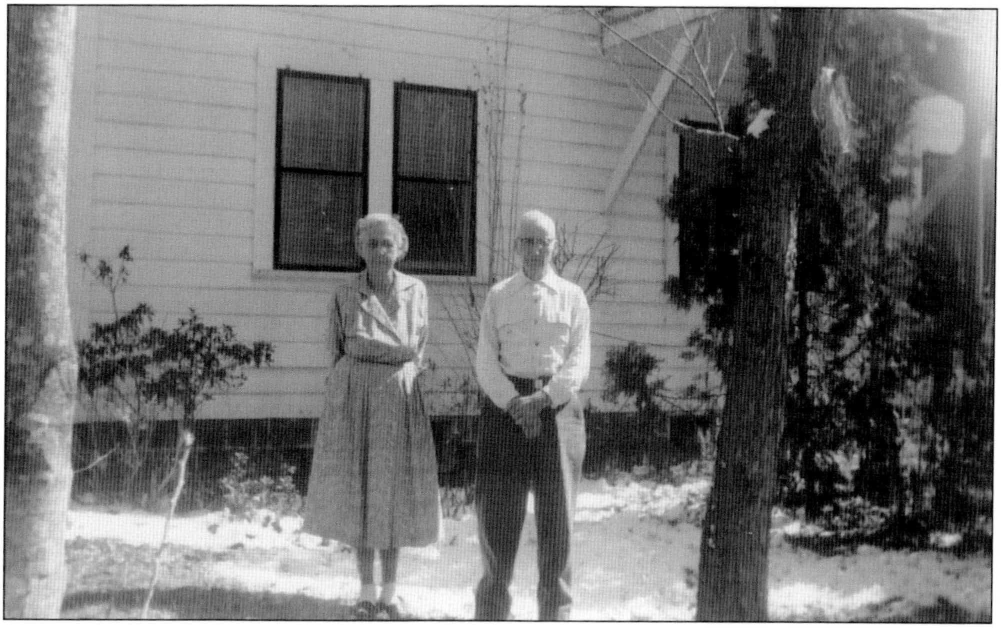

Mr. Wright built his lovely 19-room home with a basement after he built the Church of Christ building on the corner of Business 98 and Palo Alto in 1945–1946. He and his wife stand at the side of the house after a very rare snow sometime in the 1950s. (Courtesy Dorothy Wright.)

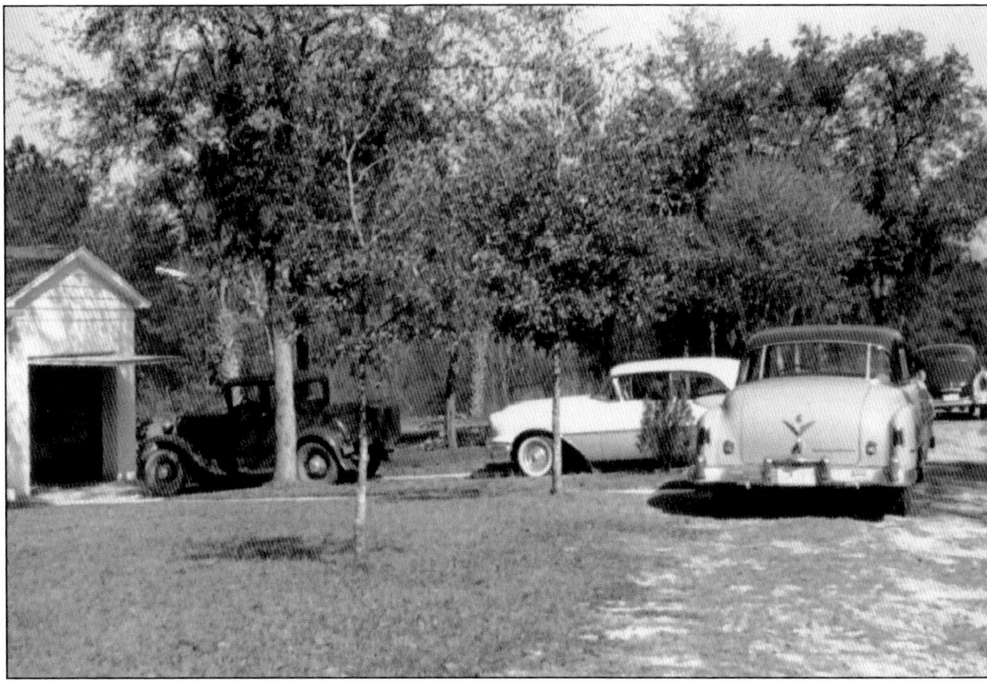

This is a 1957 view of 921 DeWitt facing east towards what is now Lannie Rowe Park. The newlyweds Lee and Donna Mattern towed Mr. Mattern's classic car from Pennsylvania. Mrs. Mattern's parents, Mr. and Mrs. R.E. Youngblood, allowed him to take their daughter to his family poultry farm only if he would agree to bring her back if she didn't like it there. She didn't and he did. They lived with her parents here.

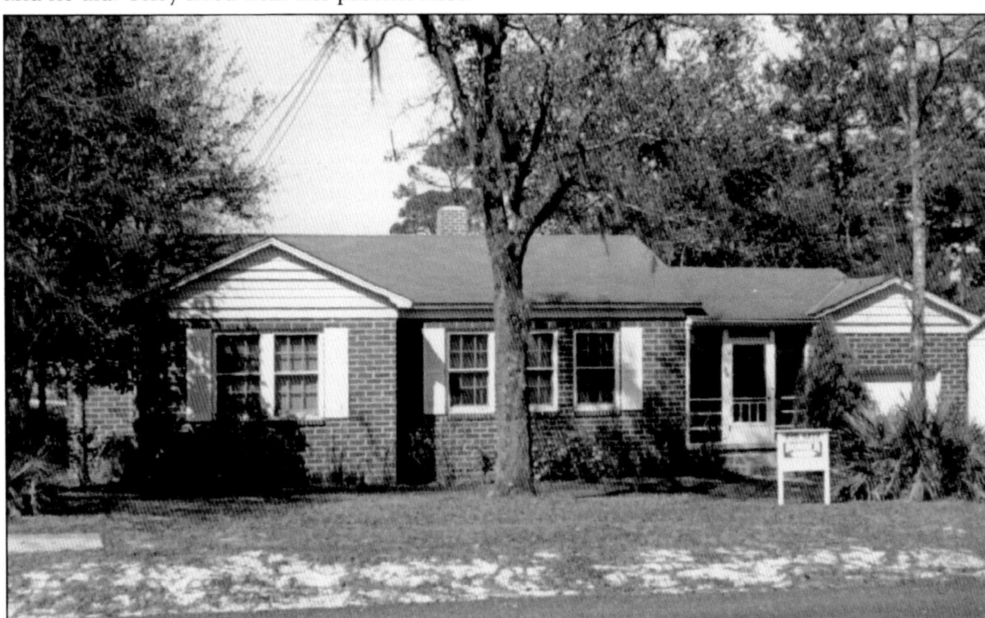

The home at 919 DeWitt was listed for sale by Bonner Realty in about 1957. Like many Cove homes, it has survived many renovations and continues to serve today as a residence.

John Wainwright and his family are shown at their home at 905 East Second Plaza. From left to right are Jan Wainwright, John Jr., John Sr., Cheryl, and mother Eileen holding baby Karen in 1954. (Courtesy Karen Wainwright O'Keefe.)

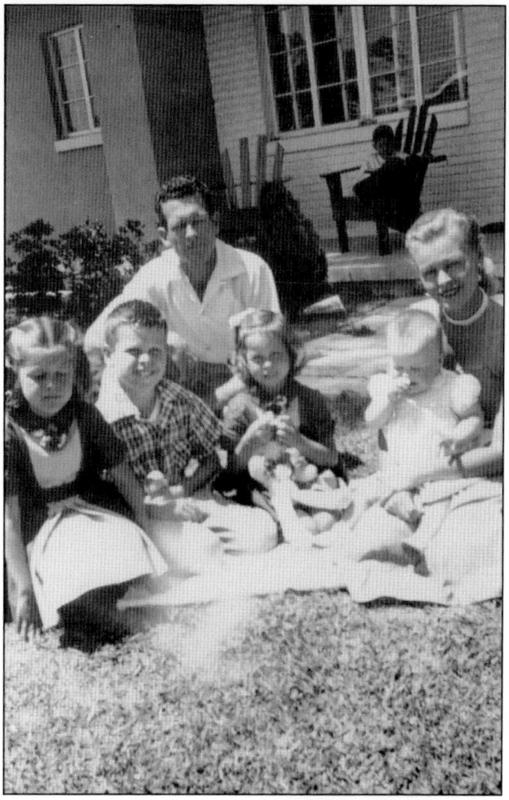

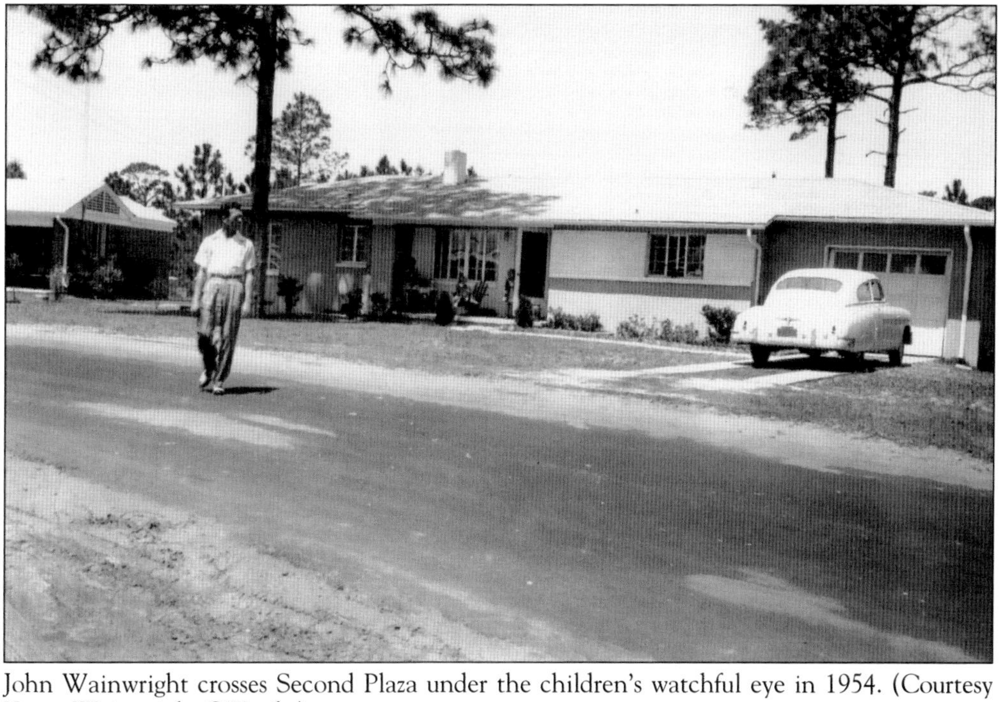

John Wainwright crosses Second Plaza under the children's watchful eye in 1954. (Courtesy Karen Wainwright O'Keefe.)

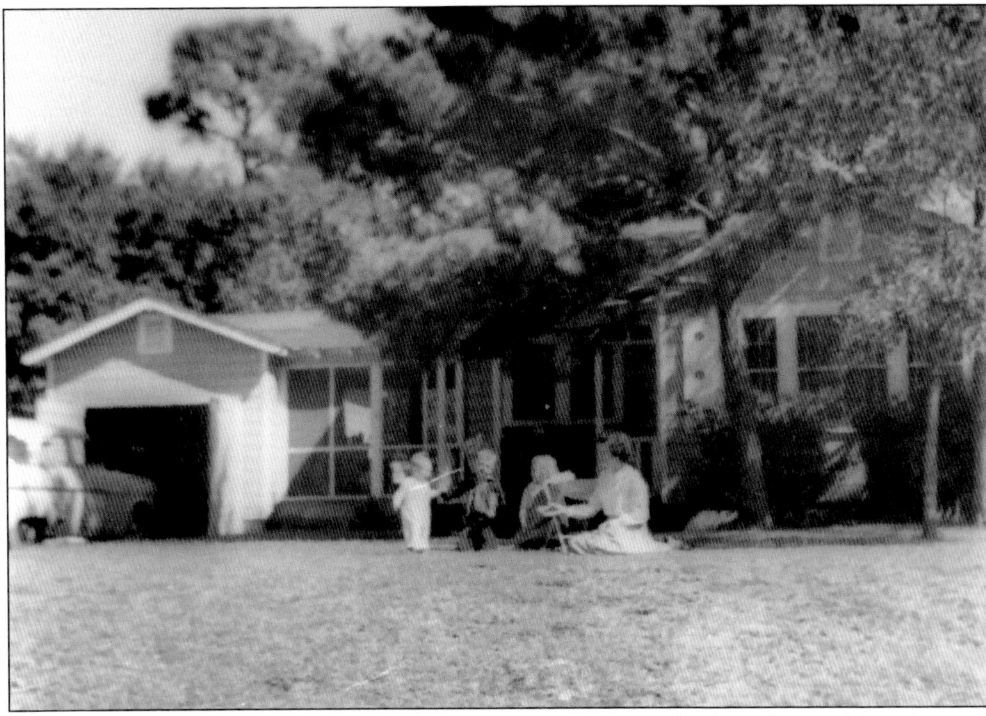

Florence Nixon and children presented an attractive scene on the front lawn of their home at 308 North MacArthur (formerly El Prado) in this early 1950s photograph. Mrs. Nixon was the wife of Dr. James Nixon who had a practice up the street near the new Bay Memorial Hospital. (Courtesy Beverly Nixon Dessault.)

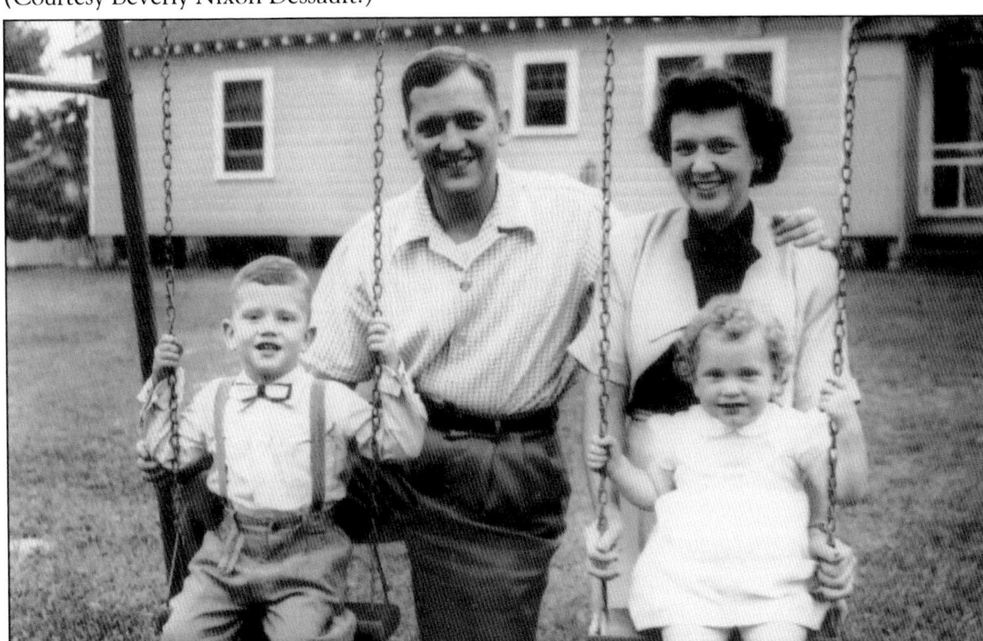

Dr. Nixon and Mrs. Nixon are pictured with Jim and Beverly in 1952 behind their house on MacArthur. (Courtesy BND.)

This snapshot was taken in the frosted drive of the Nixon's new home at 1908 DeWitt. From left to right are Janet Nixon (Dunkin), Elizabeth Ellis Nixon, and Beverly Nixon (Dessault) in the 1950s. (Courtesy BND.)

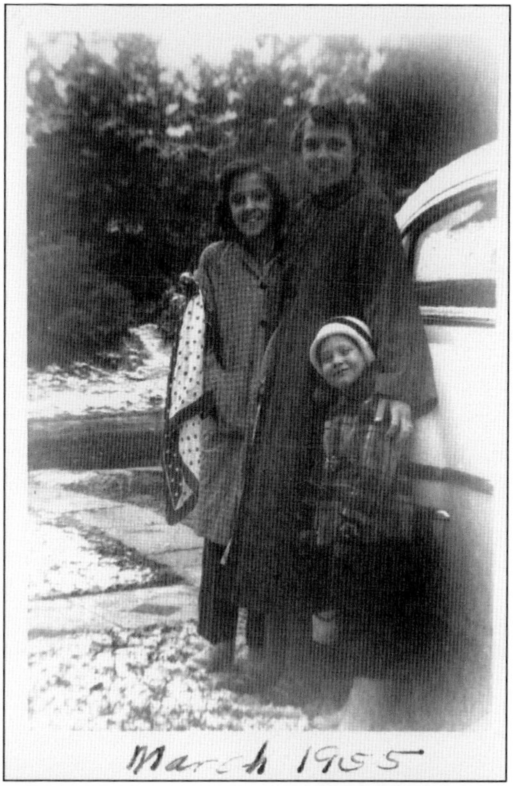

In the mid-1950s, Dr. Nixon moved his family into this modern waterfront home on DeWitt. (Courtesy BND.)

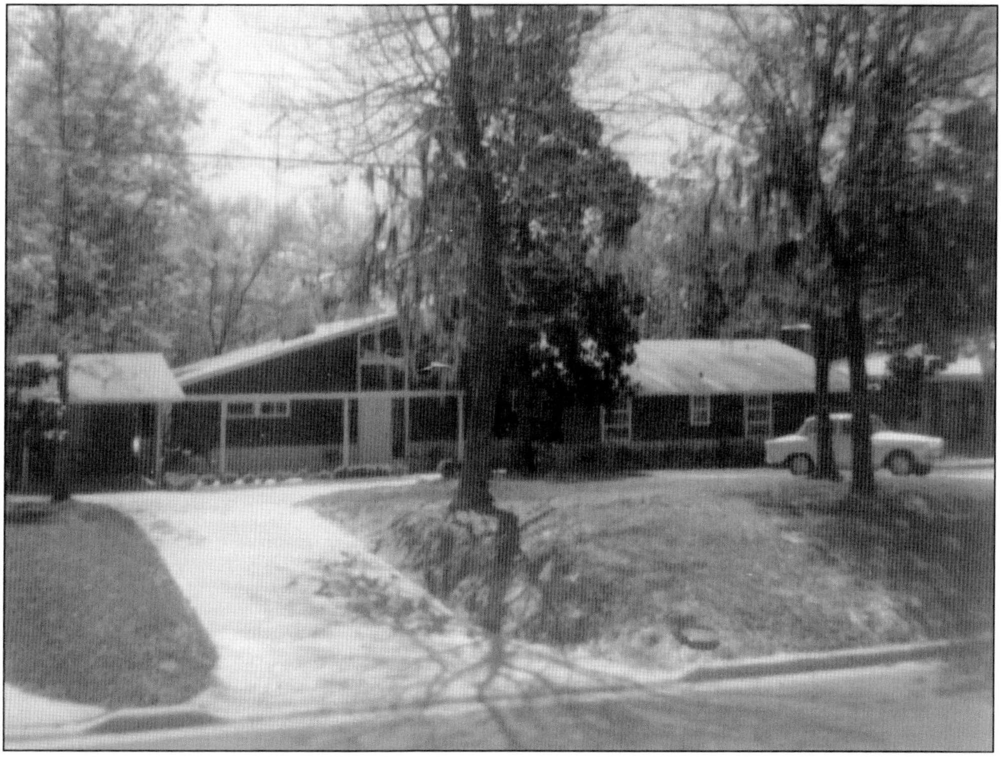

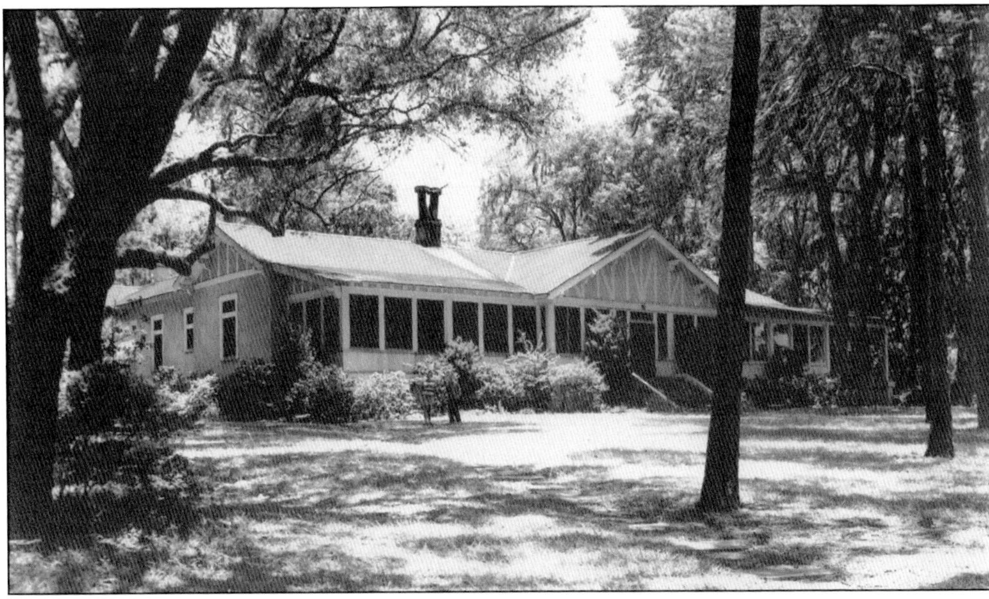

This is a view taken from the water of the old Keith place. The *Panama City Pilot* reported that work began on this home in 1919. In 1920, however, the *Pilot* stated that there were reports that Minor C. Keith was to sell all his Panama City holdings, including this unfinished home, to W.C. Sherman. Walter Colquitt Sherman, who came to the area in 1913, did buy the place and move in with his family, but his son Walter C. Sherman does not remember his late father indicating that they took possession of the home until 1926 or so. Two Sherman grandchildren are visible under the trees in this 1950s Delaney's photo. (Courtesy Tom Sherman.)

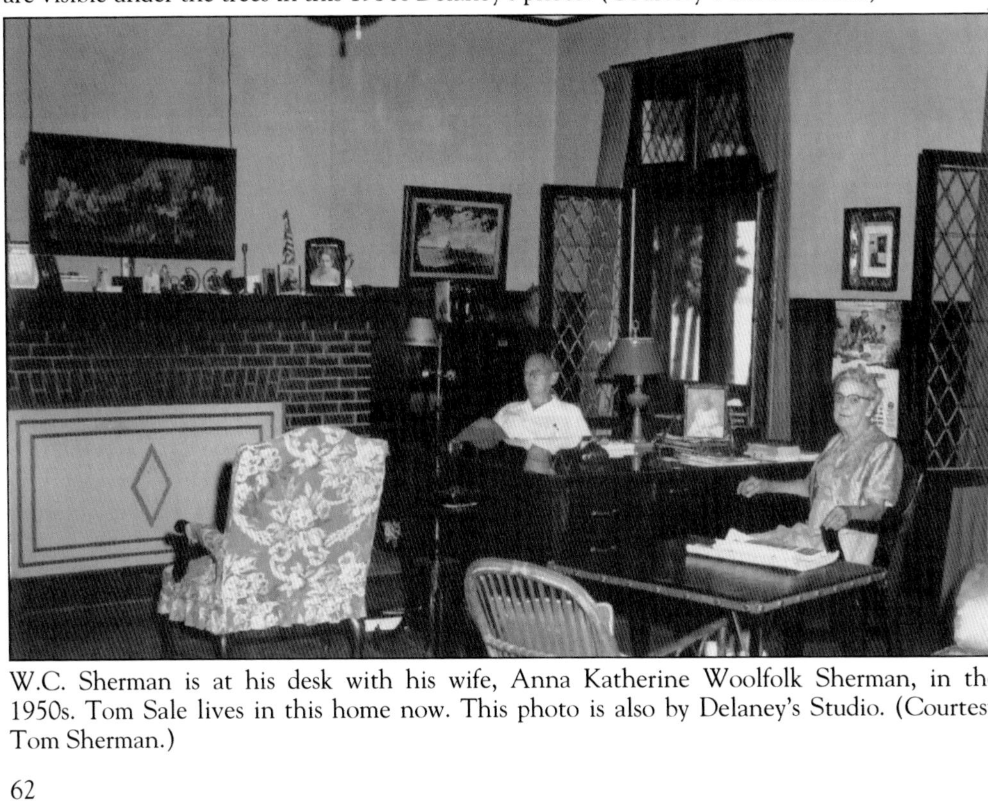

W.C. Sherman is at his desk with his wife, Anna Katherine Woolfolk Sherman, in the 1950s. Tom Sale lives in this home now. This photo is also by Delaney's Studio. (Courtesy Tom Sherman.)

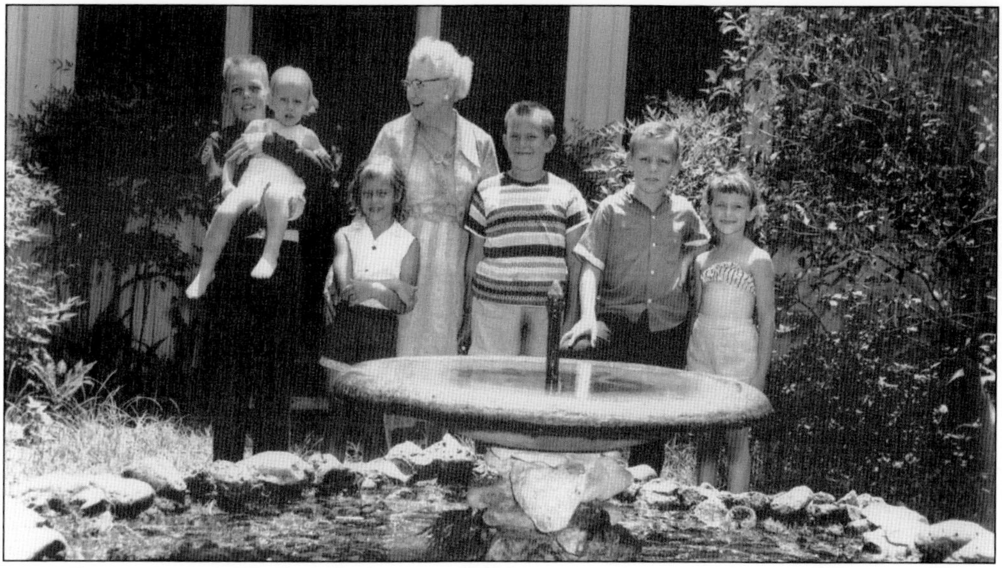

Mrs. Sherman is pictured with her grandchildren in the central courtyard. One source reported that this area originally held a swimming pool, but none of the family who spoke with the author remembered hearing anything about a swimming pool. Walter C. Sherman kindly made the following identifications: (left to right) Arthur James Lewis III (Jim), Katherine Ruth Sherman (Kathy), Mildred Elizabeth Sherman (Beth), Anna Katherine W. Sherman (Kate), John Henry Sherman Jr. (John), John Sherman Lewis, and Rosa Kay Lewis. (Courtesy Tom Sherman.)

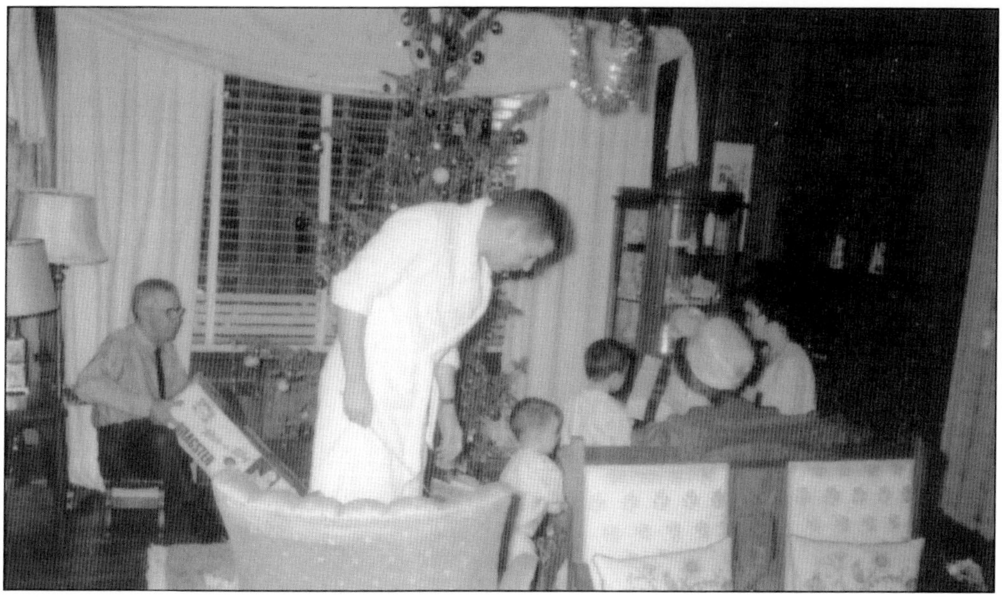

This is Christmas at the T.J. Sherman home in 1966. Thomas Jefferson Sherman II's grandchildren have fond memories of this home at 115 Bunker's Cove Road. Pictured from left to right are T.J. Sherman II, T.J. Sherman III (Jeff), young Walter, T.J. Sherman IV (Tom), grandmother Carolyn Barrett Sherman, and Mrs. Jeff Sherman (Gwendolyn Brown). Tom and Claire Sherman are currently doing an elegant and authentic restoration of this 1930s treasure. (Courtesy Tom Sherman.)

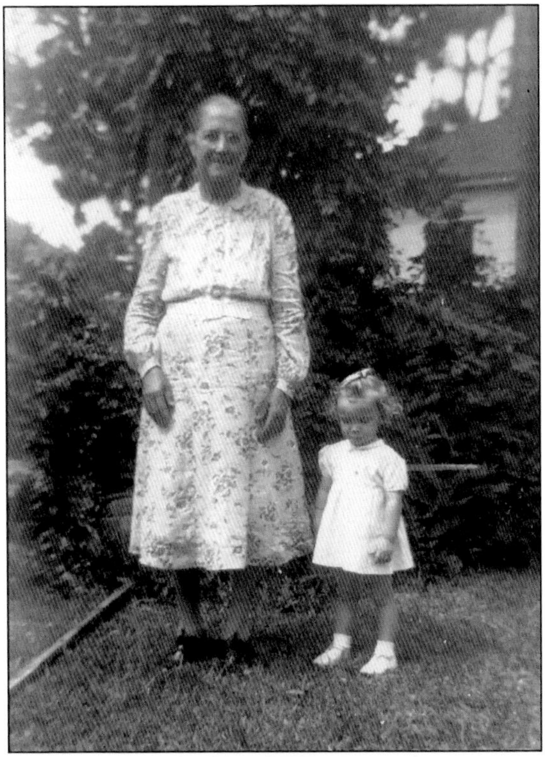

Mr. and Mrs. Andrew Martin (Lillie Bracken) bought a home on North MacArthur in 1941. This backyard scene shows Mrs. Martin's mother, Margie Bracken, with Linda Joyce Martin (Owens) about 1943. (Courtesy Mrs. L.M. Harden.)

The Martins moved to East Second Place in the 1950s. Mr. Martin operated a barbershop in the Cove Shopping Center during this time. Pictured here are Mrs. Martin, David Nelson, and Andrew Martin on Easter Sunday in 1964. David's parents, Clarence (Bugs) and Ann, sang in the choir so David sat with the Martins. (Courtesy Mrs. L.M. Harden.)

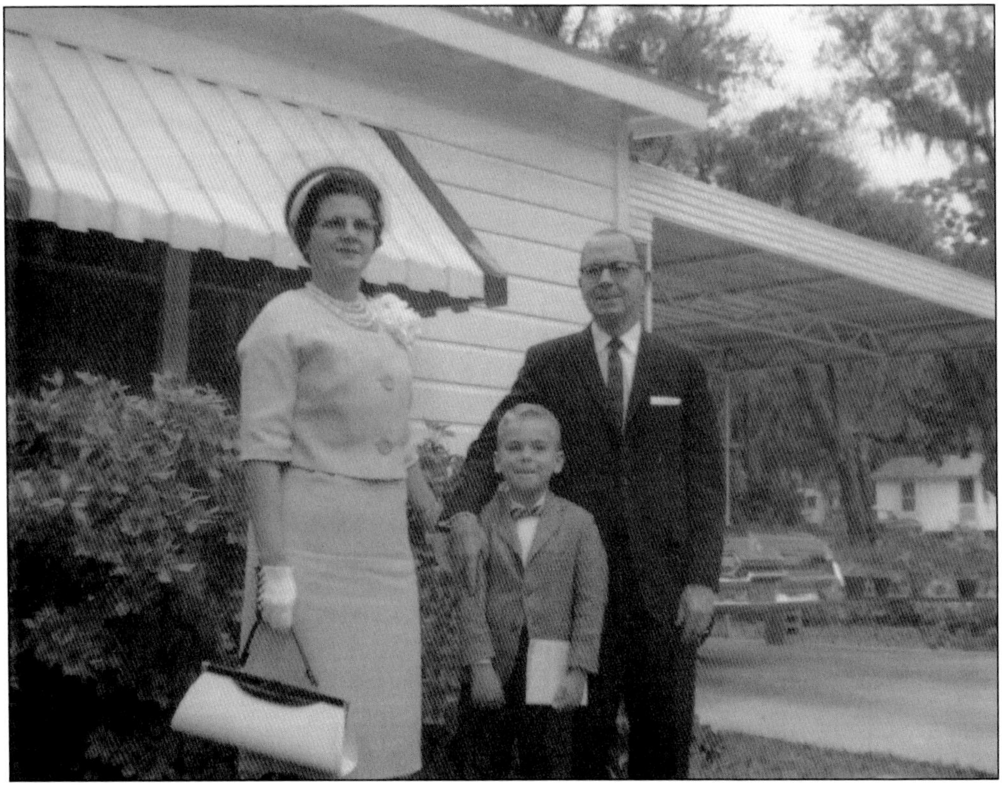

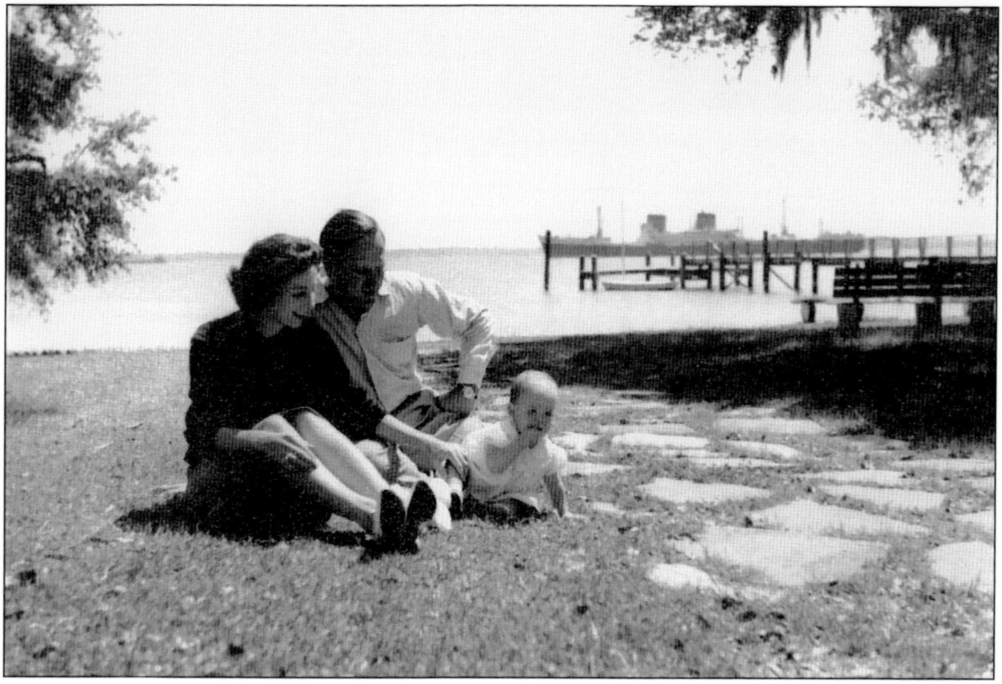

A family photo shows Phyllis and Jase Harris with baby Sealy in back of the Cove Hotel in 1959.

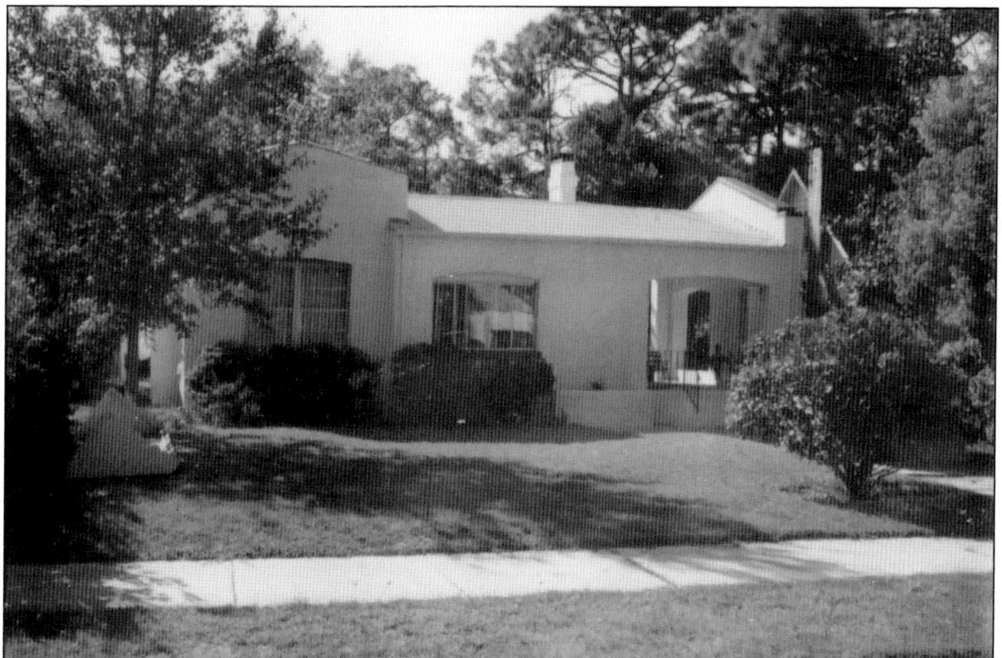

This is a curb view of 213 North Cove Boulevard on September 24, 1965, after paint and remodeling. Mr. and Mrs. Lee Mattern were able to move from her parents' home on DeWitt when they purchased this house in 1958 with a $10,000 check. This is one of the original "Spanish villas" built by H.L. Sudduth in 1927. (Courtesy Mr. and Mrs. Lee Mattern.)

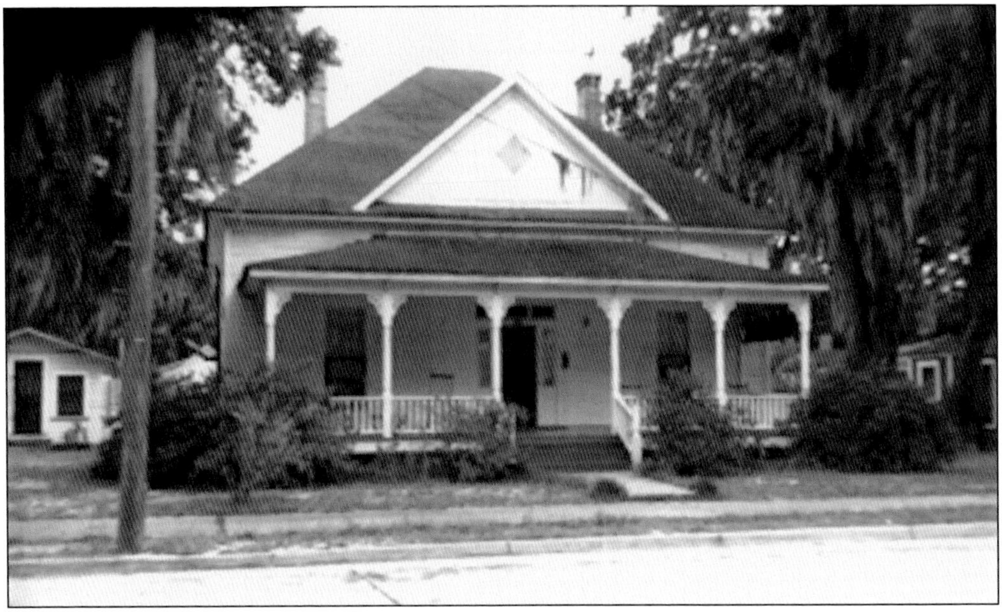

Students of Panama City history owe Dewey Smith a debt of gratitude. In 1964 he drove around town and snapped photographs of old houses, annotated the photos on the back, and dated them! The back of this photo reads, "J.W. Tiller's home, Cove section at 2nd Place P.C. FLA., He was one of the early naval store operators here, and later worked for the city, in the tax dept, untell his retirement. This home built 1909 (120 Second Place.)"

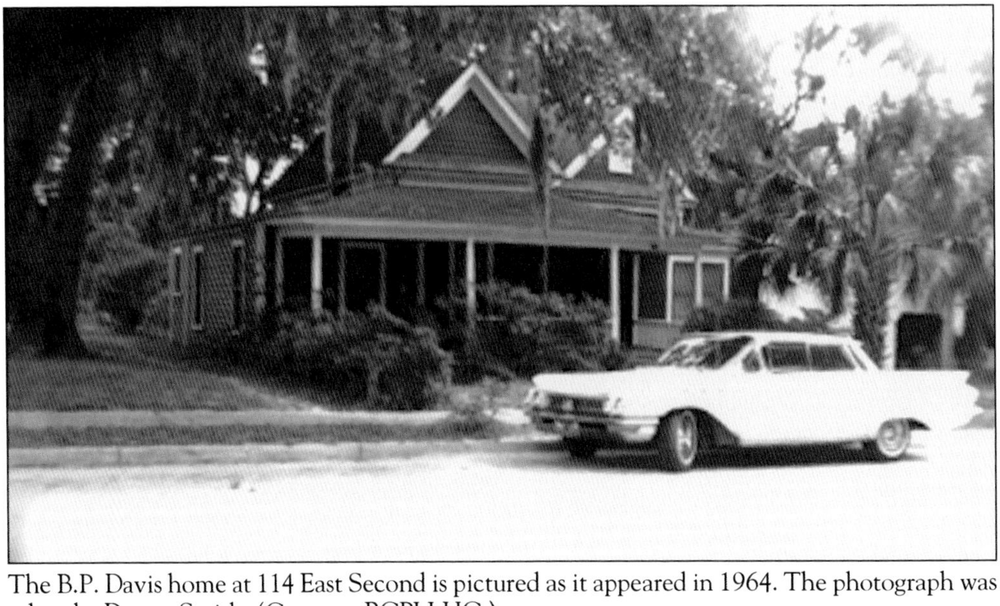

The B.P. Davis home at 114 East Second is pictured as it appeared in 1964. The photograph was taken by Dewey Smith. (Courtesy BCPLLHC.)

Ruth Howell and Mike Hauser married in 1959 and attended the University of Alabama. They stayed in this duplex across Harmon from Ruth's parents during summer breaks from school. Here Ruth holds baby Elyse (Laura having been born 15 months earlier than her sister) right before the Hausers left so that Mike could study at Stanford. This photo was taken in the early 1960s. (Courtesy RHH.)

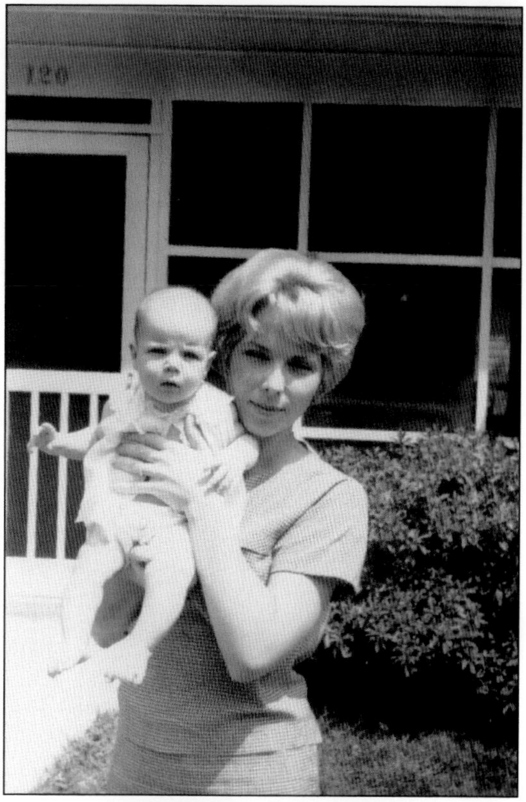

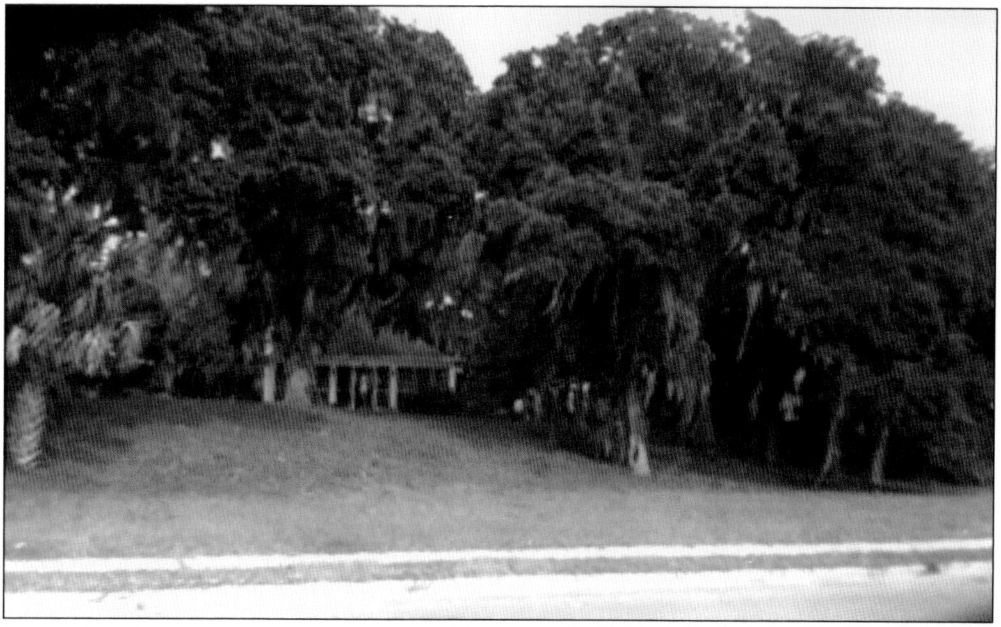

Dewey Smith wrote in neat square capital letters: "The Monty Pickens home on East Beach Drive in P.C. FLA: He was one of the early settlers here, and an accomplished musician. Pic taken 8-21-64." Baby Elyse and her husband John Fishel and their children live here now, and have really made it a gracious home. (Courtesy BCPLLHC.)

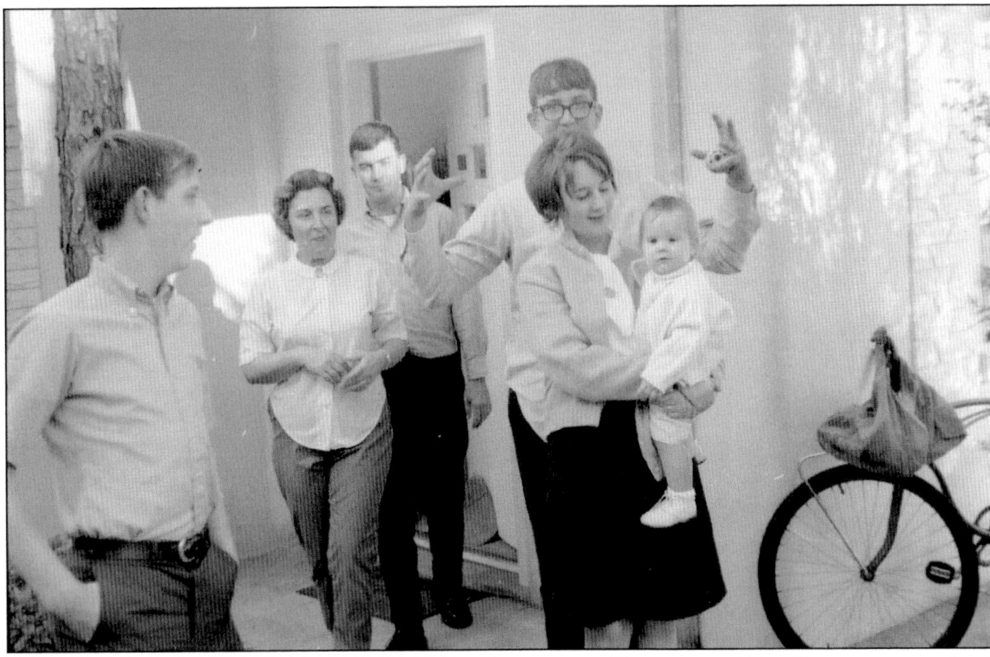

This was the beginning of a good, long Southern sendoff as niece Alice Freeman goes back to Alabama with baby Margaret. Pictured at the Hank Lawrence home at 306 Bonita in the mid-1960s are, from left to right, Bobby Lawrence, Margaret Huckabee (Huck) Lawrence, Larry Freeman, Alice Freeman holding Margaret, and Henry Lawrence behind her. (Courtesy Hank Lawrence.)

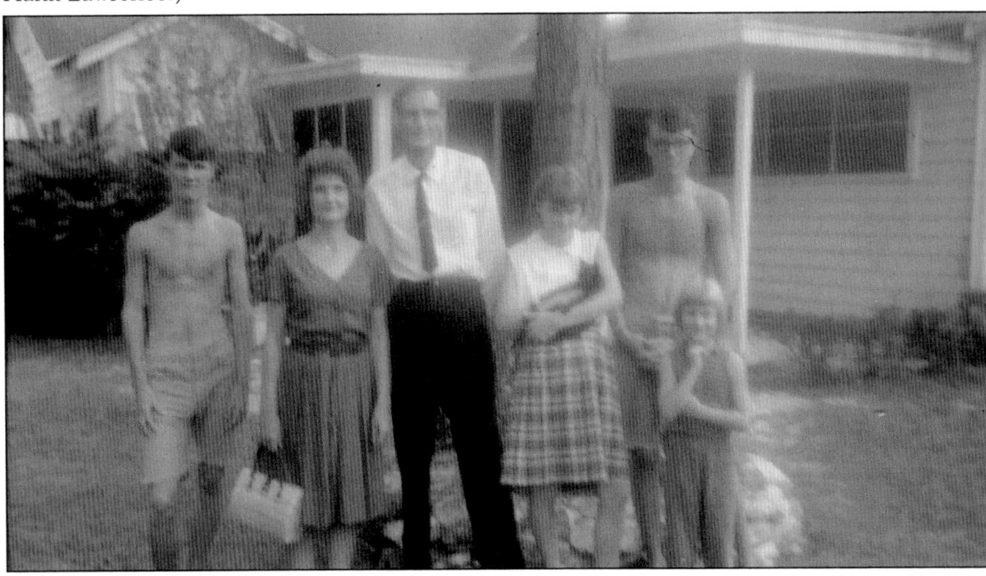

The Nellis Johnsons came to Panama City in 1957 and moved to their Cove home in 1960. Mr. Johnson sold his first cartoon nationally at the age of 17 and had his first songs played at the Grand Ole Opry at that time also. He was the wire editor at the Panama City *News Herald* as well as a syndicated cartoonist. Nellis and Reba were active in Central Baptist Church and he enjoyed playing country and western music on his many guitars. From left to right are Wayne, Reba, Nellis, Janet, Randy, and Brenda. (Courtesy Reba Johnson.)

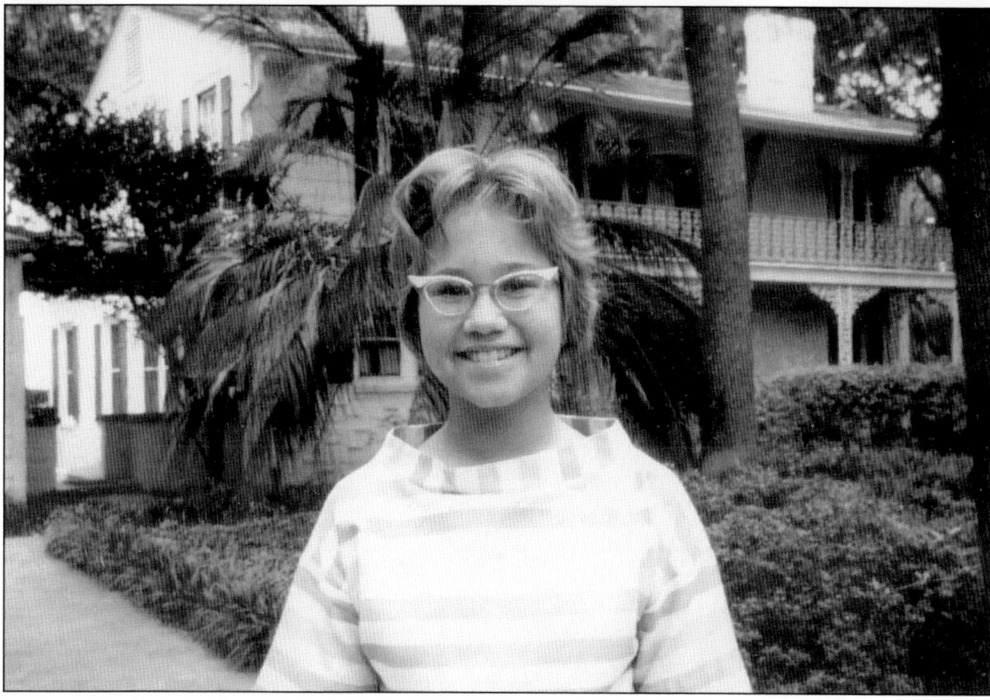

Ann Kruse (Percival) smiles winningly in front of her home on 324 Bunker's Cove Road in 1962. The Foster Kruses bought this house from Mr. and Mrs. Ray (Eve) Schmidt in about 1955. Mr. Schmidt was Panama City's first postmaster. When the Schmidts moved back, they bought the next lot and built using beautiful tile throughout. Dr. Richard Walker, a nephrologist, later purchased the Schmidt property and remodeled extensively. (Courtesy Ann Kruse Percival.)

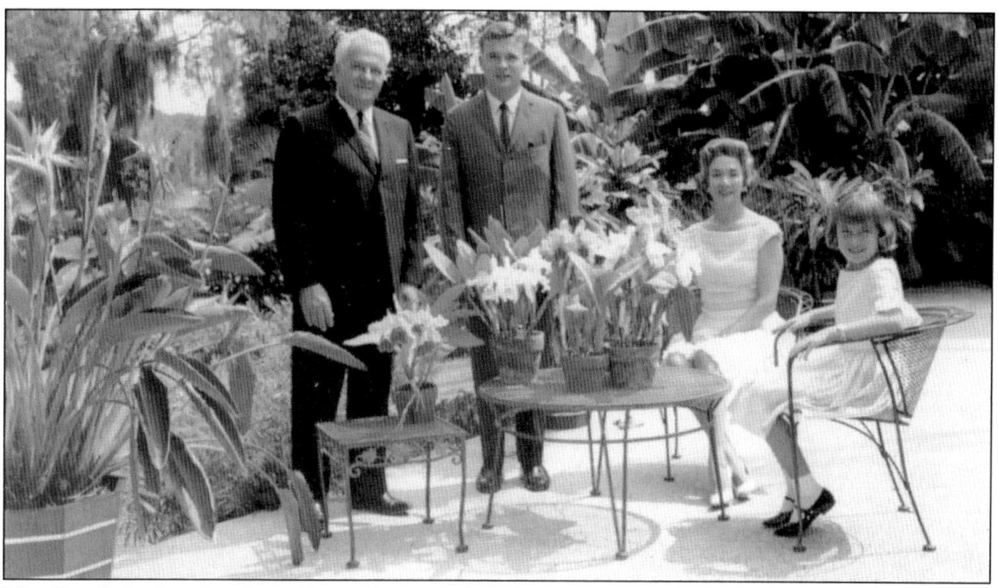

The Frank Parker family is shown here at their Bayou Court home in the 1960s. Mr. Parker was known for his beautiful orchids. Pictured from left to right are Frank Parker, son Marshall, Dorothy Sue, and daughter Helen. (Courtesy SHL.)

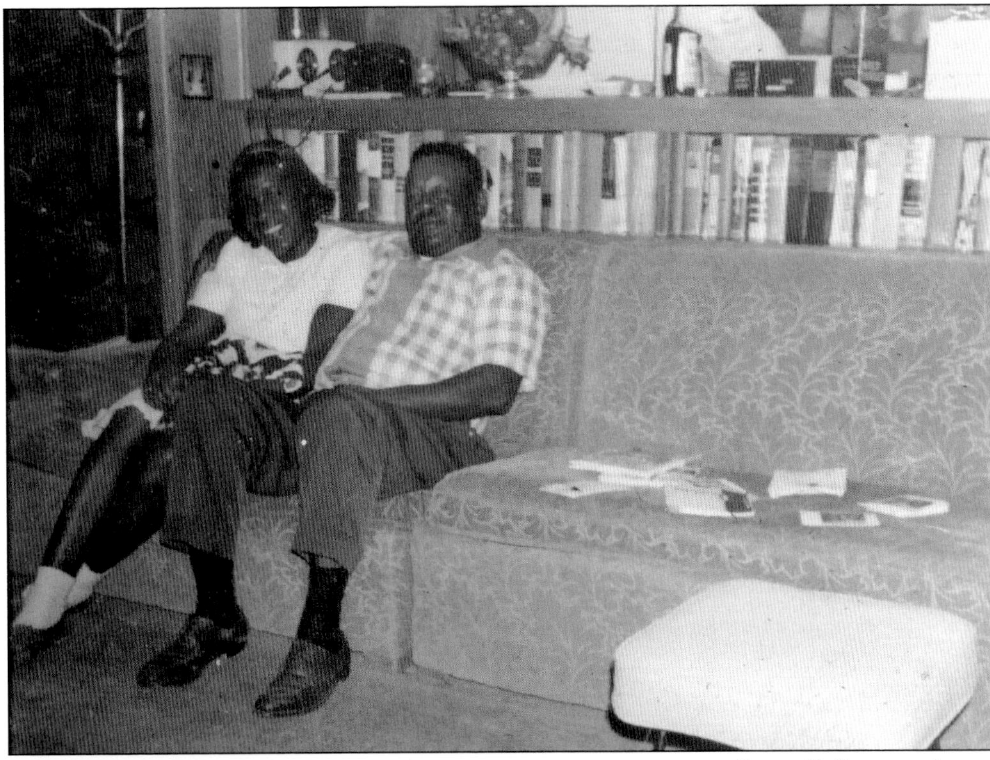

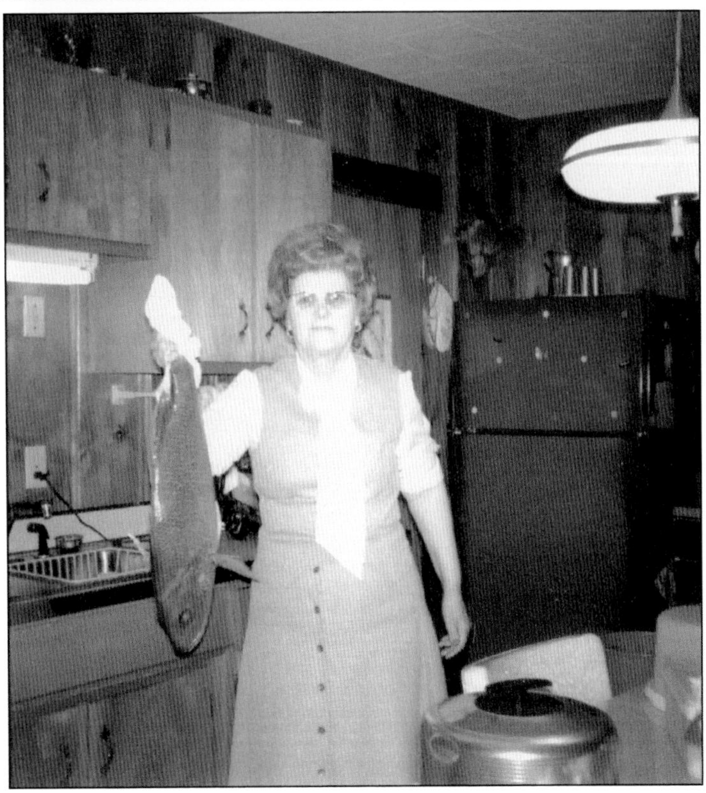

Easter Bellamy and Flambo Rambo are enjoying some quality time in the 1960s. They both worked at the Cove Hotel in its heyday. (Courtesy SHL.)

Lilly Martin (Harden) taught for years at Panama Christian School. Here she shows what the area is famous for—fresh seafood and fantastic cooks. The Martins enjoyed sharing their table with others.

Five

Our Real Home

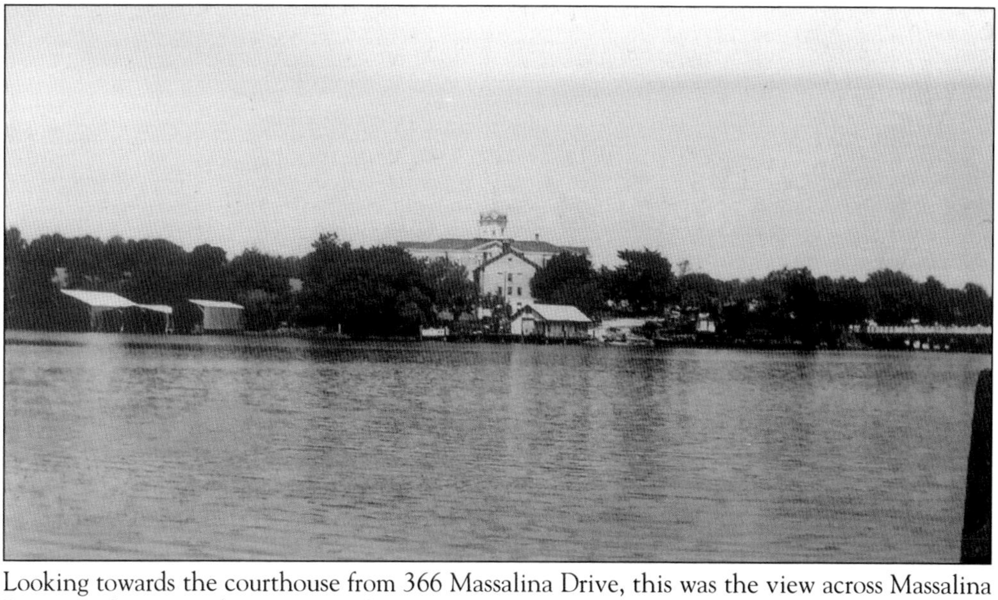

Looking towards the courthouse from 366 Massalina Drive, this was the view across Massalina Bayou in the 1940s. (Courtesy Carl Bennett.)

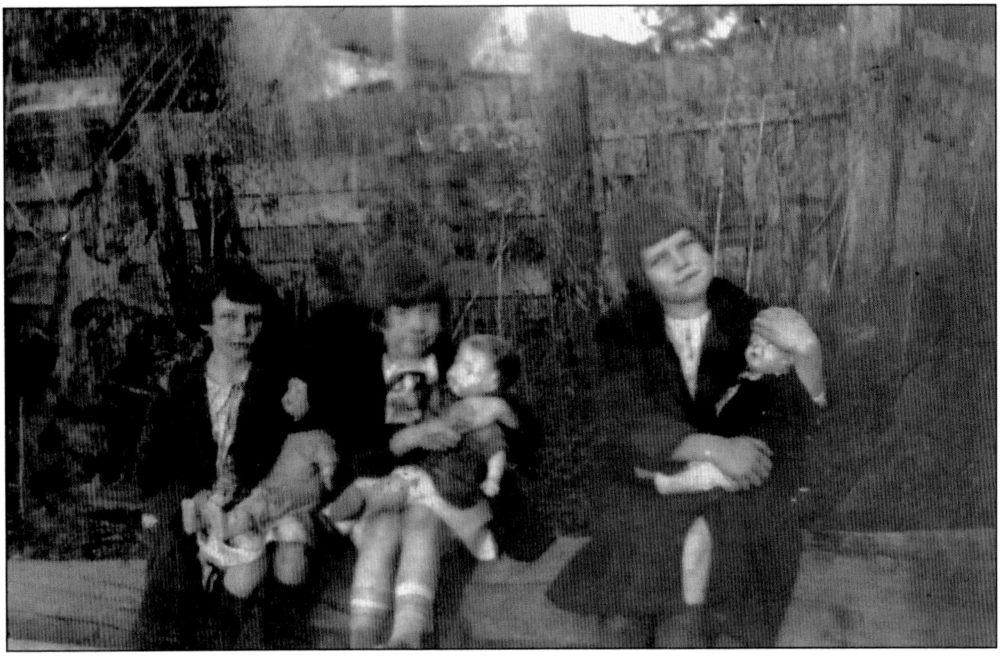

This photograph was taken at the sea wall at Christmastime, *c.* 1923. From left to right are Irene Smith (Fleming), Nellie Howell (Hobbs), and Clarice Davis, who was age six. Clarice held her hand over her doll's head to cover a hole there. Note the roofline at the top of photo. This was probably the Smith house, which is now owned by Mrs. Chester (Evelyn) Carter. (Courtesy CD.)

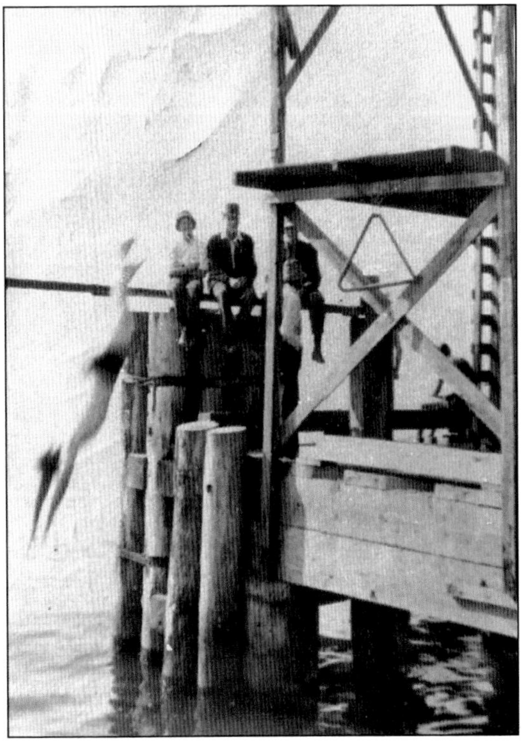

The back of this photo reads, "Dewey Smith jumping off Cove Dock." It was later amended to read, "Dewey was born in 1917. Boy looks older than age 8." Neither note is in Dewey Smith's familiar block style, so the reader may judge. (Courtesy BCPLLHC.)

Buell Murfee was born in Chipley in 1921 and moved to Panama City when he was two or three years old. This picture was taken next door to the Murfee's first home (still standing) at the corner of Harmon (named for his mother's father) and what is now Cherry Street, but was not quite a street then. The man that lived on the lot in the background was Mr. Battles, who worked with the paper and took this photograph. Buell later served his country in World War II and served The Cove as postman from 1958 to 1988. (Courtesy Mr. and Mrs. Buell Murfee.)

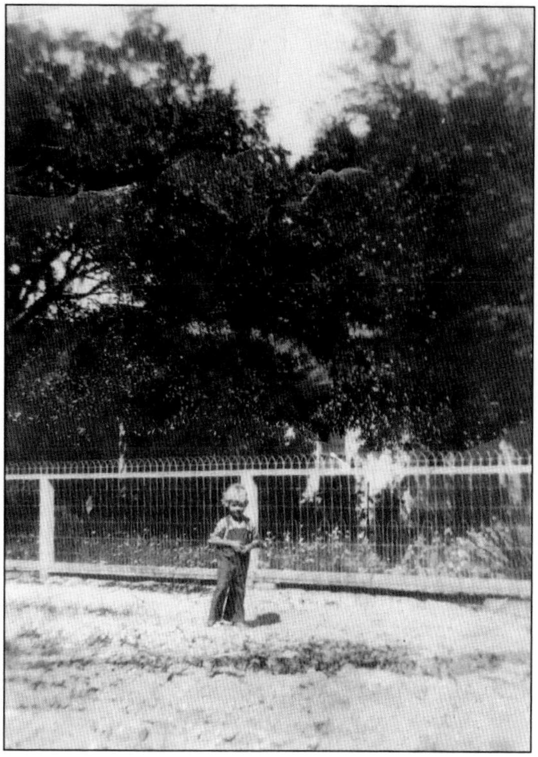

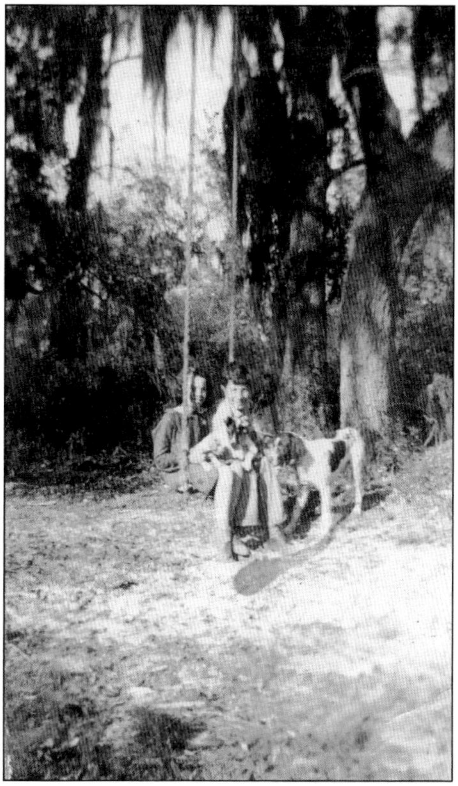

Wiley Williams built this swing for his children, Bette and Bobby, across the street from their home at 226 Olive Street in the 1930s. Buell and his family were soon to move next door to the Williams children. (Courtesy BWB.)

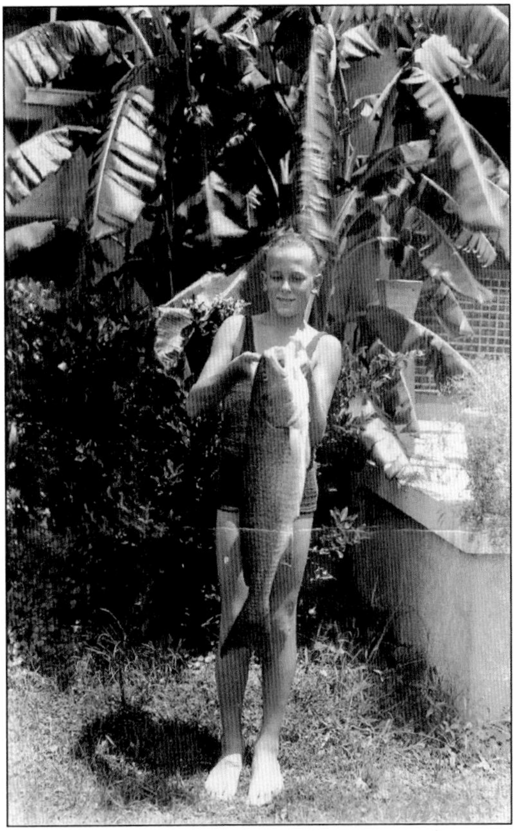

Ruby Sealy Harris's son Jase Harris is seen with a nice fish. This picture was probably taken in late 1920s. (Courtesy SHL.)

The Cove Hotel was being written about in magazines targeting hunting and fishing enthusiasts. The Sealy family had acreage in the country for good hunting, and the waters of the bay and gulf held plenty of fish. Here are a few ling, called cobia now. The men are visitors. From left to right, the first four men are unidentified and are pictured with Gene Ellis and Jase Harris. This photo dates from the 1930s or 1940s. (Courtesy SHL.)

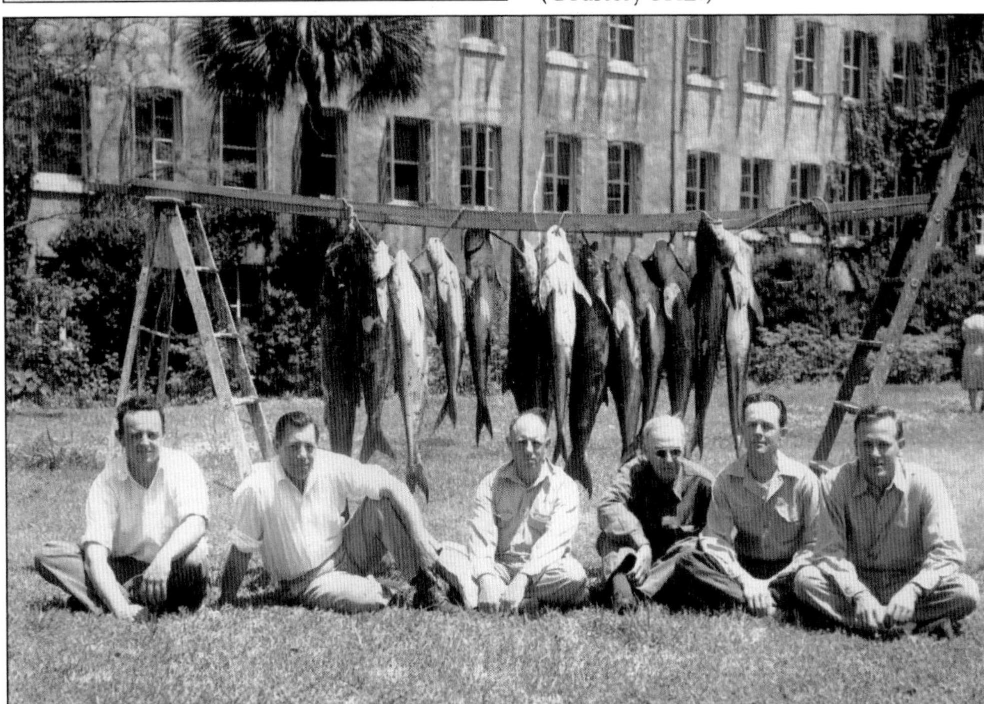

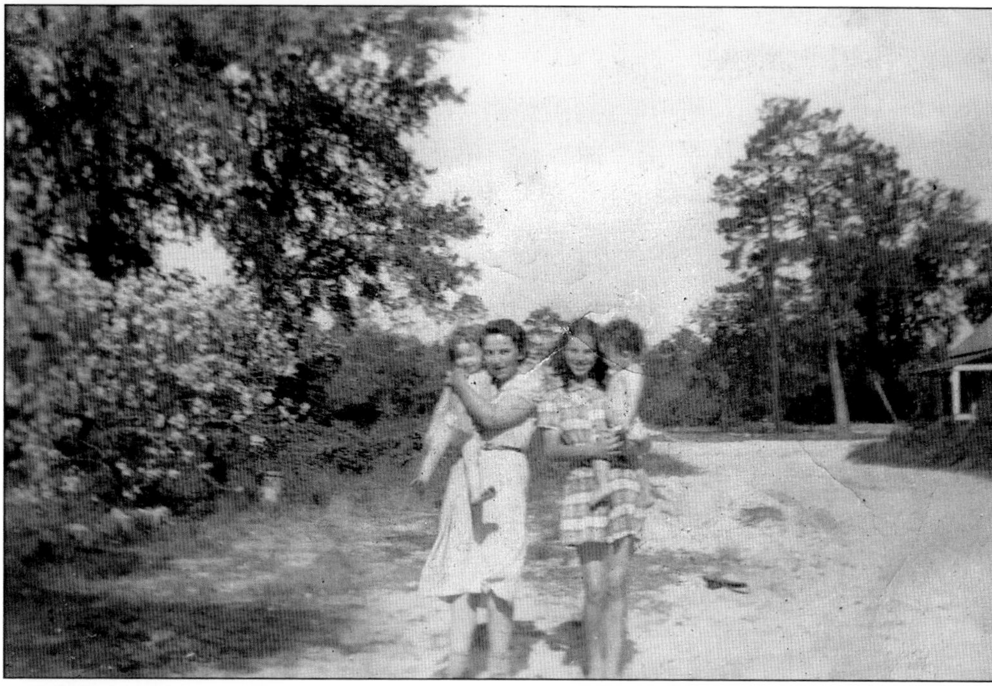

Mrs. Wiley (Dorothy) Williams is pictured here with her children on Olive Street, coming up from the bay in 1941. She holds one of her twin sons and her daughter, Bette, holds the other. The twins' names are William Lawrence, known as Pete, and Wiley Charles. (Courtesy BWB.)

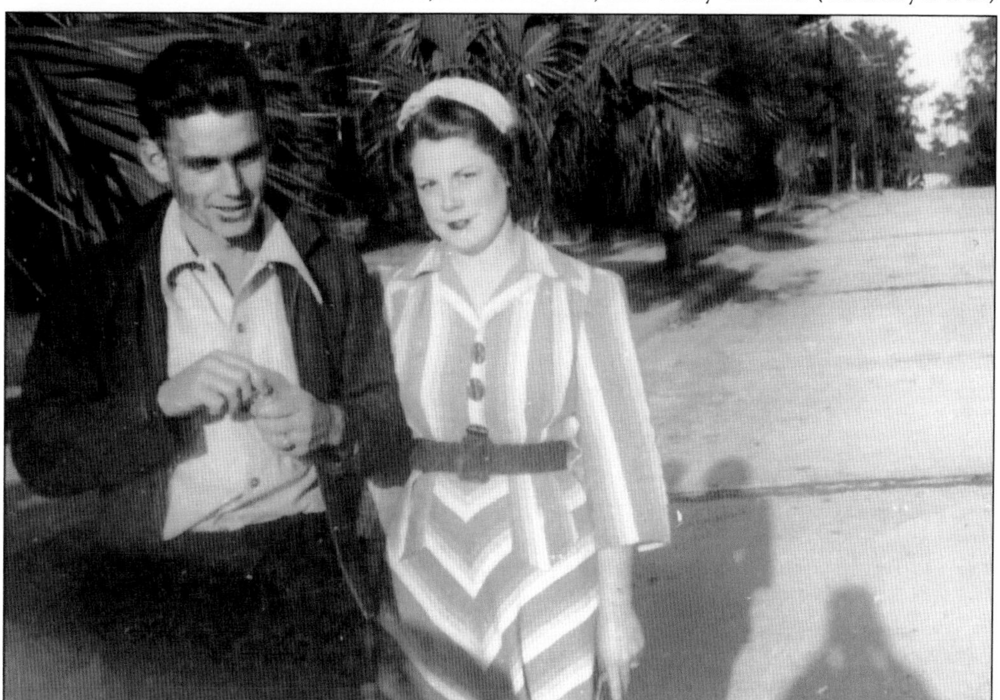

G.W. Hobbs and Nellie Howell Hobbs are at the corner of East Second Place and Beach Drive in the early 1940s. This scene is relatively unchanged today. (Courtesy CD.)

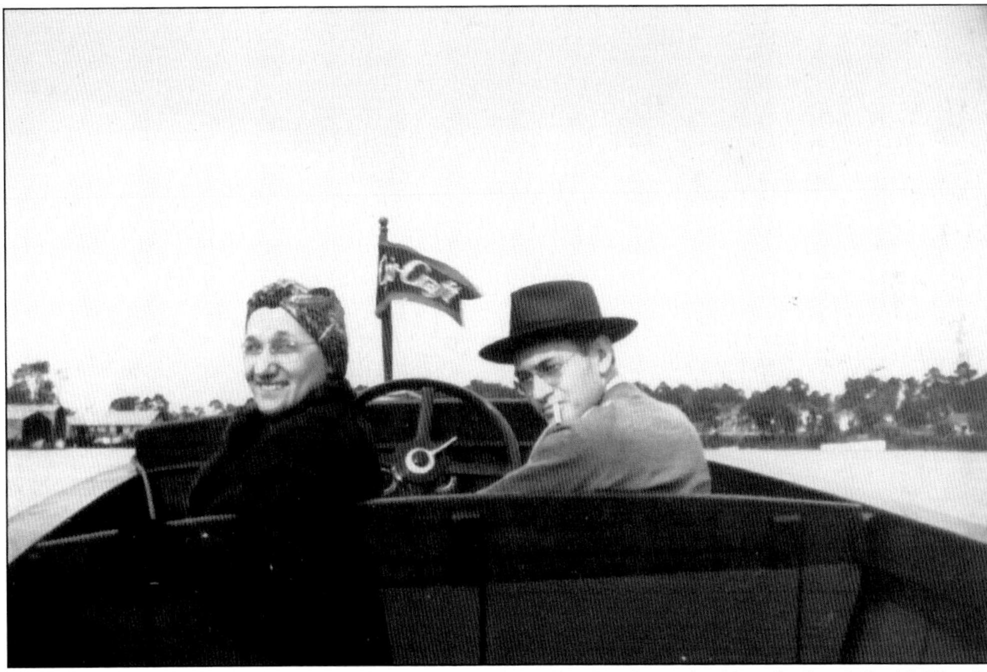

Mary Coil and Foster Kruse are shown here in the *ChrisCraft* on the Bay, before World War II. (Courtesy Ann Kruse Percival.)

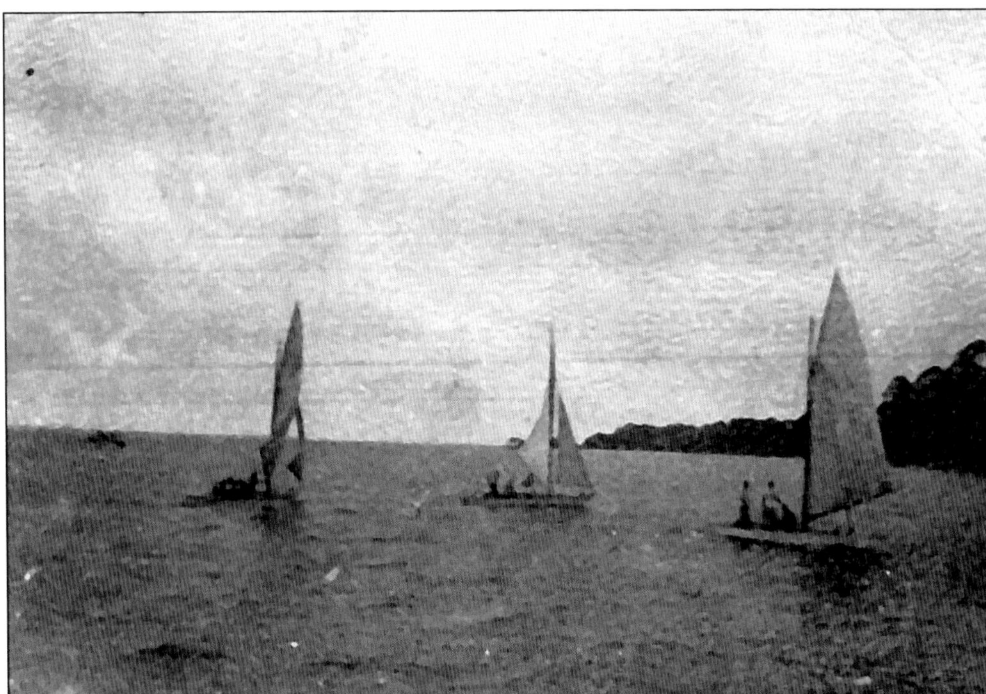

Pictured here are the fish class sailboats during the St. Andrews Bay Yacht Club Regatta in 1945. (Courtesy BWB.)

Buell Murfee and Bobby Williams bought this boat for $110, working off installments. This photo is from the early 1940s. From left to right are Gladys Hines, Bette Williams, Spencer Draughn, and Buell Murfee. (Courtesy BWB.)

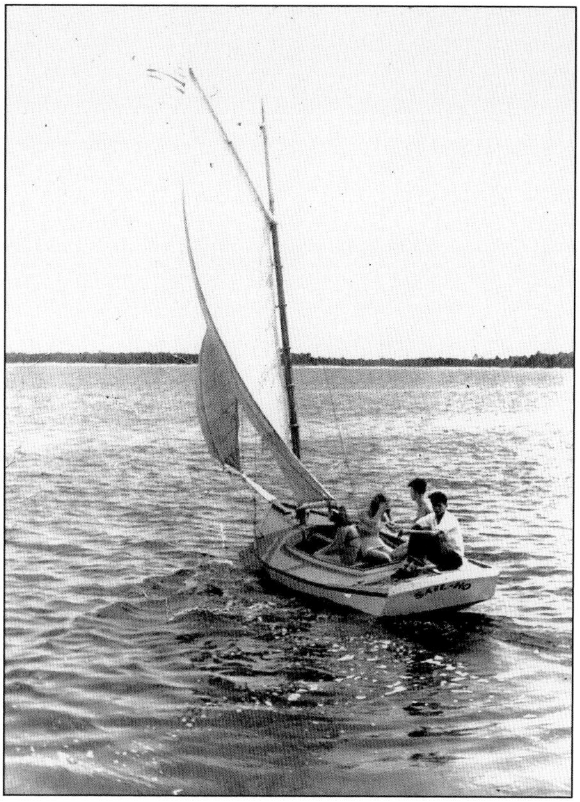

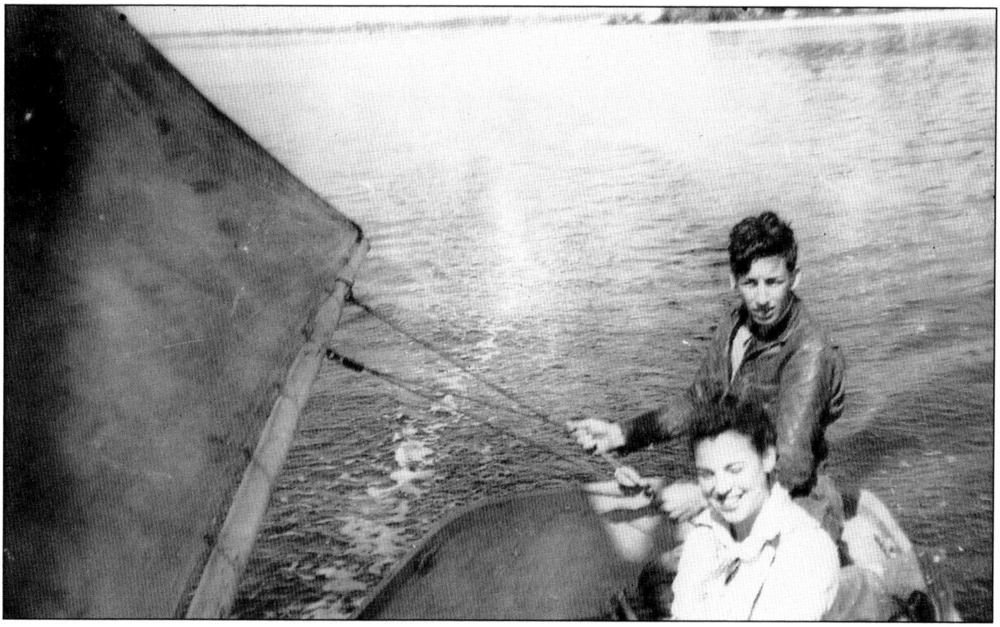

Bette Williams and Bobby Williams are photographed on the *Sail-Ho* in the early 1940s. Bobby taught Bette to sail and Bette taught Bobby to dance. (Courtesy BWB.)

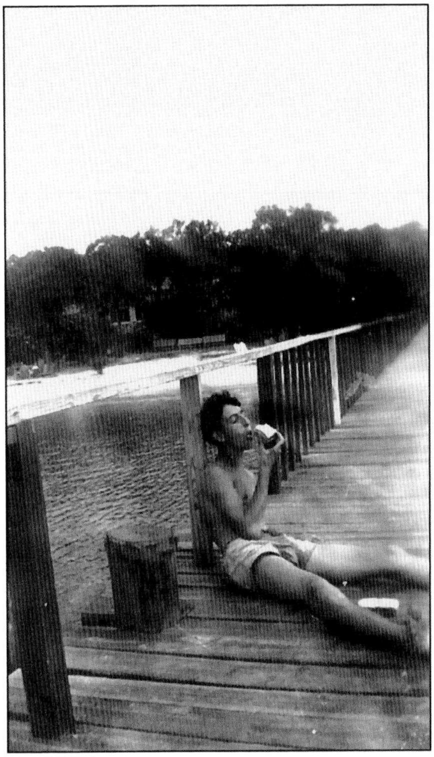

Bobby Williams rests on the pier of the Cove Hotel, *c.* 1942. (Courtesy BWB.)

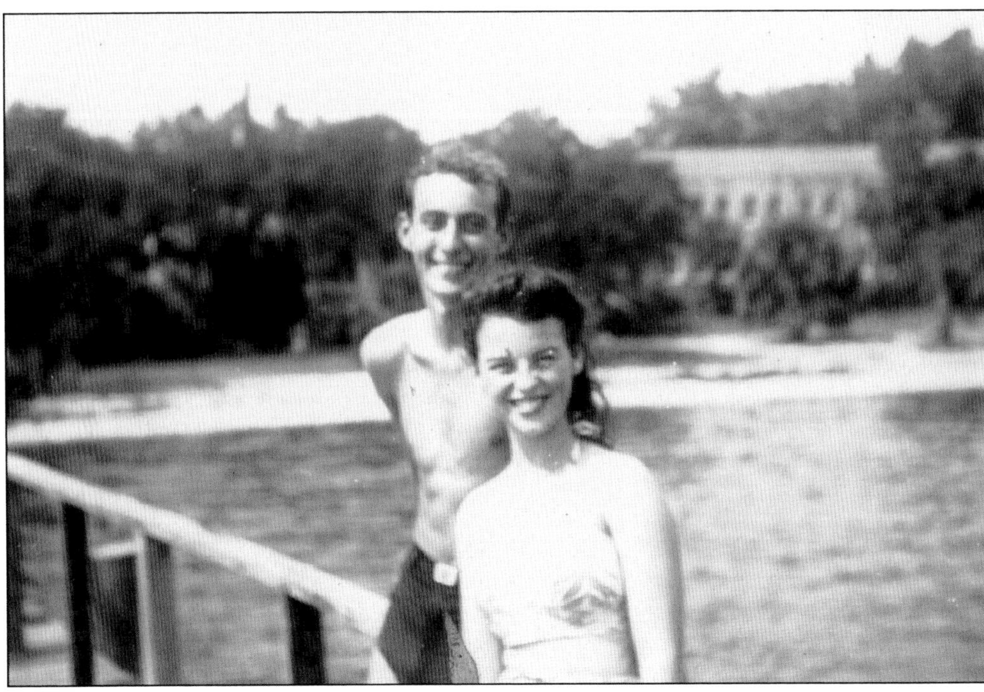

Ross Brunson and Bette Williams pose for a photograph at the Cove Hotel in 1943. (Courtesy BWB.)

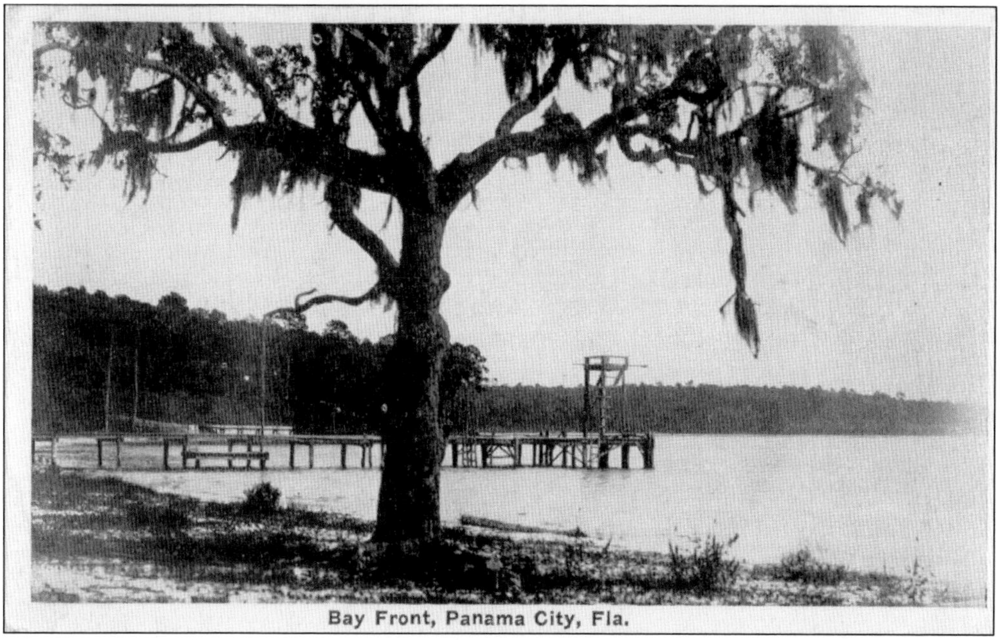

This postcard is of the city, or Exchange Club, pier. This pier at the end of Allen Avenue was out of use by the late 1930s, but the location remains popular to this day. (Courtesy Mr. and Mrs. George Thomas.)

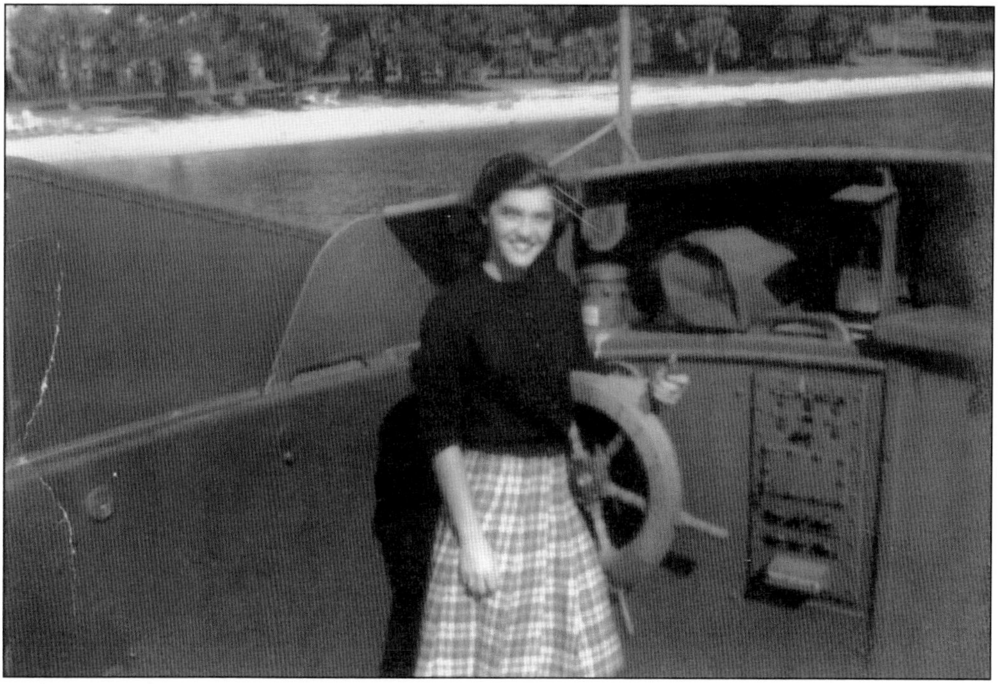

In this 1947 photo, Ann Daughtry (Lytle) is at the helm of an old World War II boat offshore of the Cove Hotel. (Courtesy Ann Lytle.)

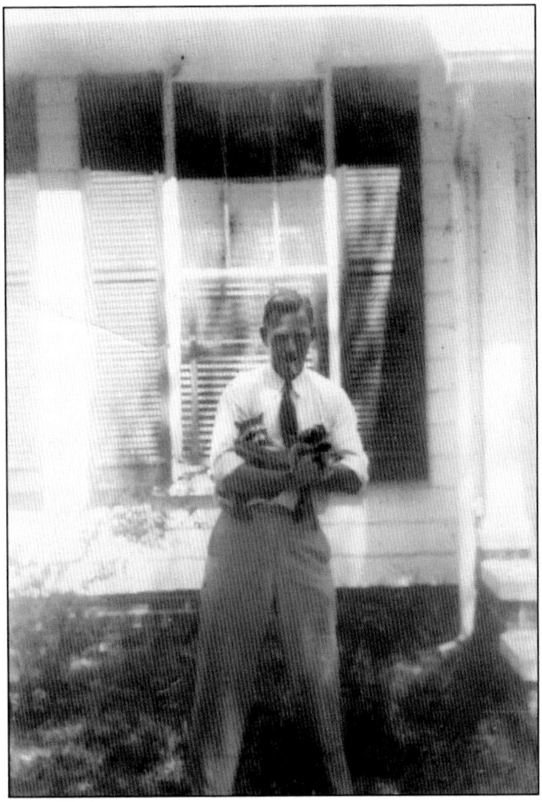

Mark Thomas poses with two furry friends in the 1930s or 1940s. (Courtesy Sarah Grace Thomas.)

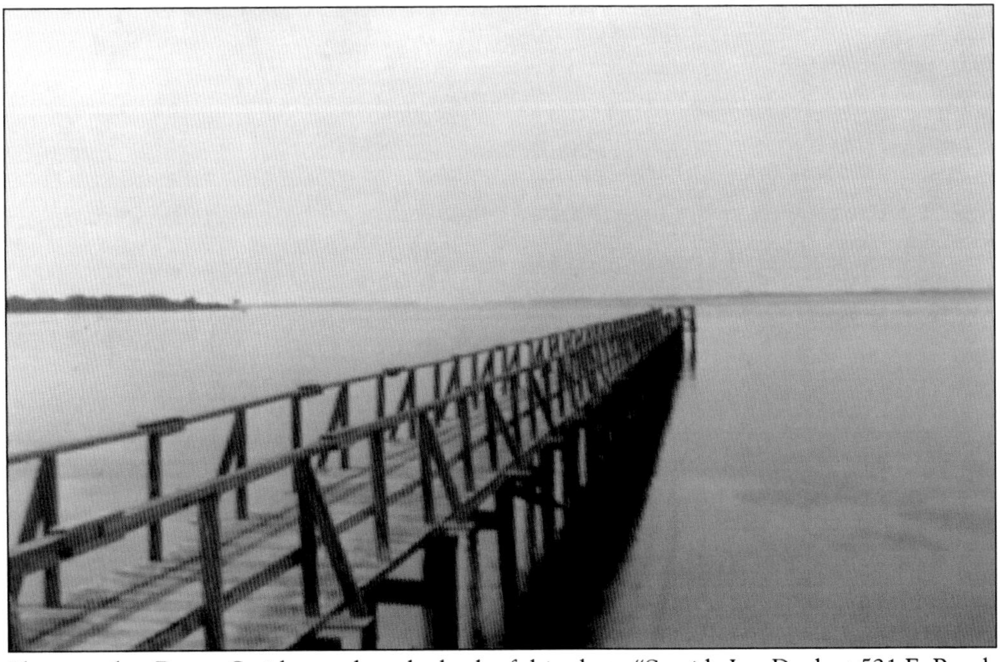

Photographer Dewey Smith noted on the back of this photo "Seaside Inn Dock at 521 E. Beach Drive A popular spot for guests, at the inn on summer days, Red Fish Point in far distance.,(left) ...PC Fla 9/13/64" (Courtesy BCPLLHC.)

This stately lady sits on the lawn next to the Wilkerson house, which stood on the lot at the corner of East Beach Drive and Second Court. She rented from the Davises in the late 1940s. (Courtesy CD.)

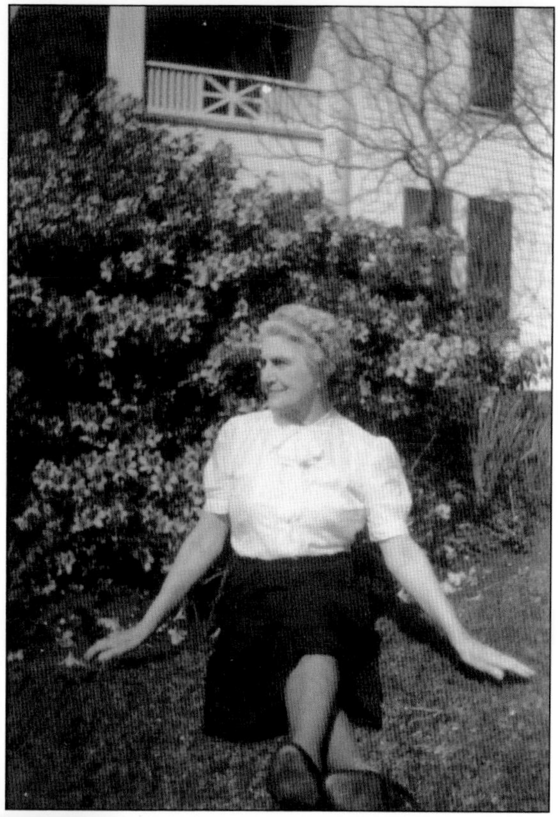

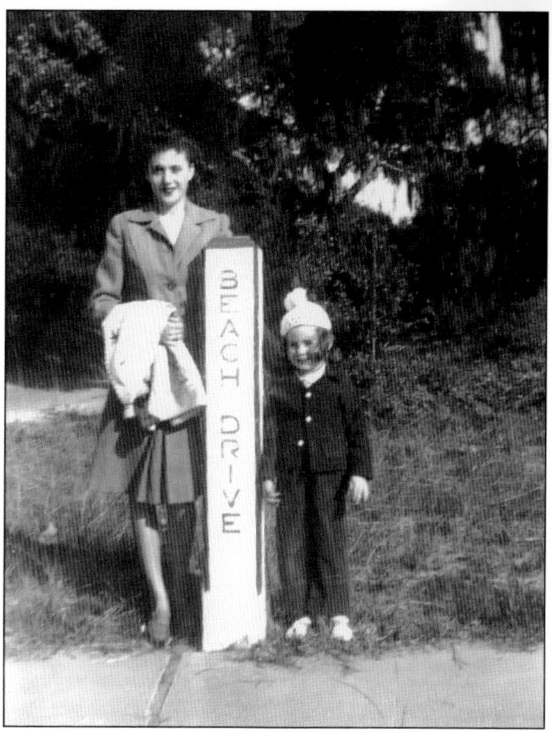

A pretty lady poses with Mary Nell Hobbs (Stone) at the corner of Beach Drive and First Court. (Courtesy CD.)

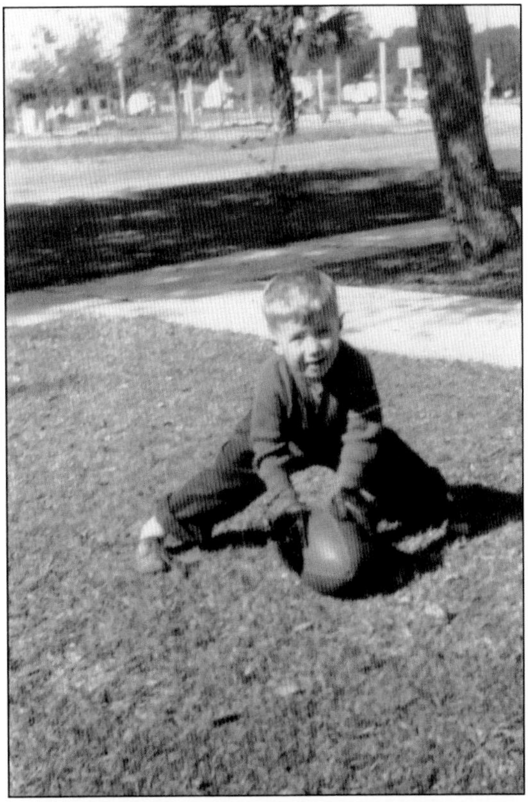

Butch Powell is pictured in the front yard of his home on 122 Hamilton in the late 1940s. (Courtesy Jane Powell Tweedy.)

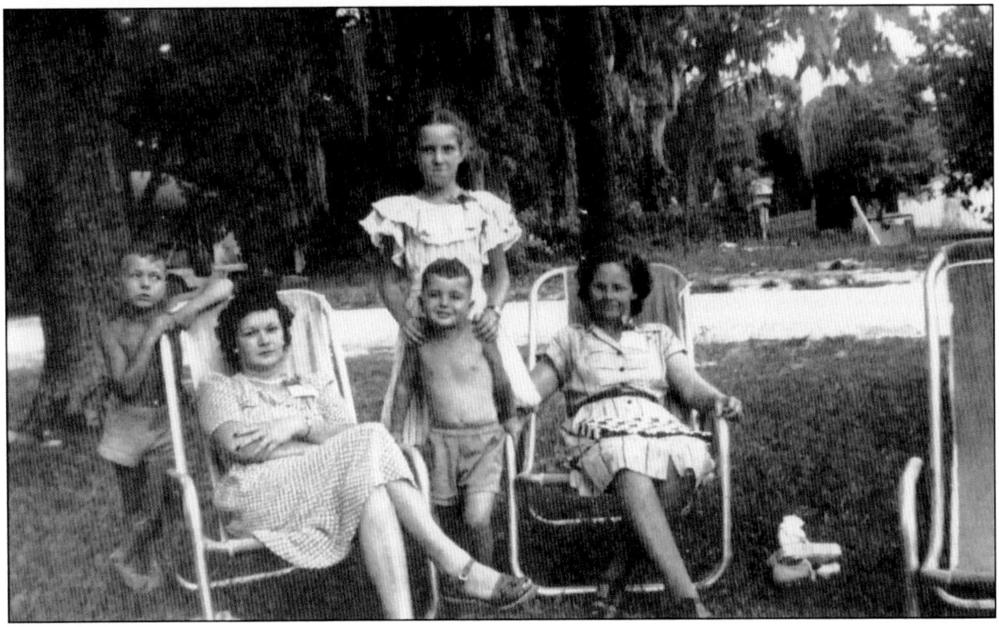

The Shriner's Parade was always well received. Here a group relaxes afterward on the front lawn of the Andrew Martins's new home on Second Place, in 1949 or 1950. From left to right are Phillip Martin, Charlotte Martin, Johnnie Martin, Betty Jo Bush, and Mittie Bush. (Courtesy Mrs. L.M. Harden.)

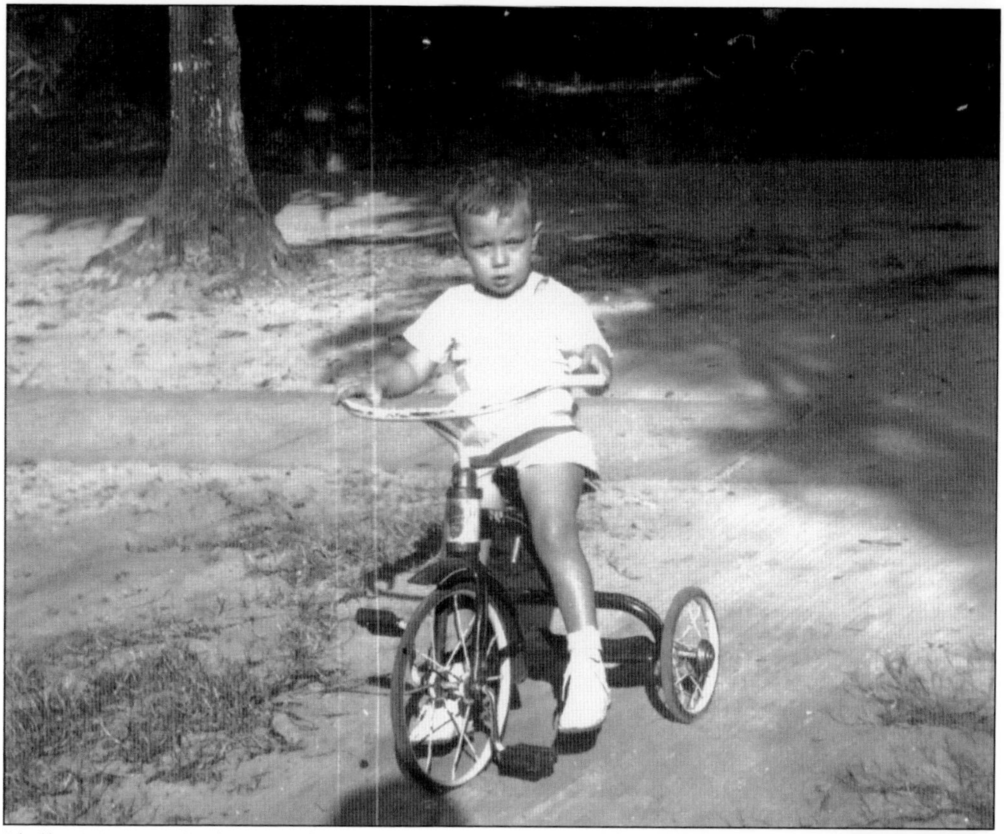

Phillip Martin rides his tricycle on Linda Avenue in the late 1940s. (Courtesy Mrs. L.M. Harden.)

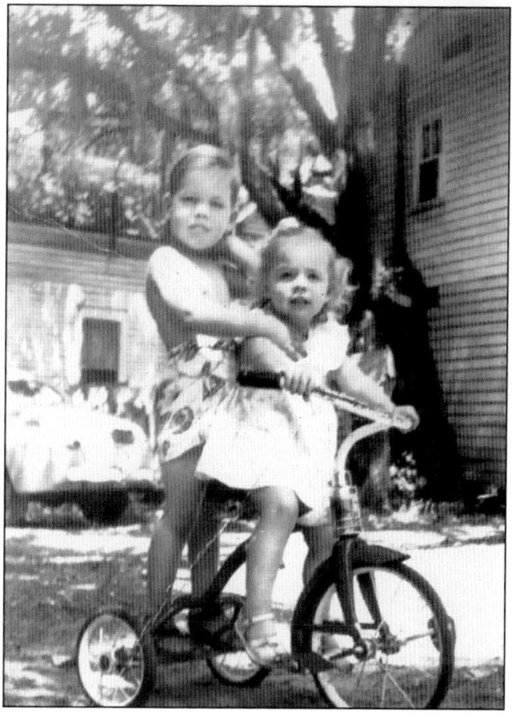

Jan Woodham lived with her family in a garage apartment between the Hobbs/Howell house and the Davis home on Second Place in the late 1940s. She loved to play outside and would call "Bobby, Bobby" for him to come out. (Courtesy Clarice Davis.)

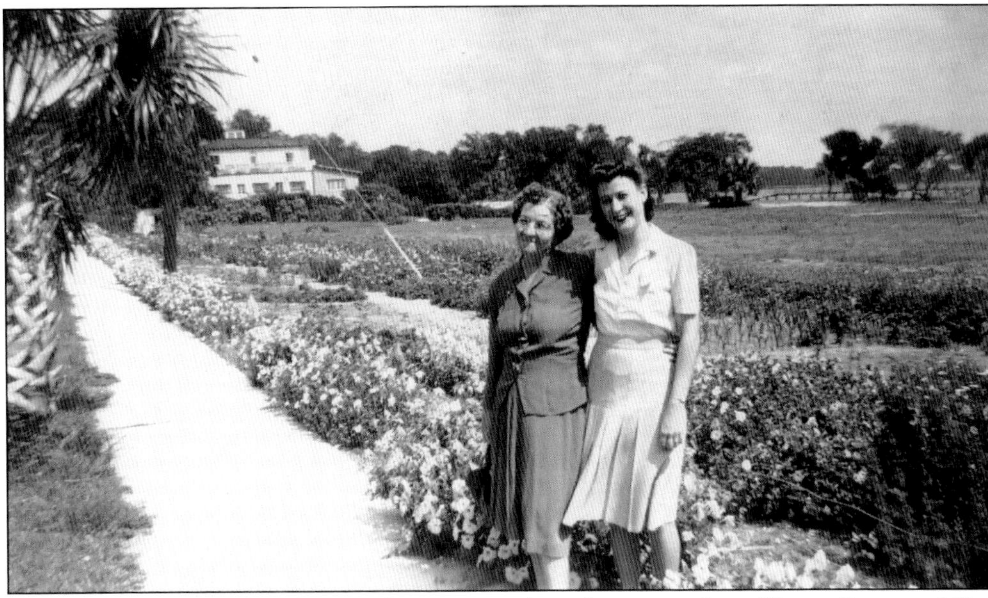

Barely recognizable today, this was the view east from the point where Cherry Street and East Beach Drive met. Jessie Davis poses with a friend of daughter Clarice. (Courtesy CD.)

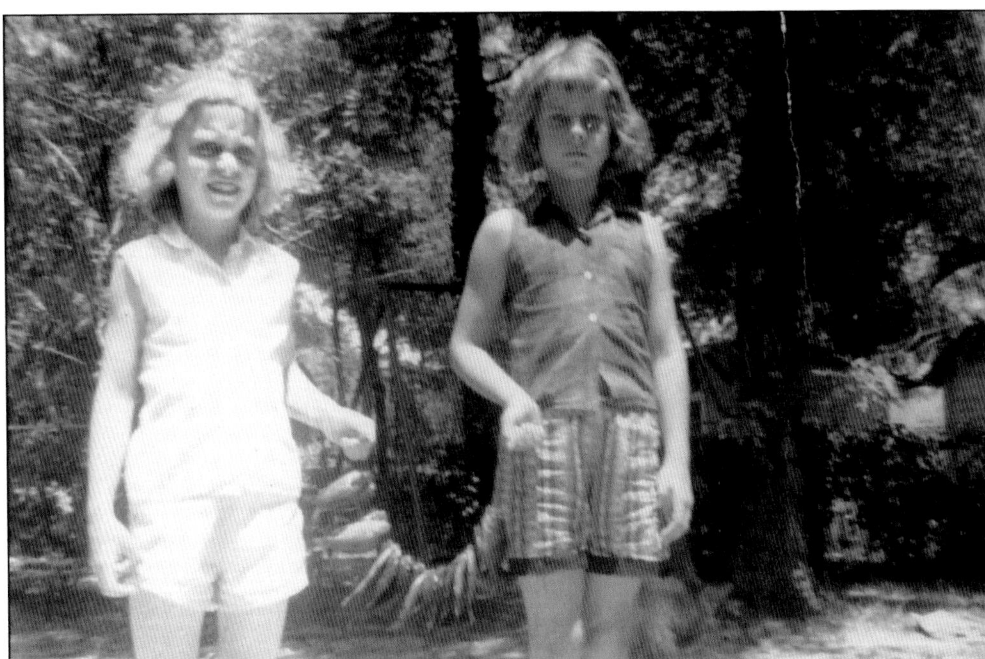

Debbie Craik and Roslyn Odum (Chandler) had a successful trip to Hentz Pond with Roslyn's dad, Robert Odum, in the summer of 1956.

The *Swamp Buggy* was built and later sold by none other than Otis Freeman in the early 1950s after he returned from World War II. This photo shows the edge of the Fourth Street Bridge (built in 1945) and the Colby Poultry office at the present site of the Bay County Correctional Institute. The home in the background with a car parked beside was inhabited by the man who read meters for Gulf Power. His wife was a Harden. (Courtesy Hellen Freeman.)

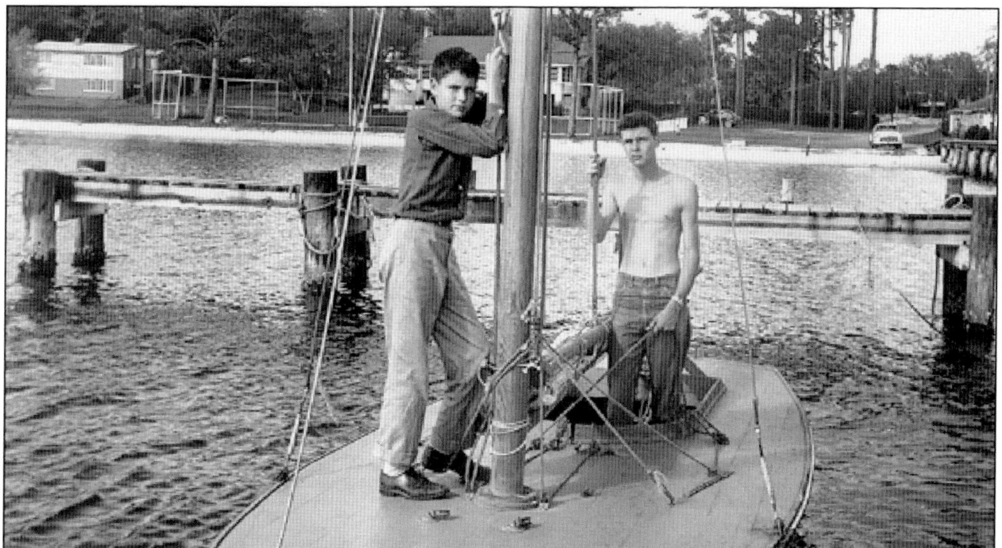

Elliott Smith and brother Mandeville Jr. are shown here on a fish class boat at the St. Andrews Bay Yacht Club in 1952. Some of the old barracks were still on the property from when it had been temporary housing for Tyndall during the early days of the airfield. Elliott moved north, and maintains a website devoted to his grandmother Martha Elliott's paintings. Mandeville stayed here and together with his wife, the former Eleanor Ann Sale, raised a wonderful family. (Courtesy Elliott Smith.)

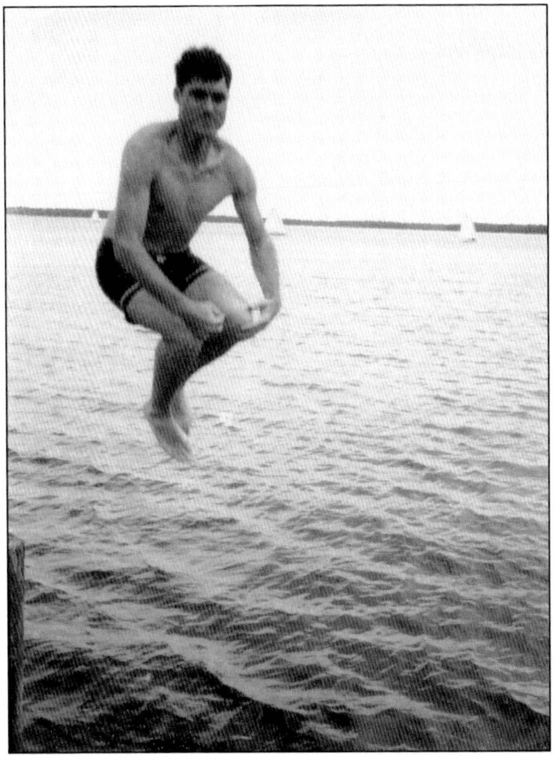

Jim Murfee jumps into the water at the Cove Hotel about 1958. (Courtesy Genear Murfee.)

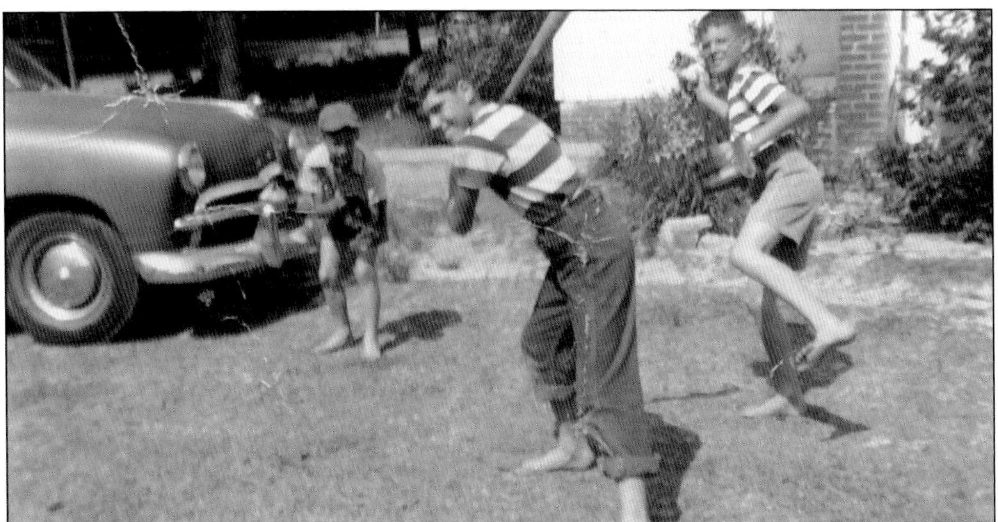

Mike Murfee, Jim Murfee and Spencer Cullen play ball in the early 1950s in front of the Murfee home on Second Street. (Courtesy Genear Murfee.)

Bill Thomas "drives" in the front yard of his parents, George and Dorothy's, home on First Court. His sister had not come along yet. (Courtesy Dorothy Thomas.)

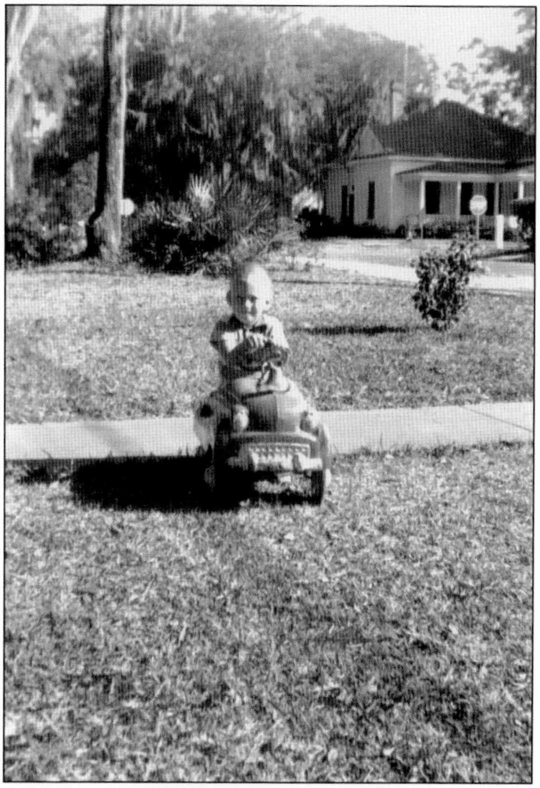

Kermit, George, and Mark Thomas are photographed after another successful turkey shoot in the 1950s. In the background from left to right are the home where the Cooks had lived in the early part of the century, the Noah Thomas home, and the Caswell Brewton home, which was later turned into apartments and still stands. (Courtesy Mr. and Mrs. George Thomas.)

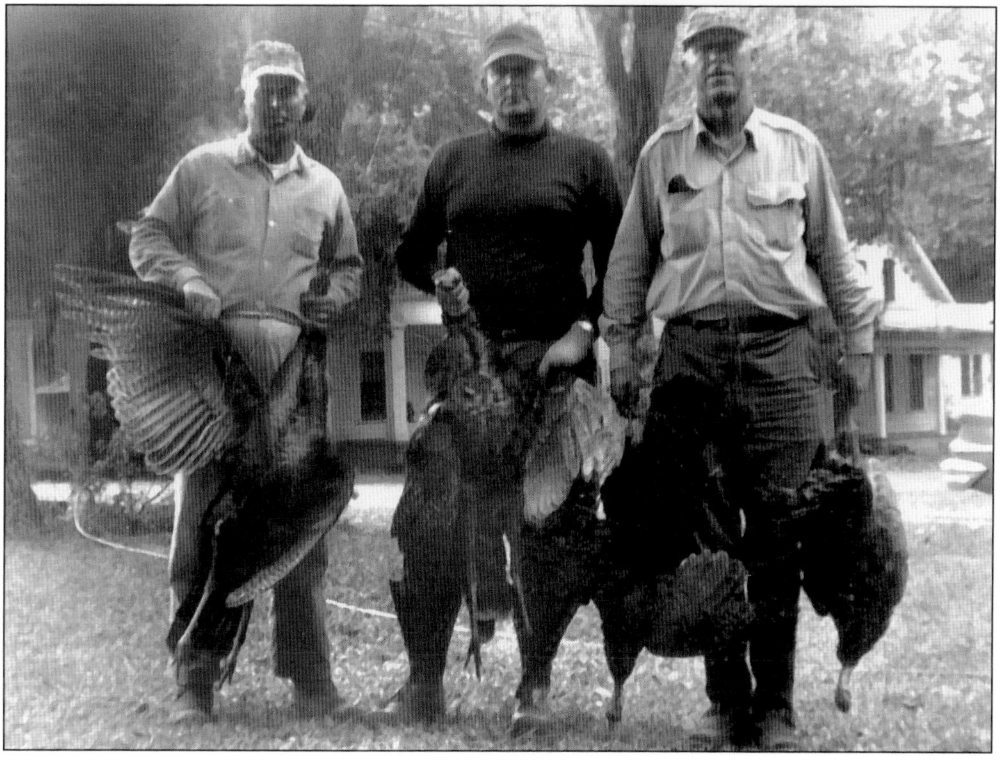

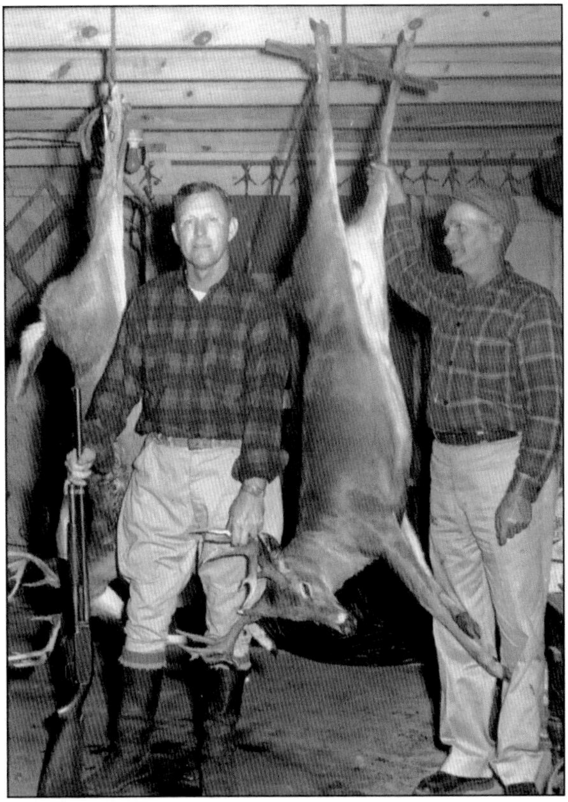

Mark Thomas and a hunting buddy are shown with two handsome bucks in the Thomas's garage. The other part of the garage housed Mrs. Thomas's kindergarten in the 1950s. (Courtesy Sarah Grace Thomas.)

Harry Thomas proudly displays a turkey in his mother's living room at 227 First Court in the mid-1960s. This was not the first wildlife Harry brought indoors. When he was younger, Harry's mother was in his room and noticed a rustling noise. She flipped up the bed skirt and found one snake, in a gallon jar with holes punched in the lid for air; one mallard duck with an injured wing; and three baby squirrels. Of course father Mark (see page 80) was able to find room for them in the garage, except the squirrels, which were allowed to remain until they destroyed the curtains in Harry's room. (Courtesy Sarah Grace Thomas.)

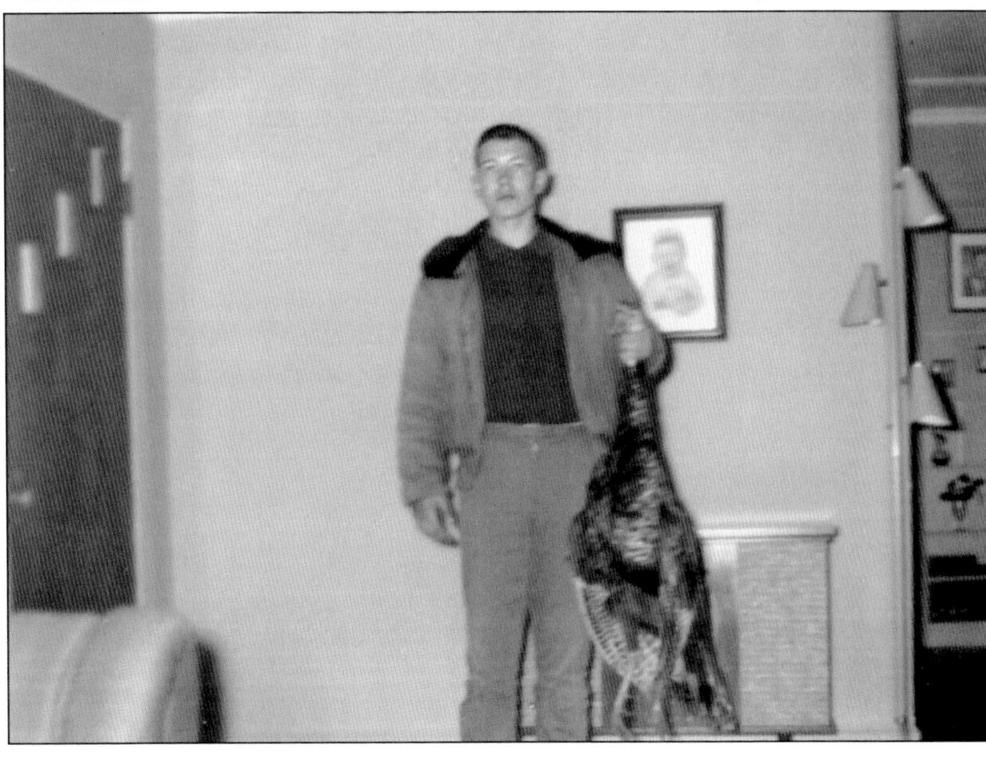

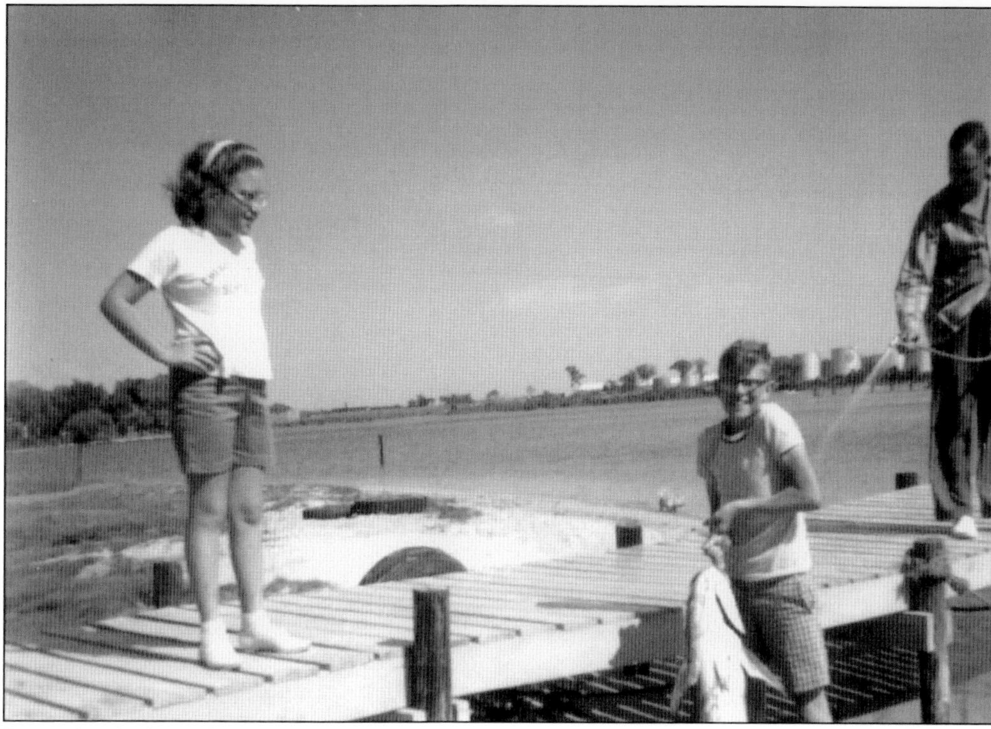

From the dock at their home on DeWitt, Judy Nixon (Dessault) and Dr. Nixon eyeball Bob Nixon's catch in the early 1960s. (Courtesy BND.)

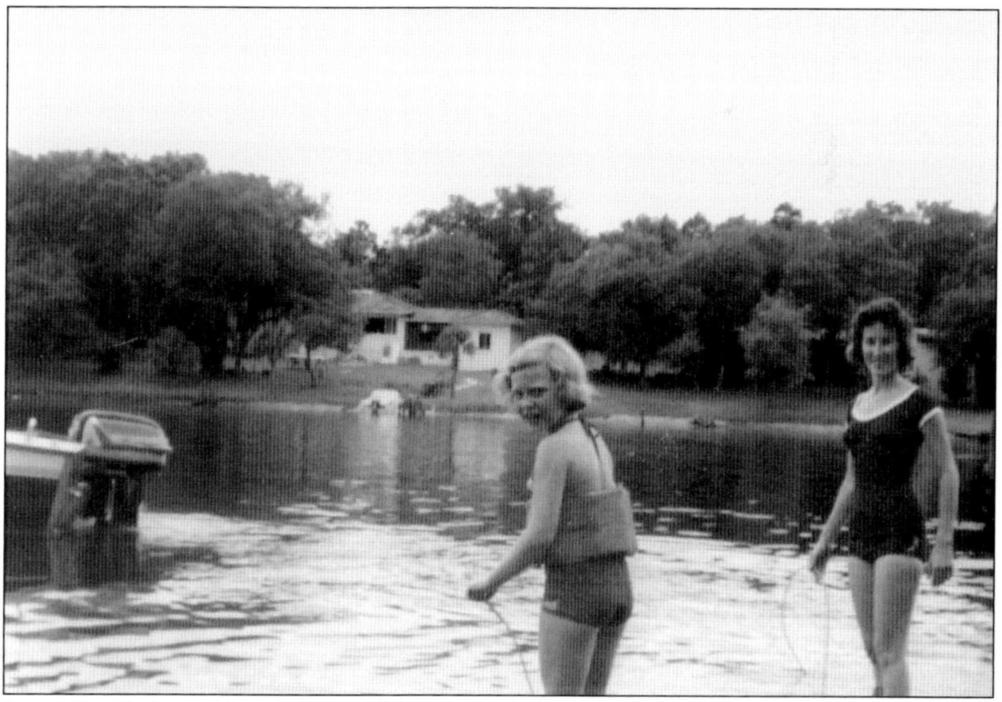

In 1959, Barbara Nixon (Dessault) gets her first skiing lesson from neighbor Marsha Wengrow (Weil.)

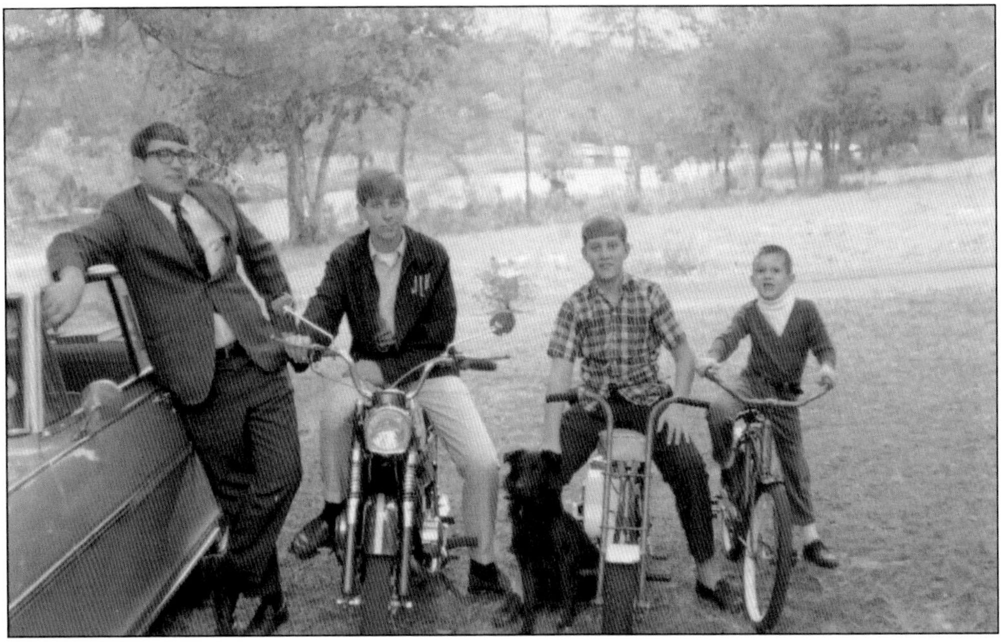

Hank Lawrence designed attractive photo Christmas cards of his family every year "until the boys' hair got too long!" Here they stood each with his vehicle of choice against an undeveloped Harris Avenue in about 1967. From left to right are Henry, Jimmy, Bobby, and Tommy. (Courtesy Hank Lawrence.)

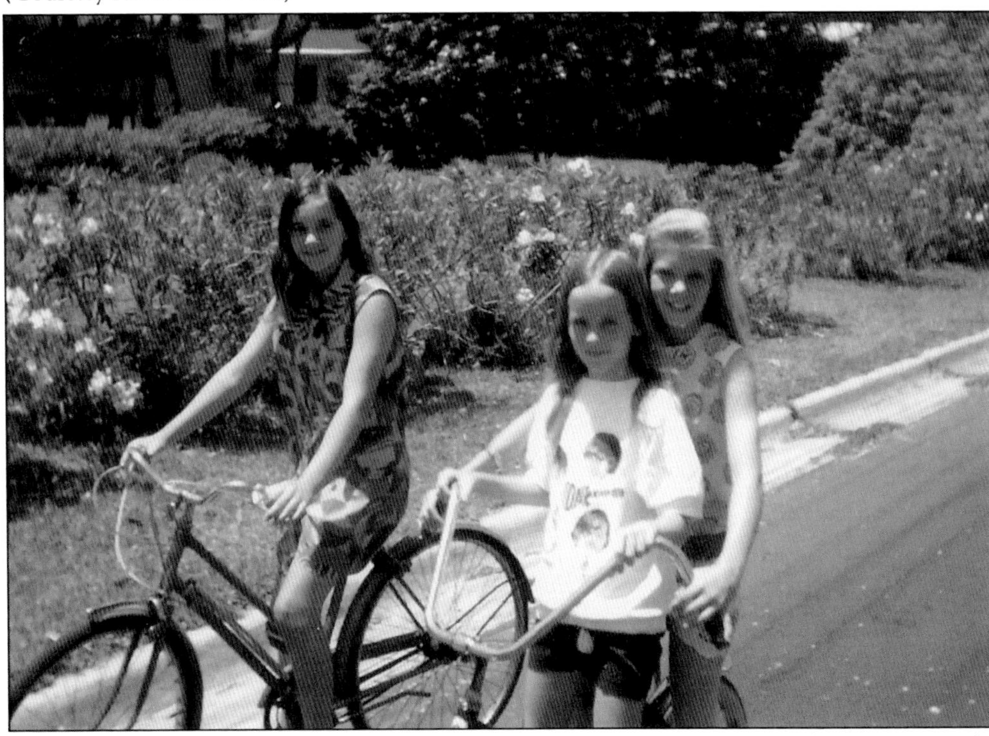

Andrea Harper, Sealy Harris, and Beth Hutt are on their Schwinns on Hollis Avenue in the late 1960s. (Courtesy SHL.)

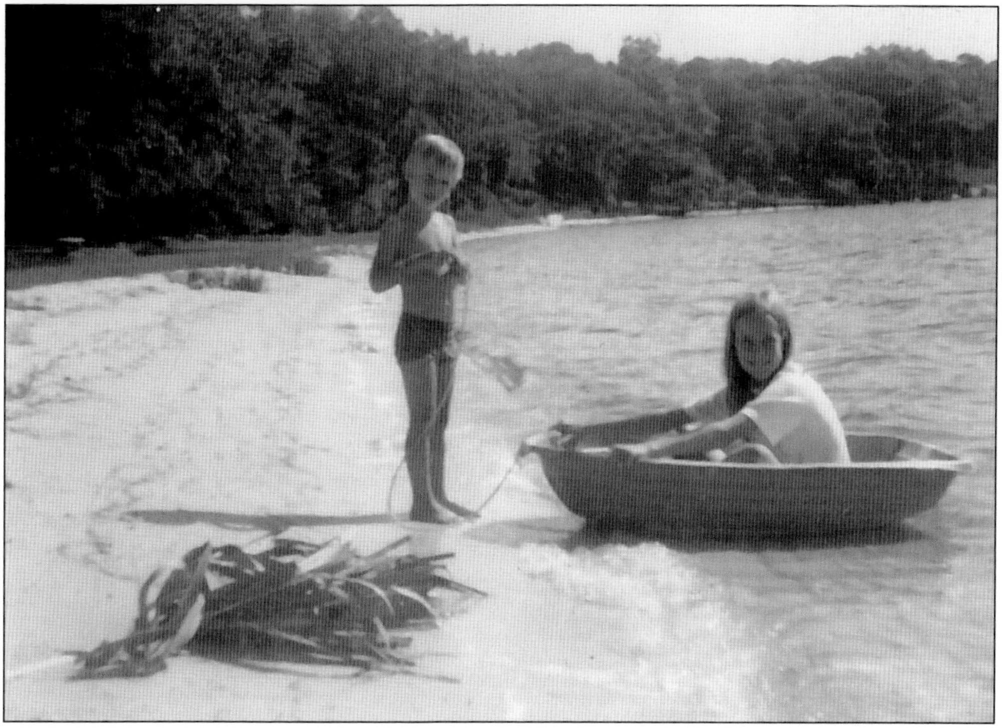

Joseph Wittmeier and Sealy Harris play in the water at Allen Avenue in 1970.

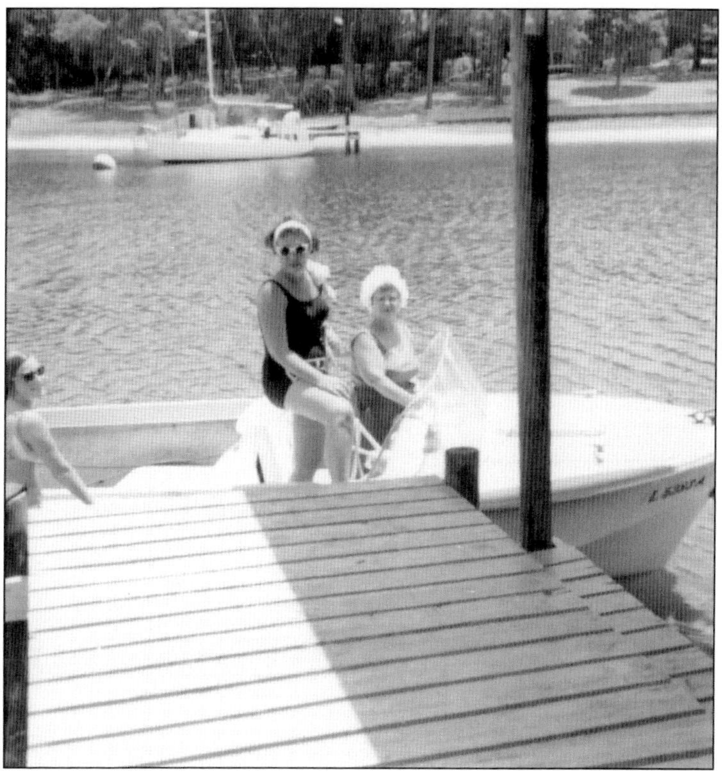

Moored at the Nixon's dock are Beverly, Florence Nixon, and her mother, Nell Aldrege, in 1967. (Courtesy BND.)

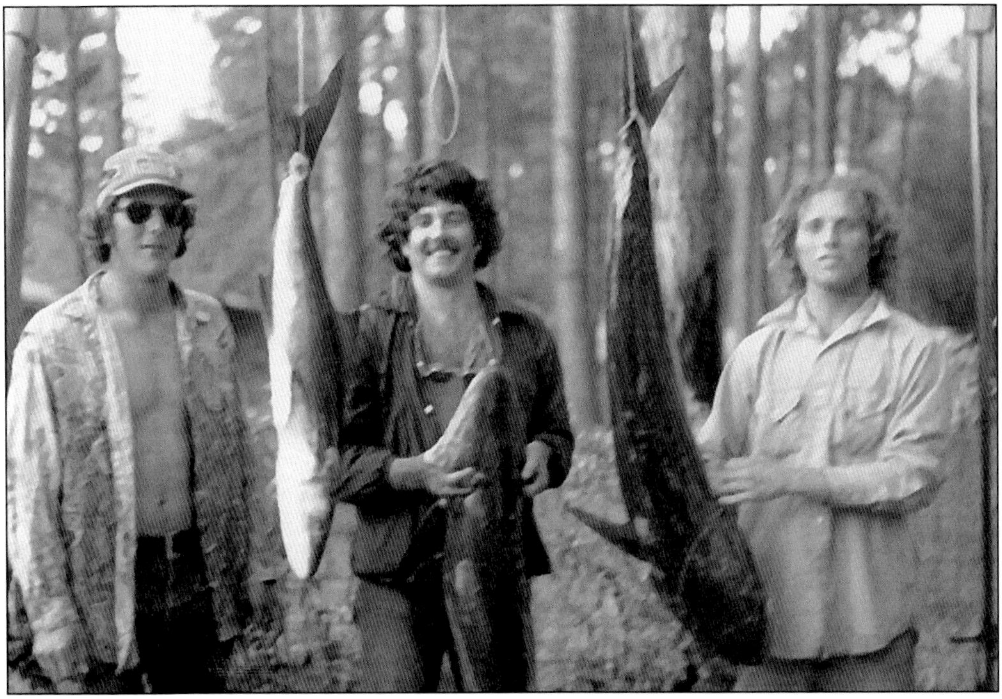

A great day fishing was enjoyed by Mark Cooper, Lawrence Ducate, and Norvin Thibodaux in 1976. (Courtesy SHL.)

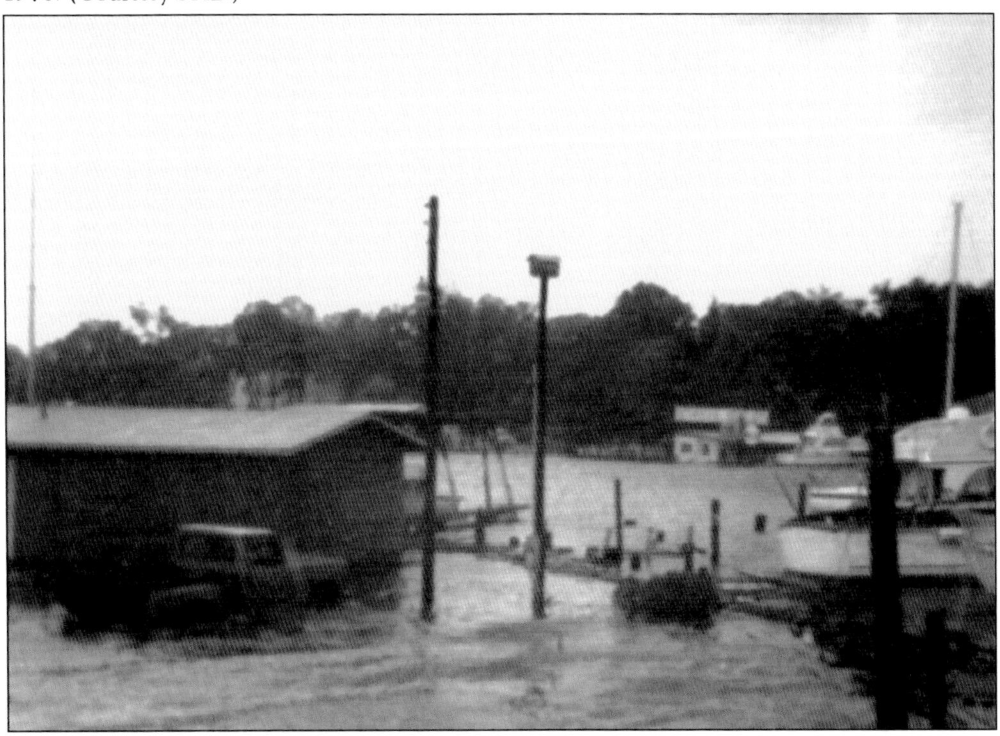

A not-so-great day for anything at Tarpon Dock was photographed during a 1970s storm. (Courtesy Jane Powell Tweedy.)

Six

CLUBS AND PARTIES

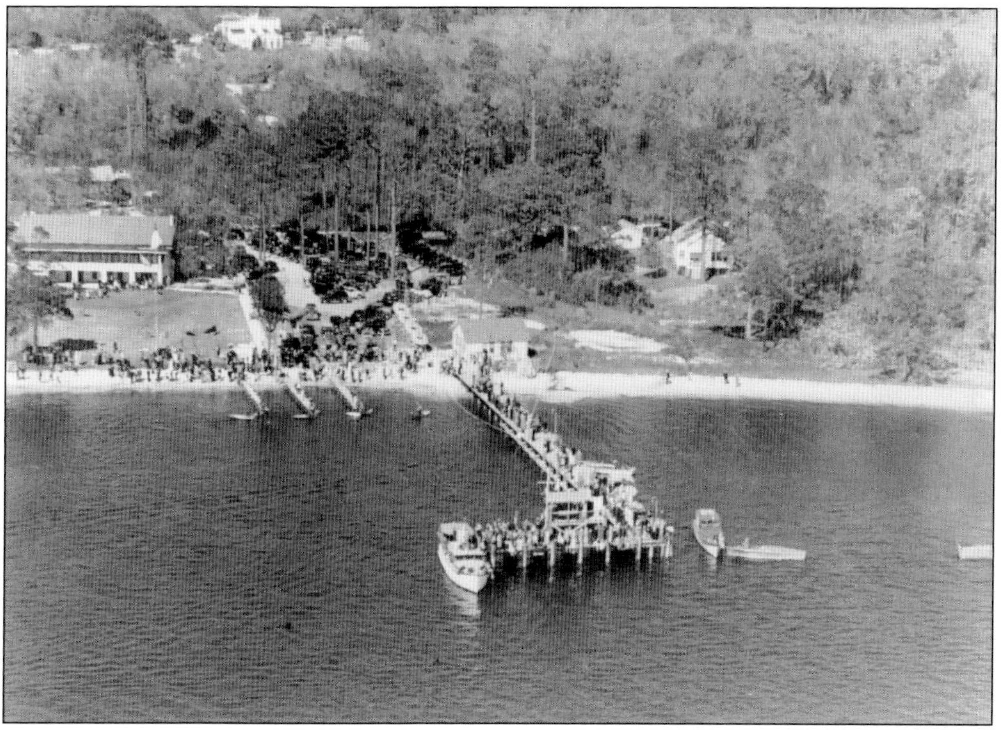

This is an aerial photo of the St. Andrews Bay Yacht Club in the 1930s. The DeWitt home, on what is now DeWitt Street, was the only other prominent structure. Mr. DeWitt covered the Spanish-American War and owned a newspaper in the North, where the family spent most of the year. He was said to be able to walk out one door to the golf course and out the other to the yacht club. (Courtesy Janis FitzSimons.)

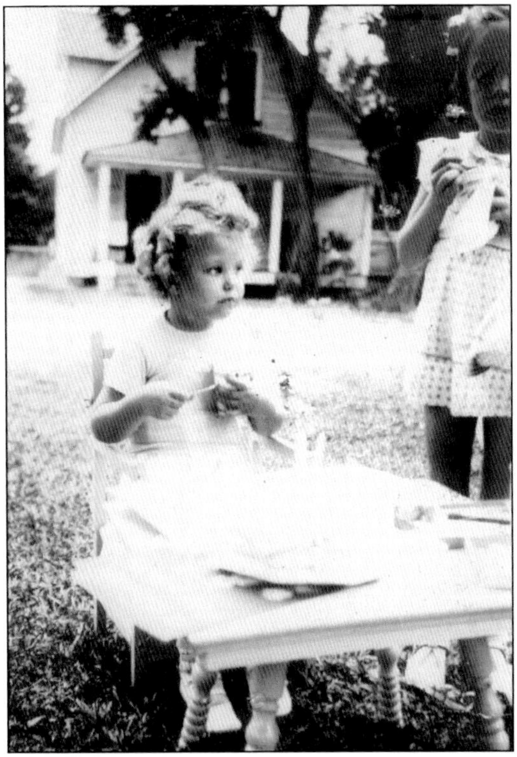

Little Miss Ruthie Howell celebrates a birthday in her front yard on Olive Street in 1942. In the background is the M.L. Harmon house, which was built, according to Dewey Smith, in 1908. "Lamp" (as Mr. Harmon was known) was the first city marshal. Lighting the kerosene street lamps in Panama City was one of his duties. (Courtesy RHH.)

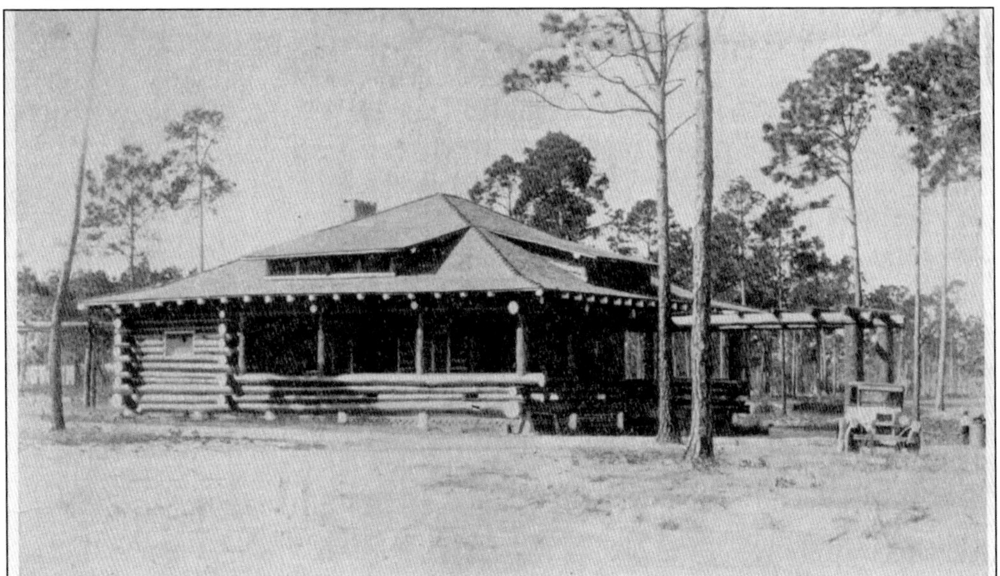

Club House, Panama, City, Fla.

This is the Cove Country Club clubhouse shown on a 1920s postcard. The property now occupied by an apartment building and Cove Shopping Center was once the golf course. The course was defunct by the 1930s, but the cabin, made from trees cut on site, lived on as a home for the dramatic arts, as well as a dance studio, until the building was replaced by Cove Shopping Center, built by Lester Jinks in the early 1950s. (Courtesy Mr. and Mrs. George Thomas.)

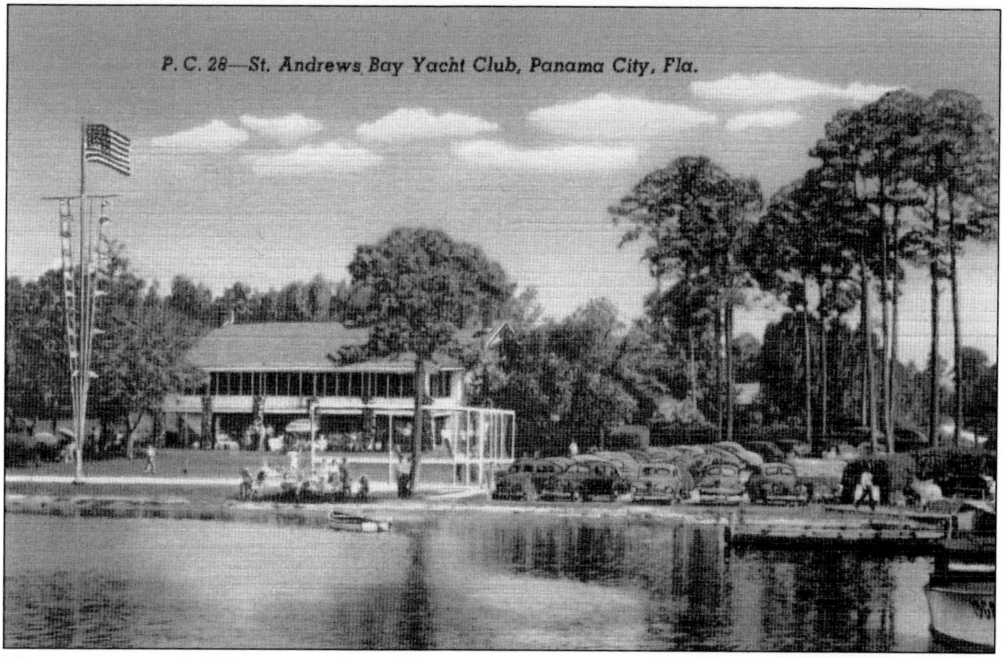

This is a postcard of the St. Andrews Bay Yacht Club. The yacht club was established in 1933 and has regularly participated in world-class events. (Courtesy Janice FitzSimons.)

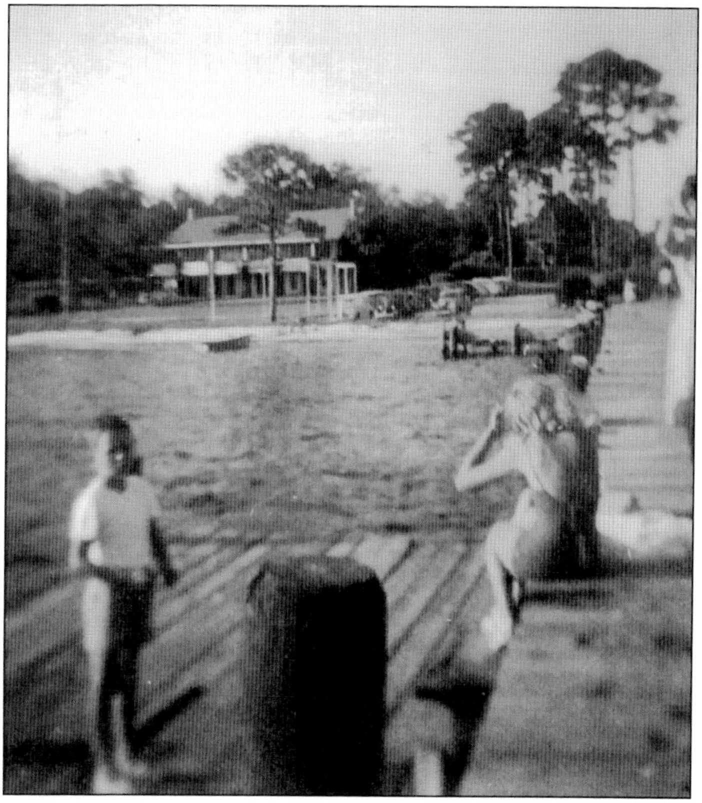

This view is from the pier toward the St. Andrews Yacht Club, taken in the 1940s. (Courtesy Carl Bennett.)

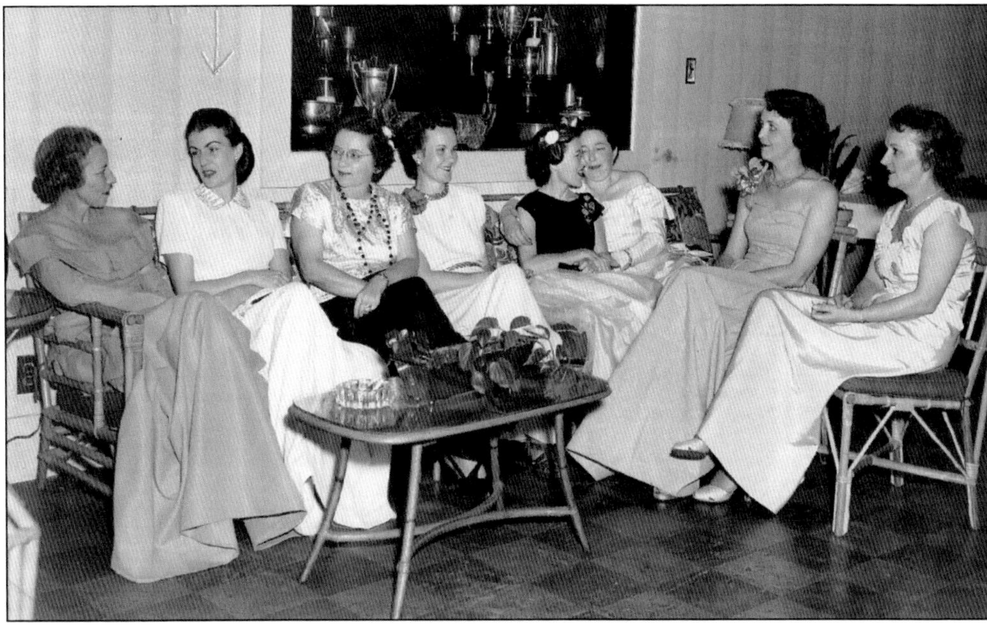

Formally attired ladies rest at a party at STABYC. From left to right are unidentified, Mary Bell Browne, Helen Kruse, two unidentified, Stella Barefield, Lois Smith, and unidentified.

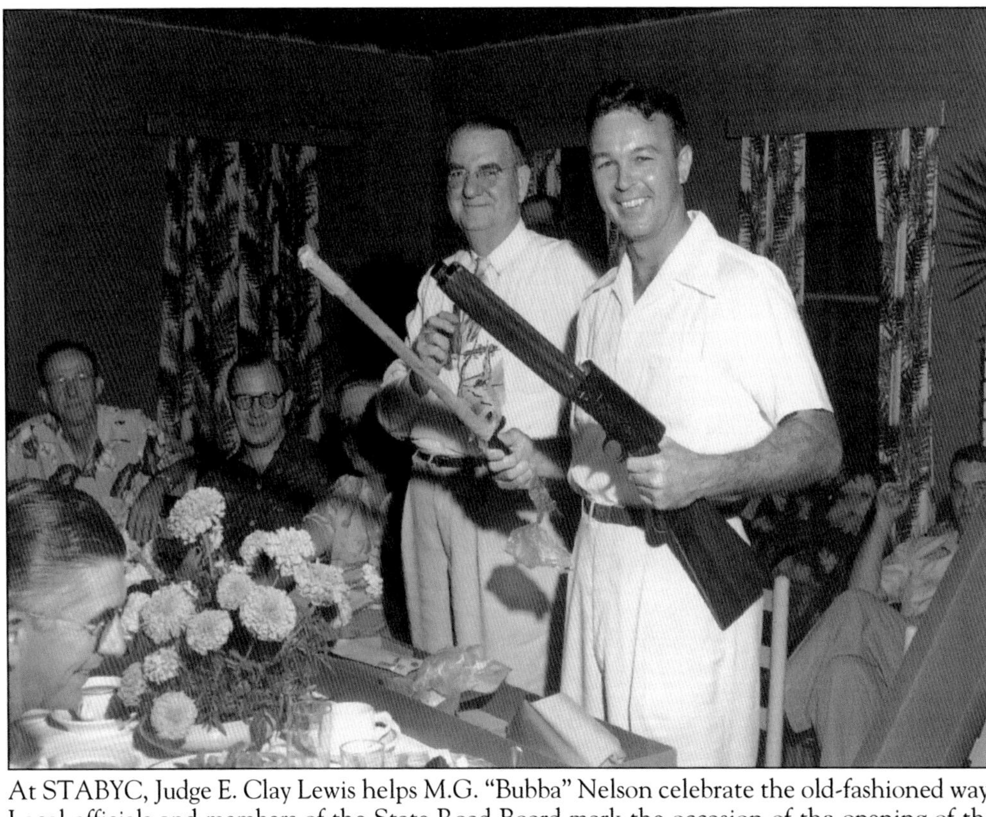

At STABYC, Judge E. Clay Lewis helps M.G. "Bubba" Nelson celebrate the old-fashioned way. Local officials and members of the State Road Board mark the occasion of the opening of the new Frank Nelson Sr. Bridge in 1951. (Courtesy Sara Grace Thomas.)

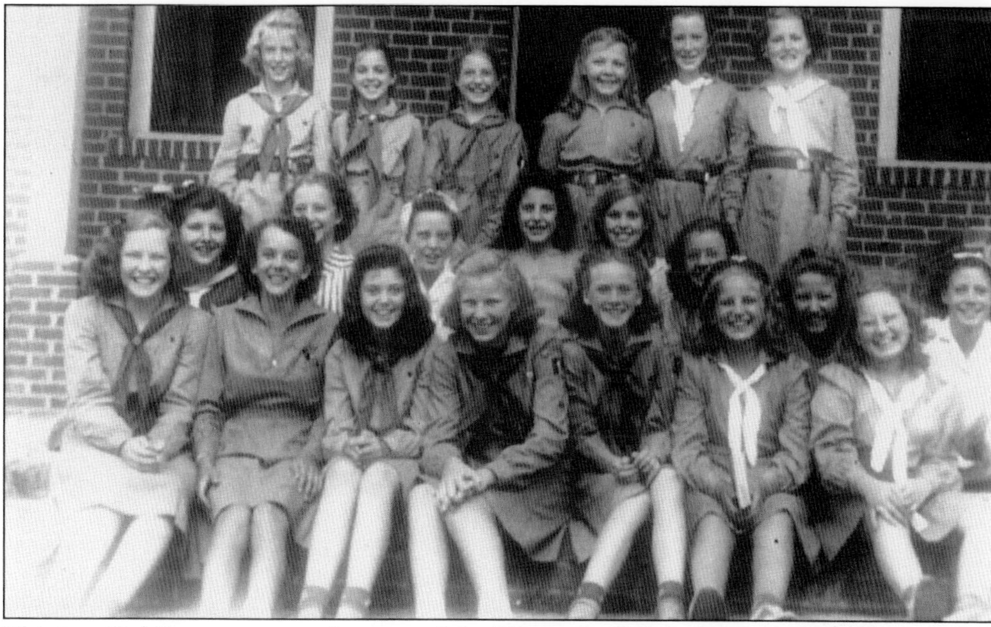

This is a Girl Scout troop on the steps of the Women's Club building on Cove Boulevard in 1942. H.L. Sudduth offered three lots to the Women's Club after the group sold their bayfront building to the Elks Club in 1935. The present building dates from 1936, but has undergone several expansions. The scouts are, from left to right, (front row) Helen Harrison, Jan Morgan, Glen Wilson, Martha Still, Betty Earle Van Horn, Jane Becker, and Anna Glen Robertson; (middle row) Louise Davison, Imma Ruth Lindsey, Marjorie Williams, Betty Anne Wamble, Ada Herman Perkins, Jo Carolyn Campbell, Audry Wiselogel, and Ann Everett; (back row) Angeline Russ, Joan Wilson, Virginia Dennis, Lora Harrison, Katherine Holland, and Annie Jane Milton. (Courtesy Jane Becker, BCPLLHC.)

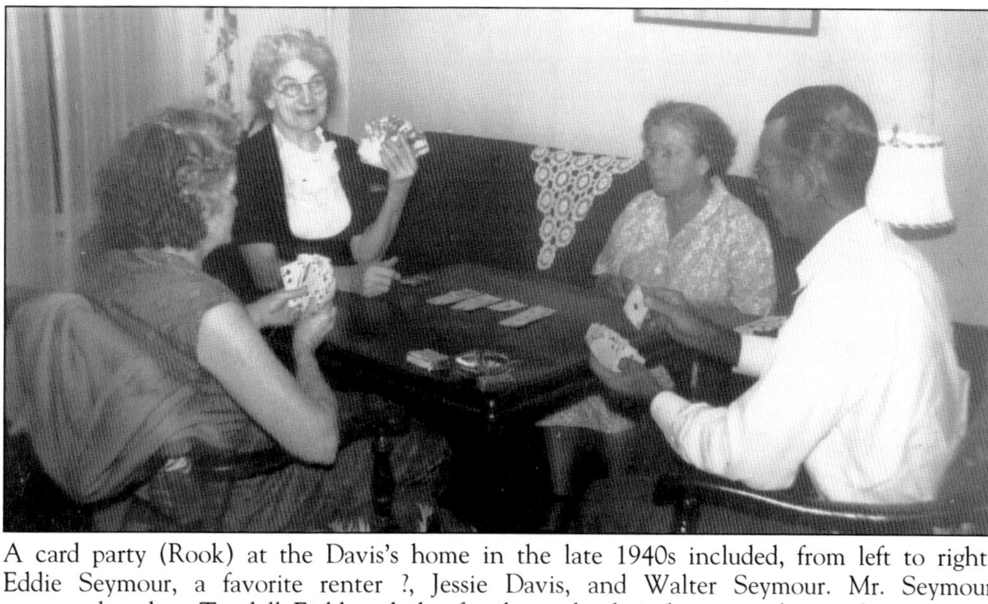

A card party (Rook) at the Davis's home in the late 1940s included, from left to right, Eddie Seymour, a favorite renter ?, Jessie Davis, and Walter Seymour. Mr. Seymour was employed at Tyndall Field and the family made their home at the southeast corner of Harmon and Second Place.

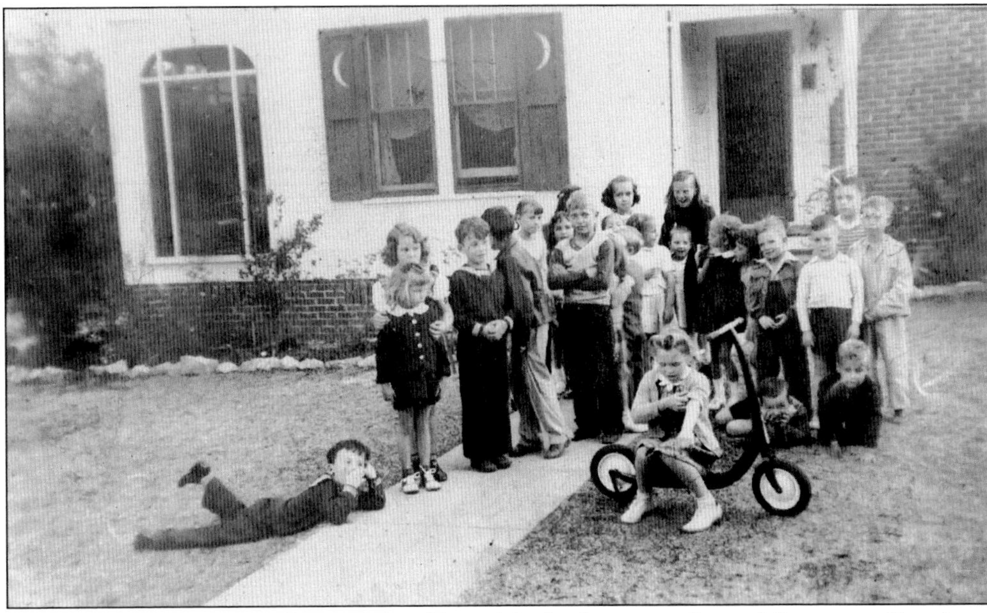

In this 1946 gathering in front of the Glenn Murfee home on Second Street, or "Incubator Avenue" as it had been referred to for obvious reasons, Charles and Pete Williams are the boys wearing sailor suits, Barbara Mullins sits on her scooter, and Glenda Goodson is the tallest in the picture, wearing a dark dress. (Courtesy Genear Murfee.)

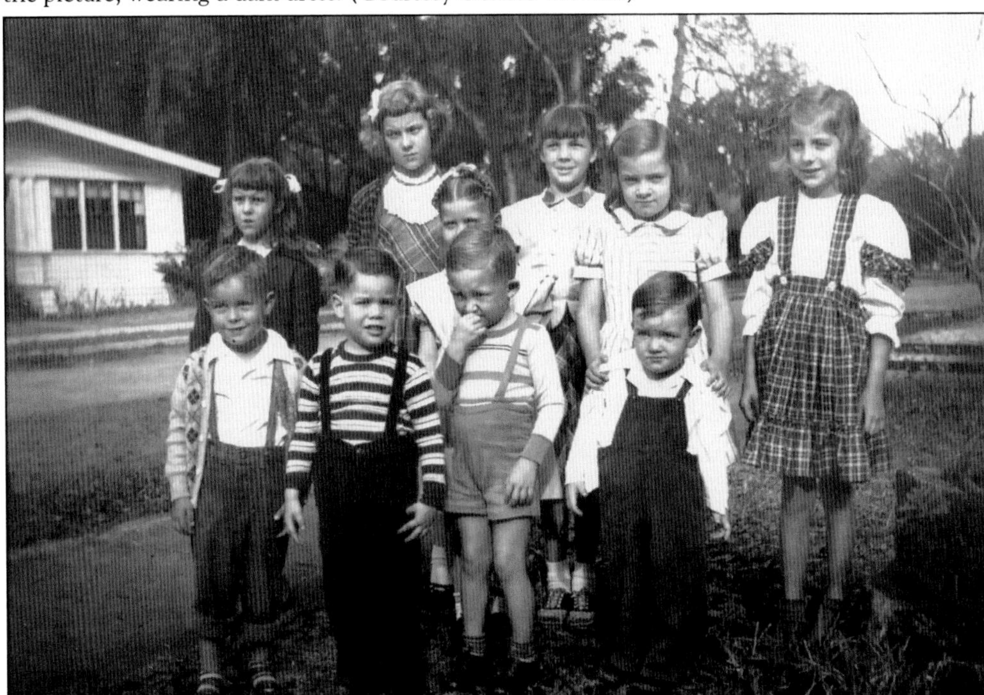

This is Bobby Davis's birthday party in 1949. The guests are, from left to right, (front row) Lewis Howell, Bobby Davis, unidentified, and Mike Hobbs; (back row) Marie Howell, Ruthie Howell, ? Zelm, Carol Seymour, unidentified, and Wanda Harmon. (Courtesy CD.)

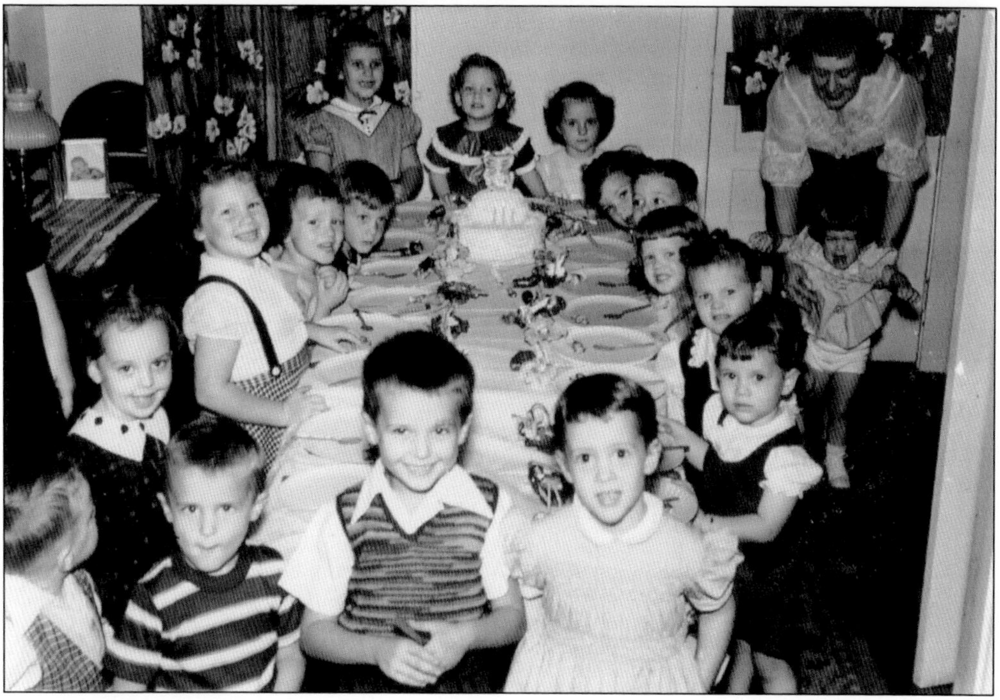

Now we know why they called them the Baby Boom generation! This is Beverly Nixon's third birthday in 1953 at her home on MacArthur Avenue. (Courtesy Beverly Nixon Dessault.)

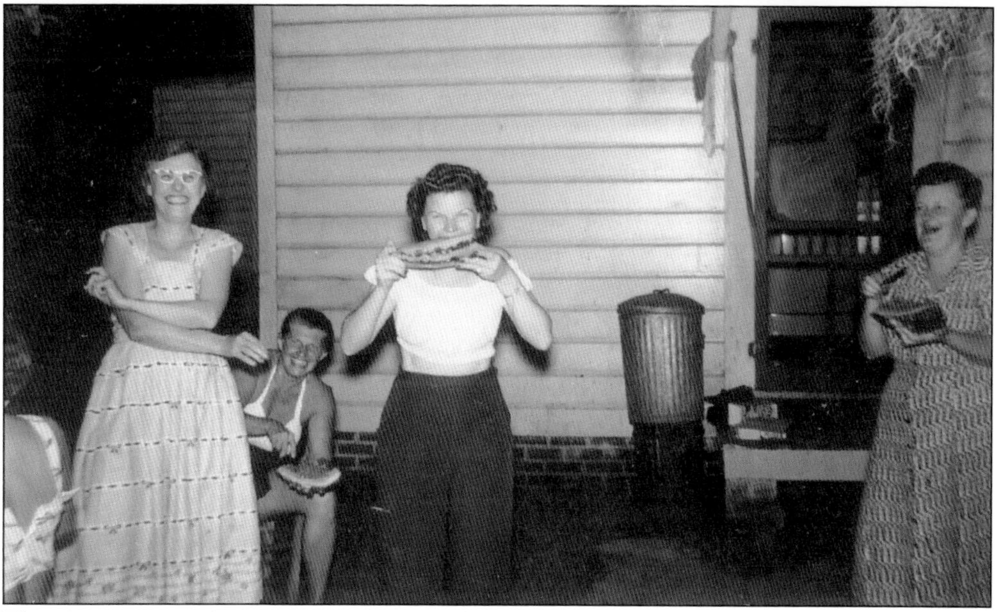

The "Come as You Are Party" was very popular in the 1950s. Homemakers would phone a group of "girls" or simply drive to their home and "kidnap" them. The partygoers would have to attend just as they were dressed at the time they were called upon. Here are members of the Rebecca's, a church group, at the back of Pastel Allan's home at East Second Place. The Mitchell Harrises live here now. From left to right are Effie White (standing), Marty Douglas, Clarice Davis (with watermelon), and unidentified. (Courtesy Mrs. L.M. Harden.)

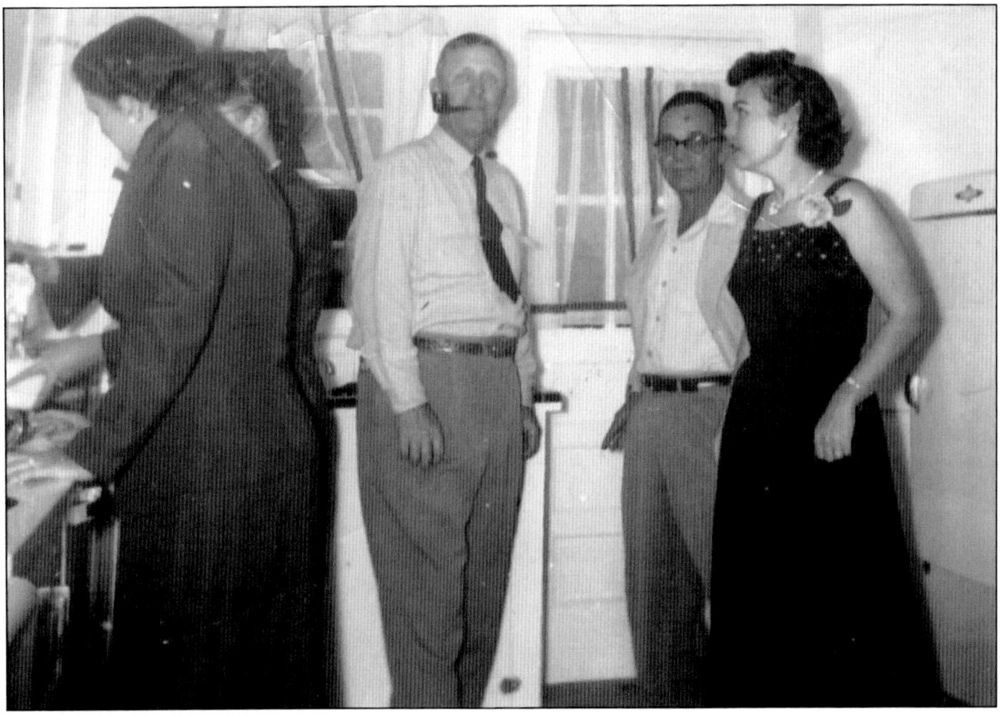

Every good party ends up in the kitchen, such as this one at the home of Mark and Sarah Grace Thomas at 227 First Court in the 1950s. From left to right are unidentified, Thelma Knowles, Mark Thomas, Frank Knowles, and Sarah Grace Thomas.

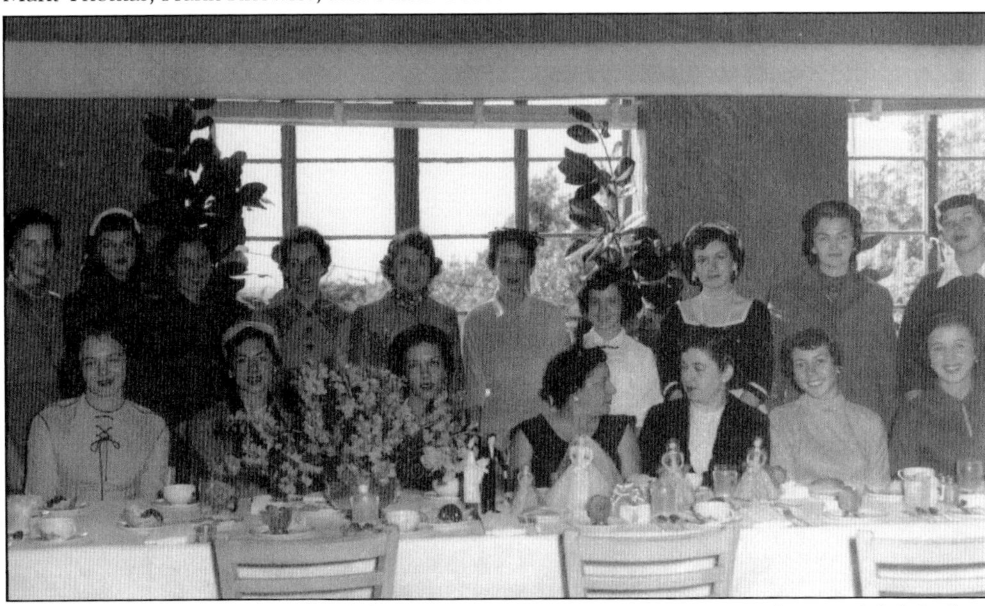

Several Cove ladies, members of the Junior Service League, prepare to drive to Mobile for a Children's Theatre conference. The Junior Service League was founded in Panama City in 1951 and has served the area since through events such as Holly Fair and children's clothing distribution. Pictured are Mrs. U.J.W. (Lucy) Peters, Mrs. A.M. Lewis Jr., Mrs. William Cook Jr., and Mrs. Frank Z. Jemison.

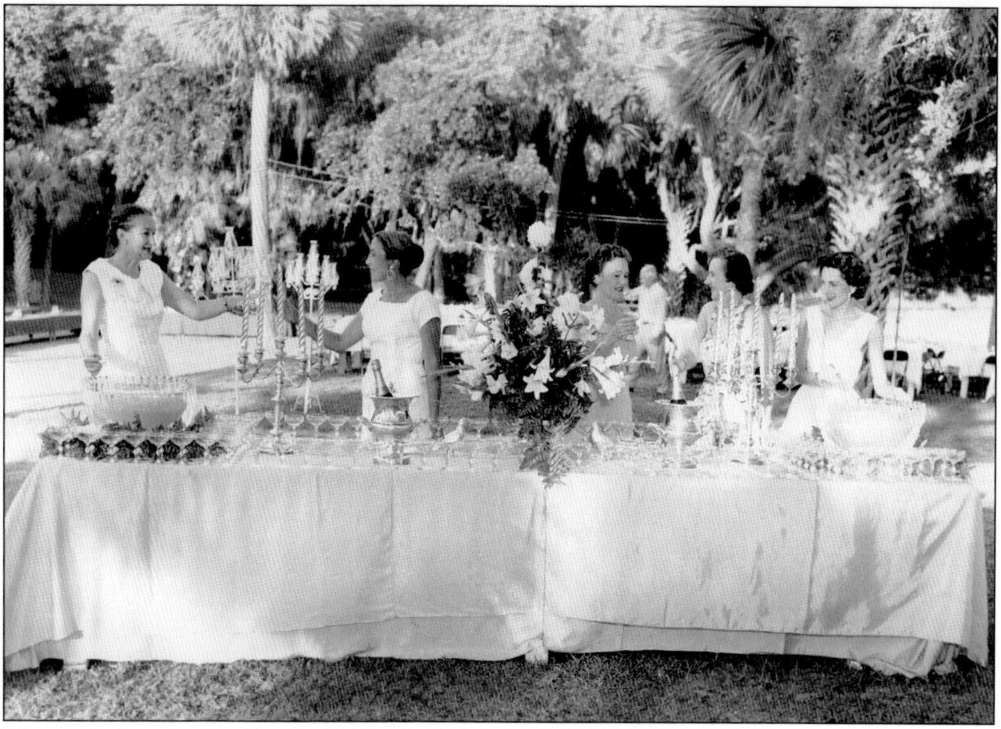

Elegant ladies prepare for the Banker's Banquet. Ruby Harris gave these on the lawn of the Cove Hotel for several years during the 1950s. (Courtesy SHL.)

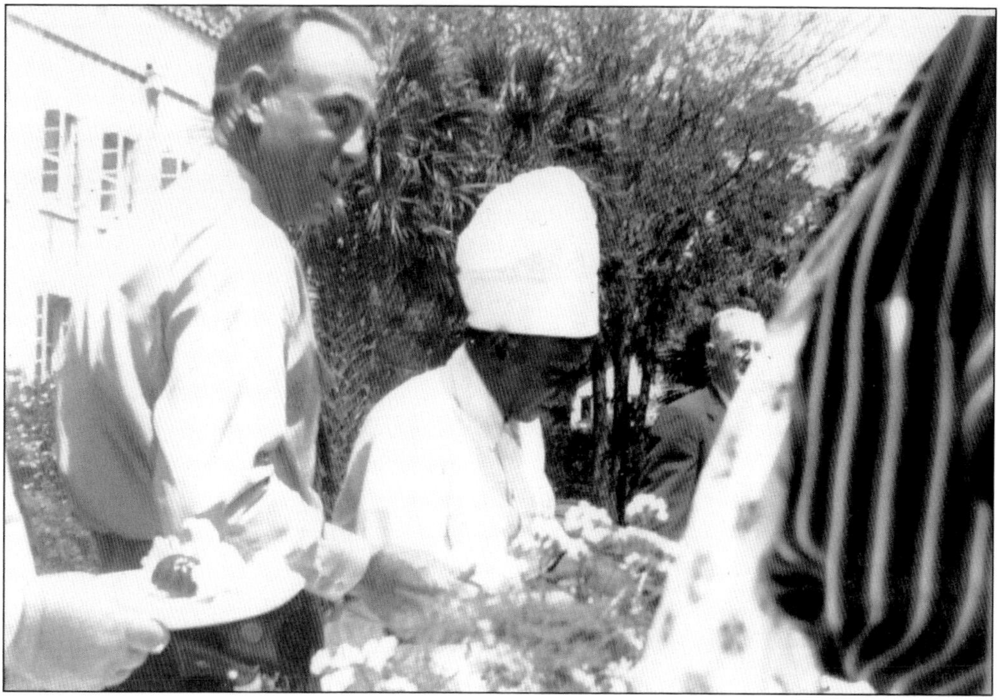

Sam Jones worked at the Cove Hotel for many years. Here, he presides over a Banker's Banquet. (Courtesy SHL.)

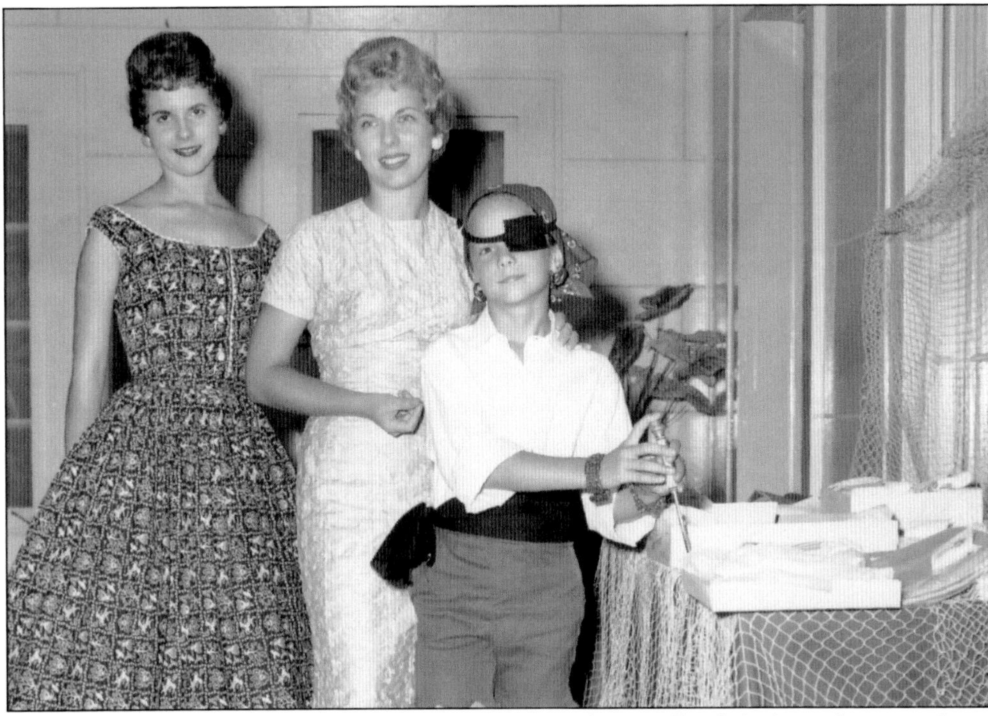

In an attempt to capture young Gwen's interest, Mrs. Sidney Daffin, left, devised a pirate theme for a bridal party she held in honor of Miss Ruth Howell, center. Gwen Howell is on the right. (Courtesy RHH.)

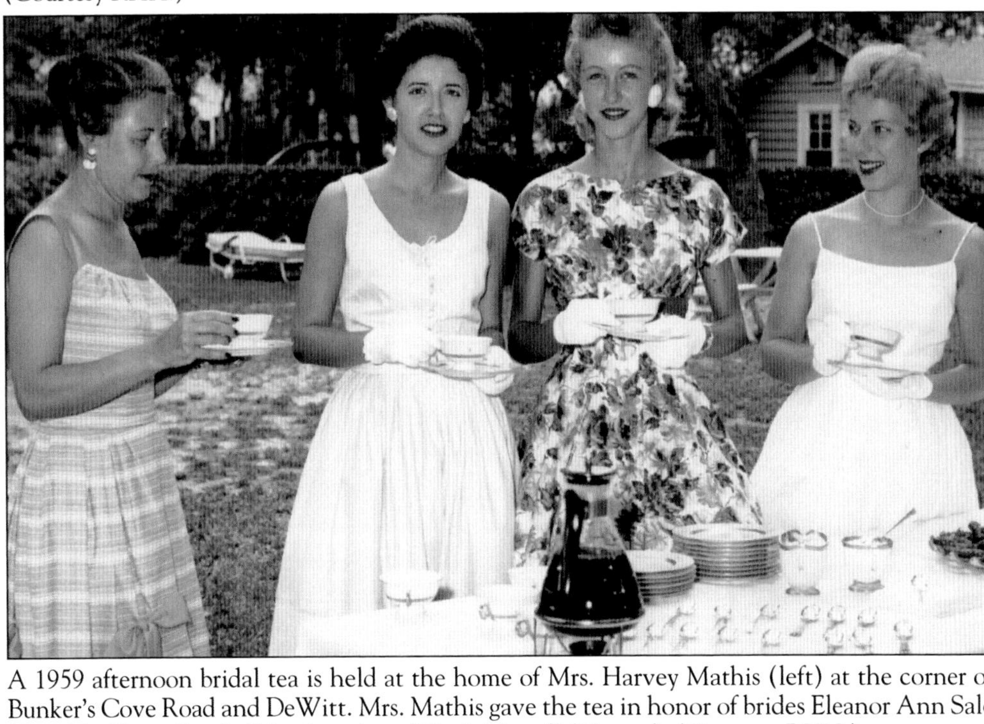

A 1959 afternoon bridal tea is held at the home of Mrs. Harvey Mathis (left) at the corner of Bunker's Cove Road and DeWitt. Mrs. Mathis gave the tea in honor of brides Eleanor Ann Sale (Smith), Claire Smith (Merchant), and Ruth Howell (Hauser). (Courtesy RHH.)

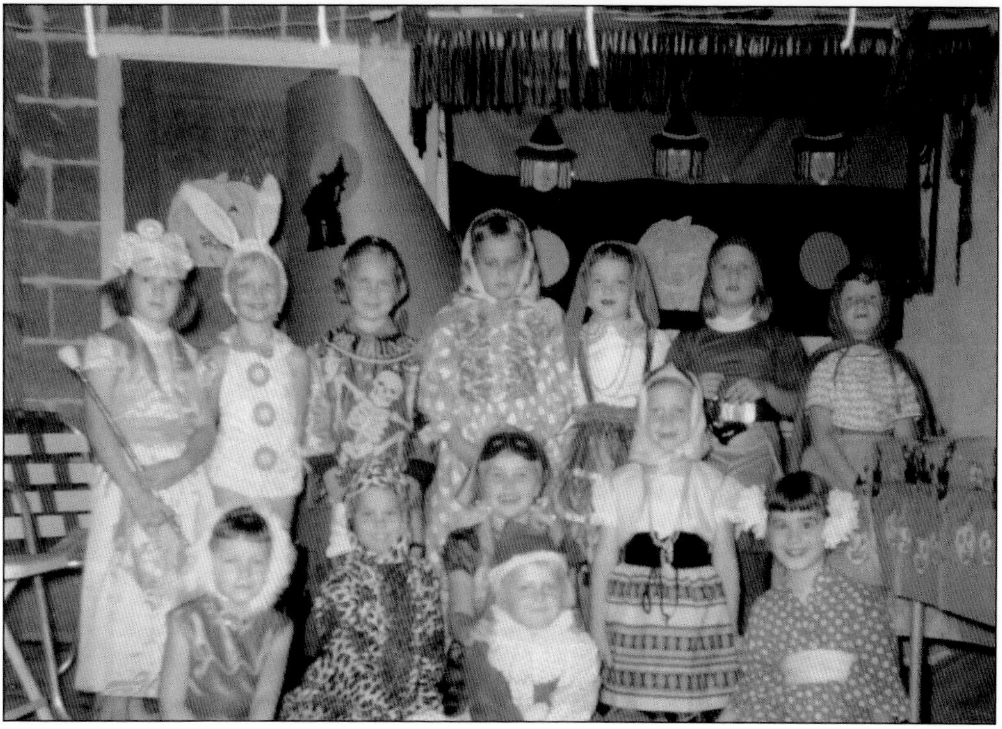

Halloween can still be fun in The Cove when you know your neighbors. This late 1950s group showed off their costumes for the camera. Cheryl Wainwright was the leopard and Karen Wainwright O'Keefe was the clown. (Courtesy Karen Wainwright O'Keefe.)

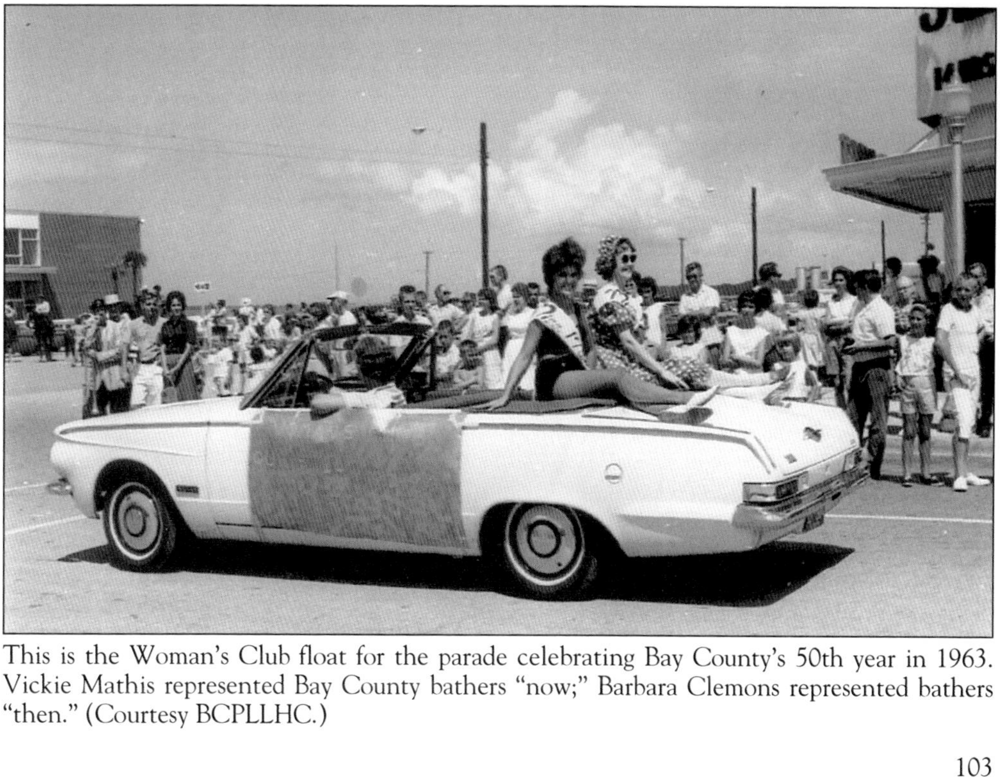

This is the Woman's Club float for the parade celebrating Bay County's 50th year in 1963. Vickie Mathis represented Bay County bathers "now;" Barbara Clemons represented bathers "then." (Courtesy BCPLLHC.)

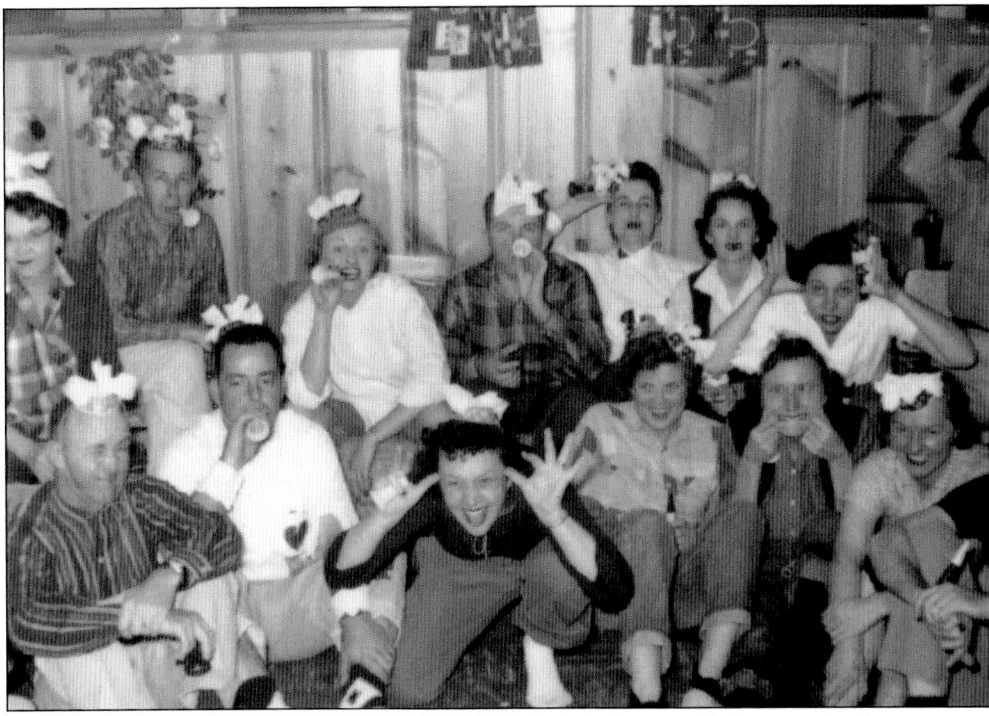

Flo Nixon loved to entertain. A typical fun-loving group wears silly hats in the downstairs of the Nixon house on DeWitt Street on New Year's Eve in 1959. (Courtesy BND.)

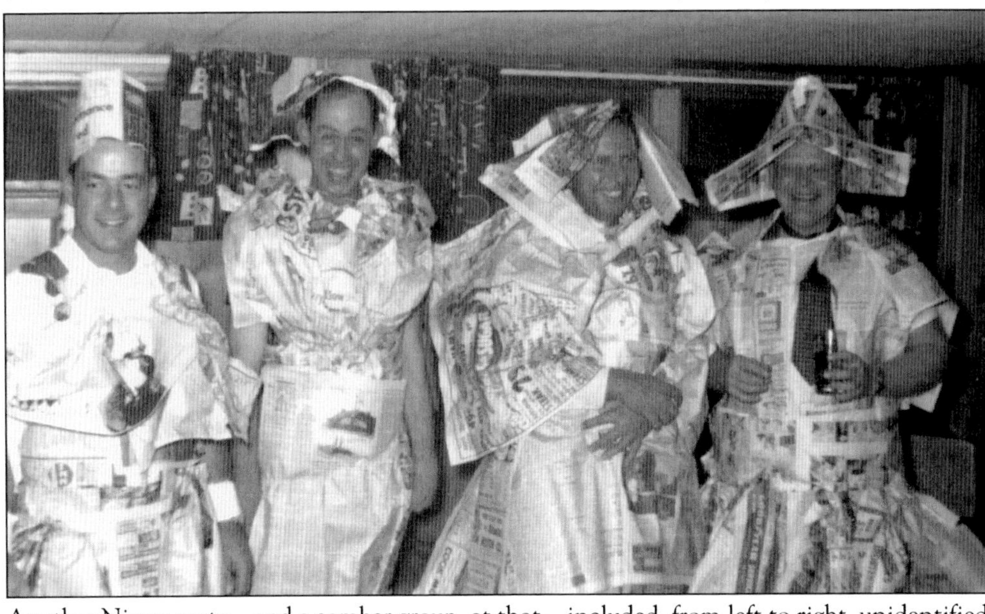

Another Nixon party—and a somber group, at that—included, from left to right, unidentified, Fred Turner, unidentified, and Miller Epps. Mr. (later judge) Turner would make quite a different impression several years later. The landmark 1963 Supreme Court case *Gideon v. Wainwright* had its beginnings in Bay County. When the Supreme Court ruled that indigent felony defendants must have defense council at public expense, Fred Turner represented Gideon at the retrial and won an acquittal. (Courtesy BND.)

This is the cover of the 1952 St. Andrews Bay Jr. Yacht Club Membership directory. (Courtesy SBC.)

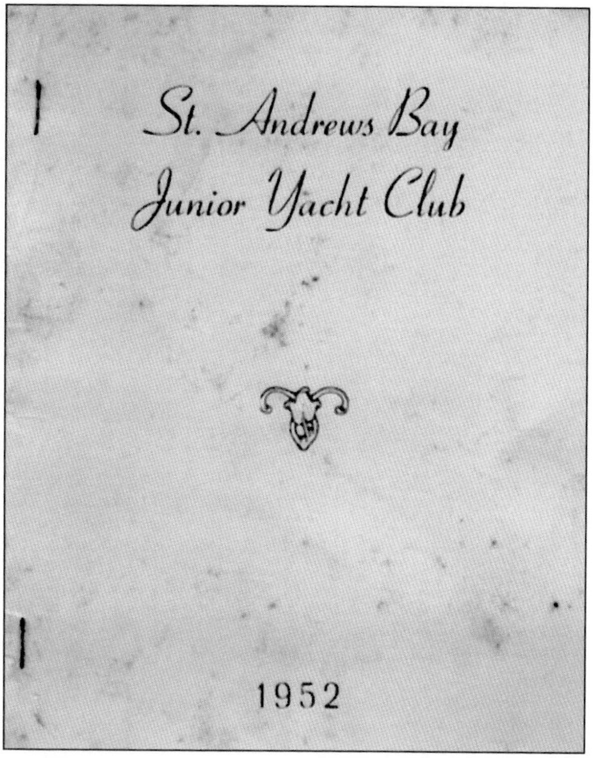

Off to the Jr. Yacht Club party in 1961 are, from left to right, Paul Cieielski, Beverly Nixon, and Bobby Nixon. (Courtesy BND.)

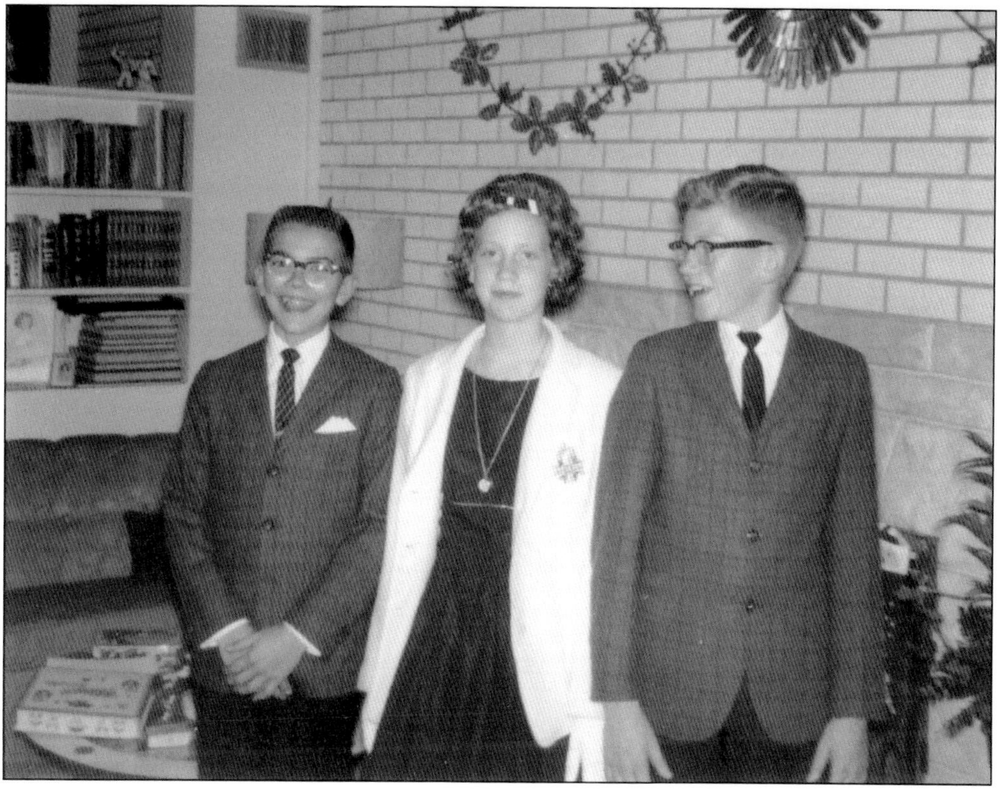

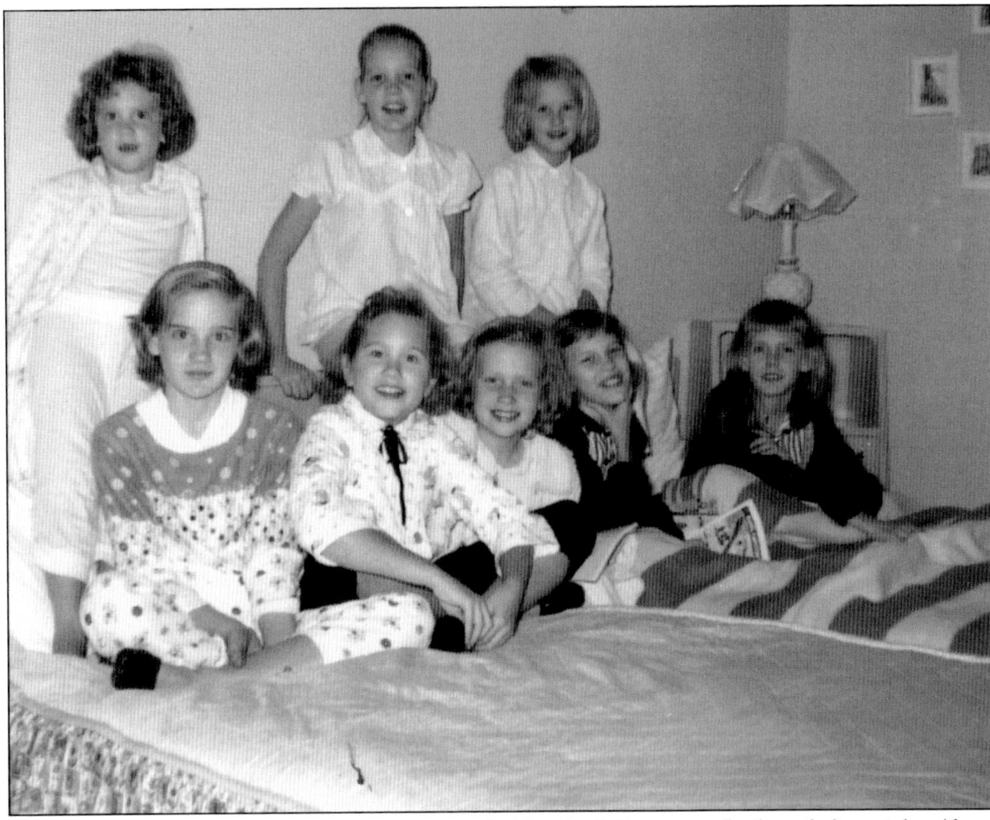

A third-grade slumber party in 1960 was attended by the following girls, from left to right: (front row) Cissy Daffin, Ann Kruse (Percival), Beverly Nixon, Shirley Rowell (Ramsey), and Martha Wadell; (back row) Judy Nixon (Dessault), Wanda Allen (Emblom), and Kathy Ullman (Barr). (Courtesy BND.)

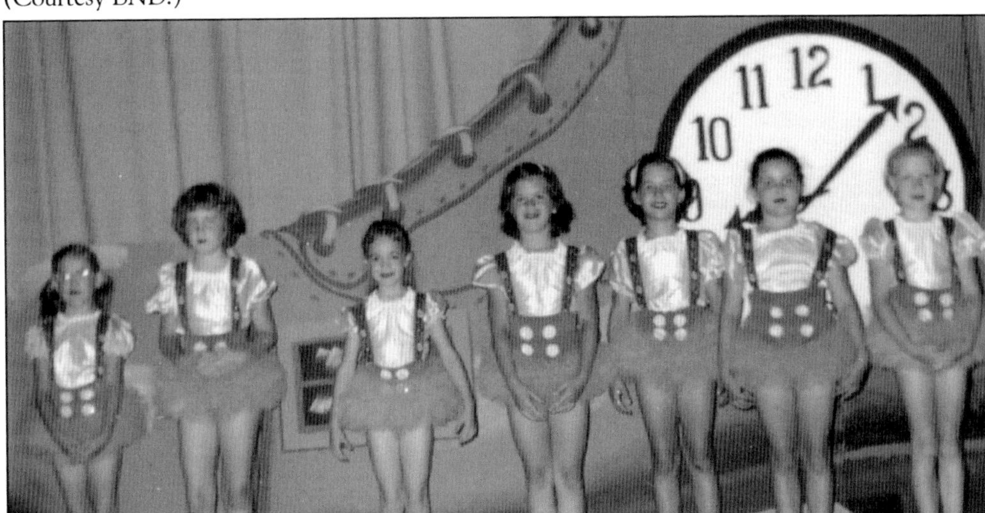

Virginia Sweet's School of Dance met one house southwest from the corner of the intersection of Cherry and Palo Alto Streets. Catherine Thomas, on the far right, participates in a recital. (Courtesy Sarah Grace Thomas.)

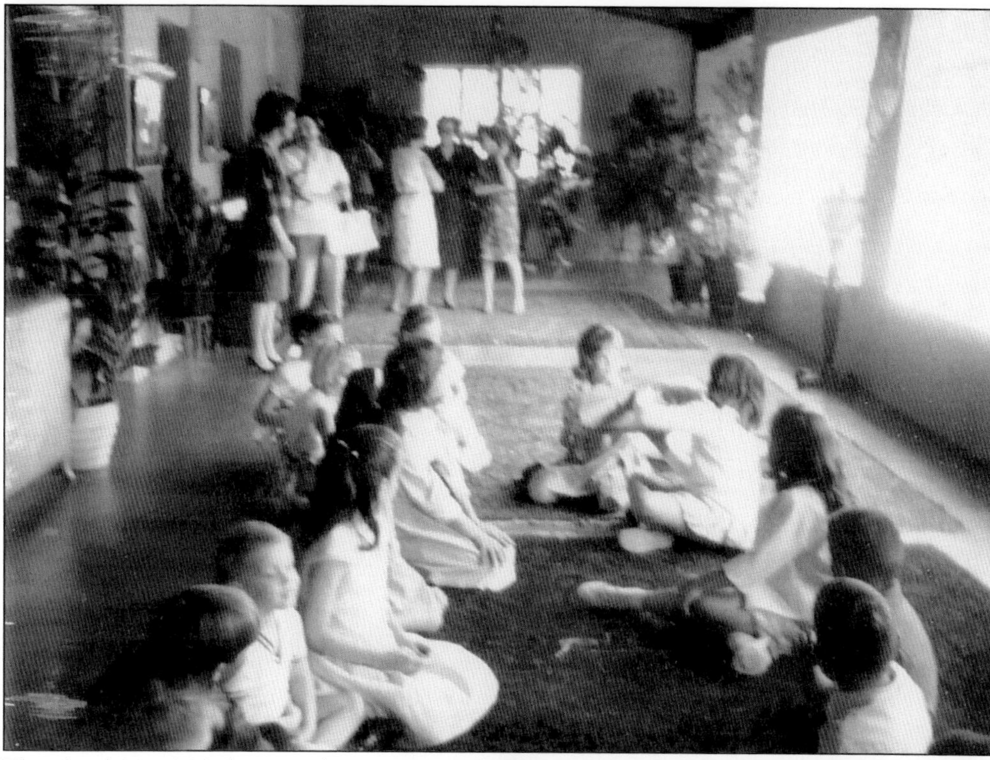

This April 11, 1966 photograph shows Sealy Harris's birthday party at the Cove Hotel. The children are playing pass the parcel.(Courtesy SHL.)

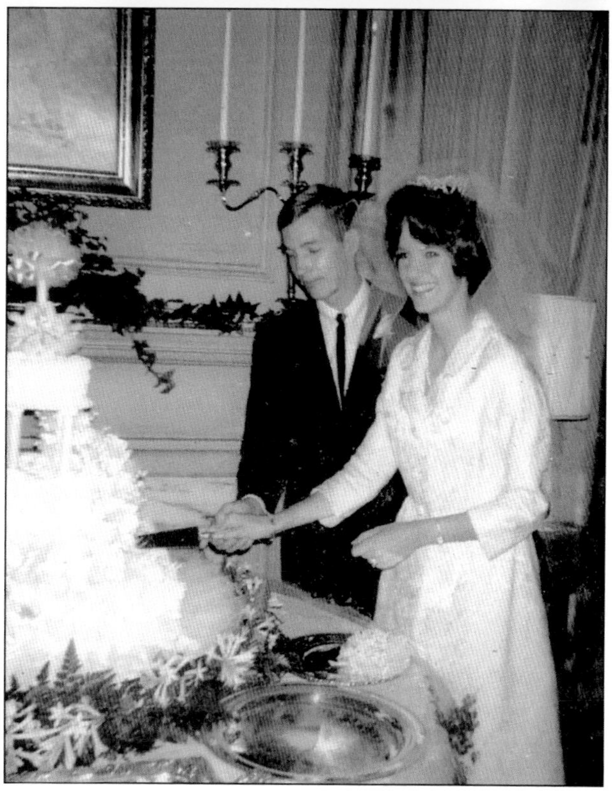

Ruth Rambo's lovely wedding took place at the Cove Hotel in November 1965. (Courtesy SHL.)

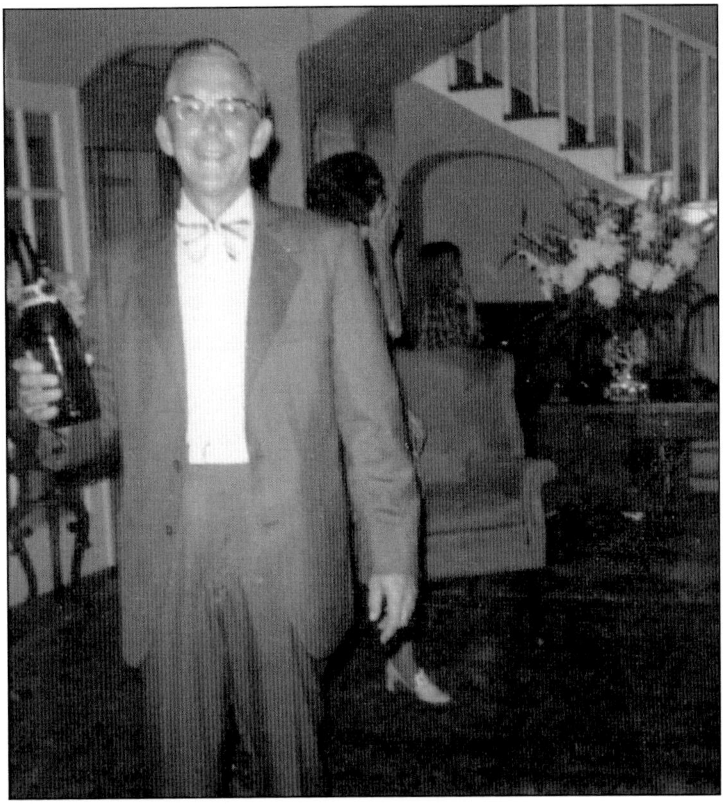

John Hutt was known for his sense of fun and his bow ties. He is seen here in the 1960s. (Courtesy SHL.)

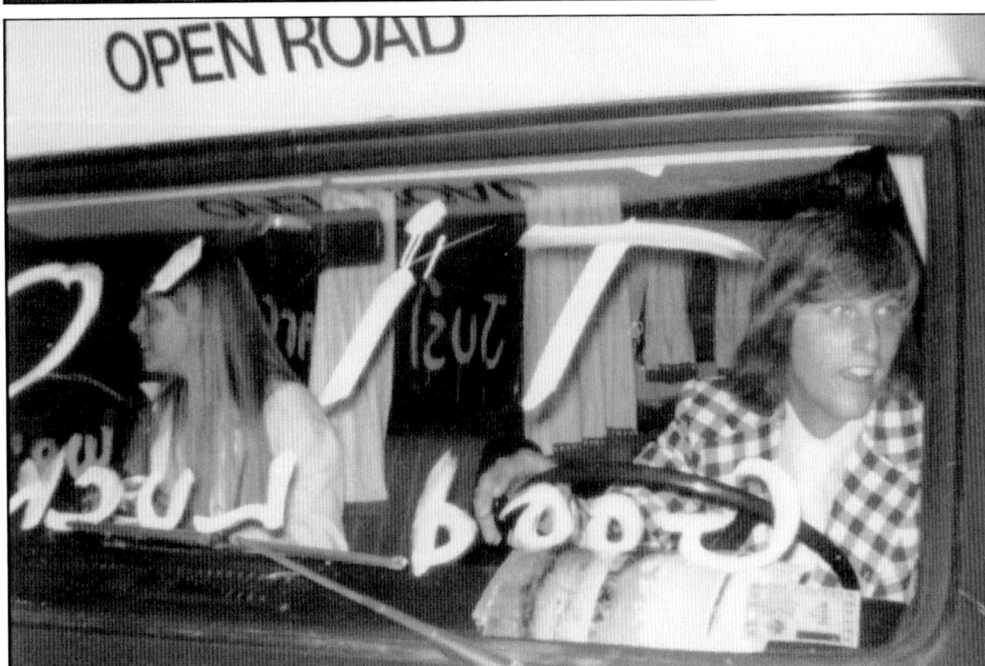

Beth Hutt and Jimmy Lawrence were married in June 1975 and raised their three children on Hollis Avenue. (Courtesy Hank Lawrence.)

Seven

SCHOOL

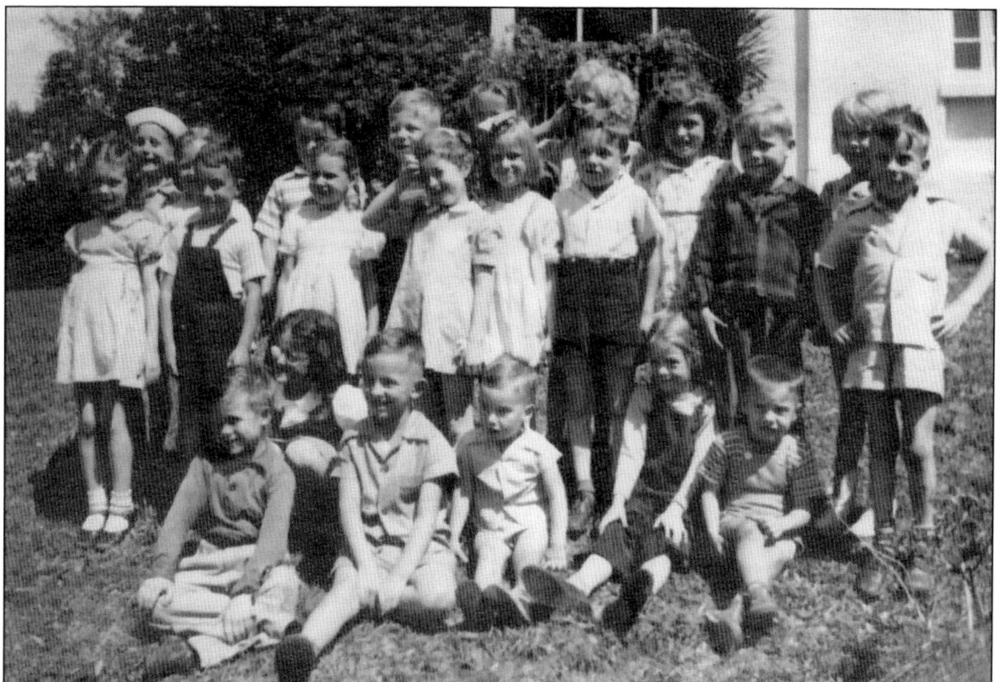

The first-grade class of Cove School in 1943 went to Mrs. Allen's for a field trip. Included in this photo are Dee Mathis (Redding) (fifth child from the left, sitting), Salie Allen Browne, (left, standing) next to Charlie Lahan wearing a sailor's hat, and Annette Youd (eighth child standing from left). (Courtesy SBC.)

Cove School News

.. 1, NO. 5 — PANAMA CITY, FLORIDA, MONDAY, APRIL 30, 1945 — PUBLISHED MONTHLY

EIGHT GRADE CLASS

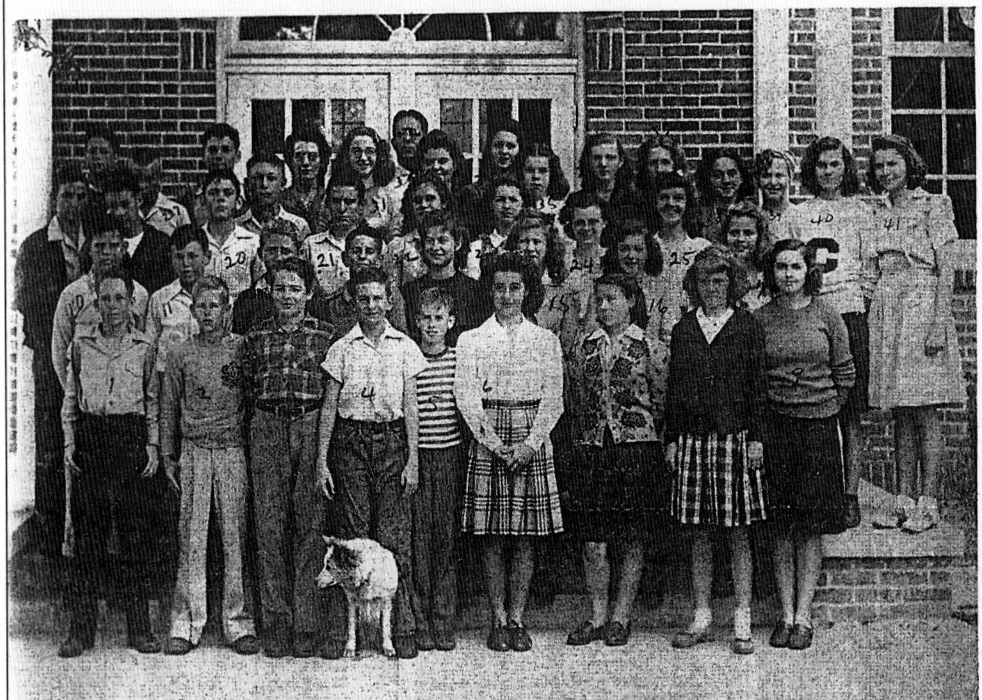

HE EIGHTH GRADE LAST WILL AND ESTAMENT

Ve, the members of the Eighth ade, being supposedly of sound nd, wish to bequeath our pet pressions and habits to the mbers of the Seventh Grade.

To the Seventh Grade as a a whole we will our teachers, od as gold!

To Bobby Higdon, Billy Comer lls his desire to be a roamer.

Betty Wilkins wills her freckles d shining hair to pretty, little ncy Blair!

Sonya Wiselogel wills her lovely ape to Carolyn Zichelback.

Ellen Ham wills her complexion hich isn't false) to Erma Nell use.ton.

"Babs" Baldwin leaves to Karen Timeroth her power as a high-stepping majorette.

George Rushe, who still isn't tame, leaves Monroe Morris his super-brain.

George Williams in making his will, leaves his girl to Paul Steele.

Jerry Wiggins wills his position on the Student Council to Shirley Bradshaw.

Betty Jean Barrett leaves to Carmel Roberts her little habit of starting arguments.

Floyd Fogle, who is always neat, leaves Desser Langley his big feet.

Billie Dove Cain leaves her loud

HISTORY OF THE COVE SCHOOL EIGHTH GRADE

We, the Eighth Grade of 1944-1945 of Cove School, wish to show our appreciation to our teachers, Mr. Rushe, Mrs. Skender, Mrs. Price and to our principal, Mrs. Bridges, by thanking them for their teaching and guidance throughout the past year.

Our class activities started off with a bang! September 8, 1944, Mr. Rushe began by teaching us Science and Math. Mrs. Irene Skender taught us Literature, English, Spelling and History. Mrs. Sandillos coached the girls in Physical Ed. and Mr. Rushe coached the boys, while Miss Erma Whittle entertained us with other social activities.

Skender but were happy to obtain Mrs. Price, who teaches Mrs Skinder's subjects.

Our class officers for the past year were:

President—Virginia Dennis.

Vice-President — Billie Dove Cain.

Secretary—Floyd Fogle.

Treasurer—Martha Ann Gibson

We helped our country through our school by aiding the Junior Red Cross, the Community Chest the Sixth and Seventh War Loan Drive and several other organizations.

Our main athletics during the school year were volley ball, basketball and soft ball for the girls

This is a copy of Cove School's April 30, 1945 newsletter. (Courtesy BCPLLHC.)

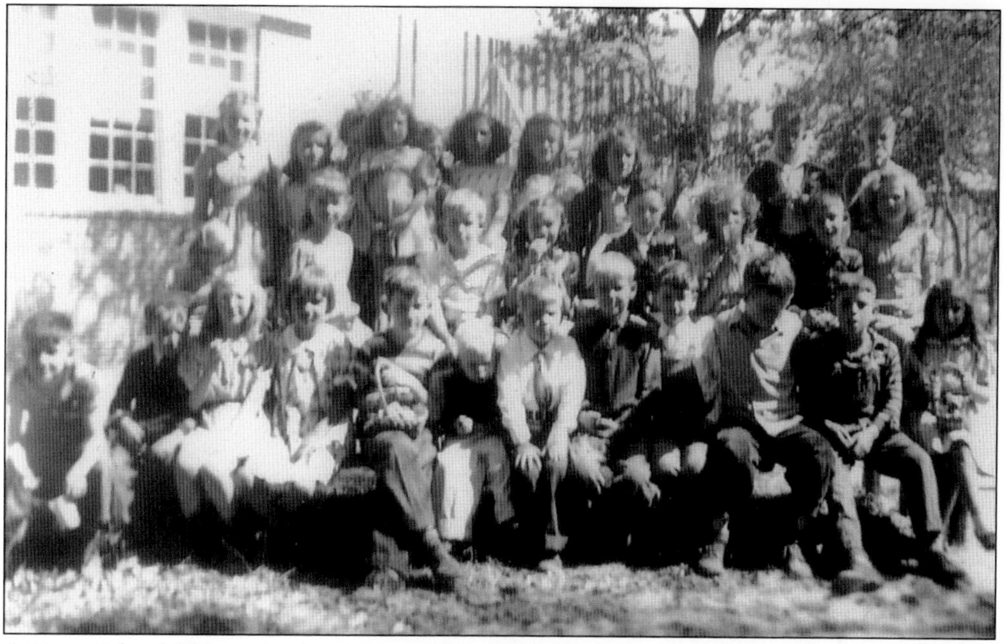

A Cove School fifth-grade class is pictured in 1944. (Courtesy Carl Bennett.)

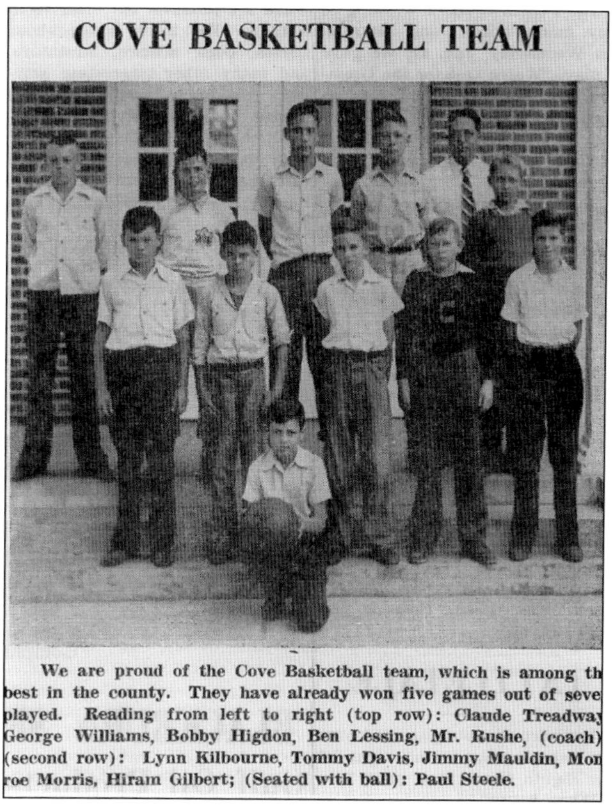

COVE BASKETBALL TEAM

We are proud of the Cove Basketball team, which is among th
best in the county. They have already won five games out of seve
played. Reading from left to right (top row): Claude Treadwa
George Williams, Bobby Higdon, Ben Lessing, Mr. Rushe, (coach)
(second row): Lynn Kilbourne, Tommy Davis, Jimmy Mauldin, Mon
roe Morris, Hiram Gilbert; (Seated with ball): Paul Steele.

This is a copy of the Cove School News featuring a photo of the Cove School Basketball Team of 1945. (Courtesy BCPLLHC.)

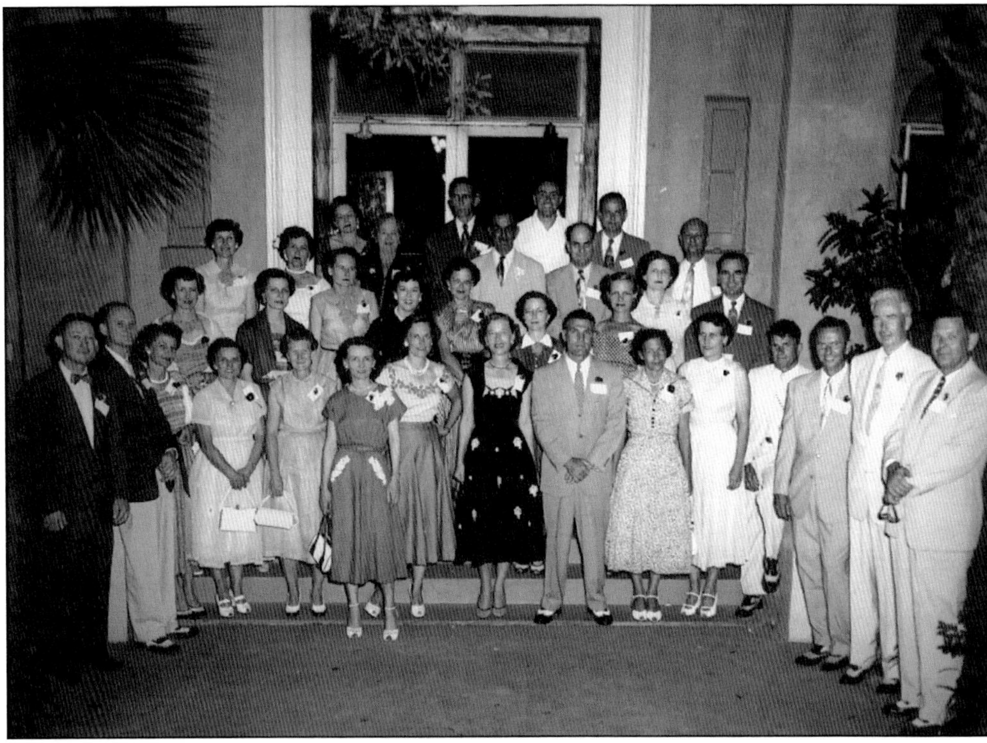

The Bay High Class of 1930 meets for a reunion on the front stairs of the Cove Hotel in 1950. (Courtesy BCPLLHC.)

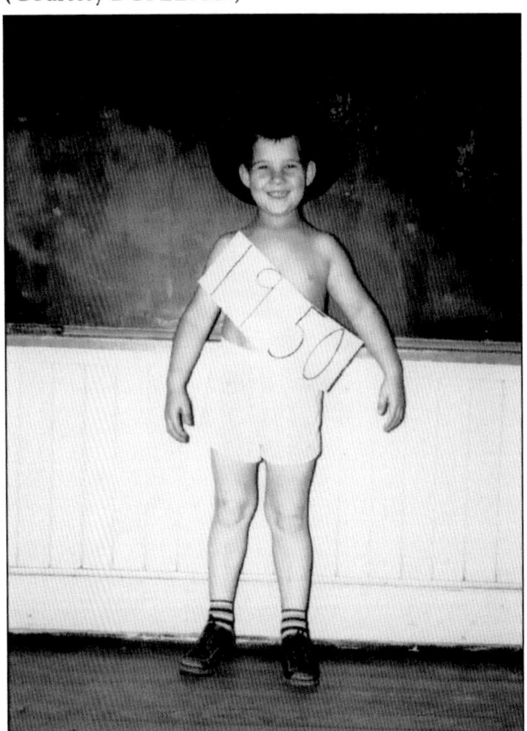

Lynne Green portrays New Year's Day in a Parade Of Holidays at Cove School in 1950.

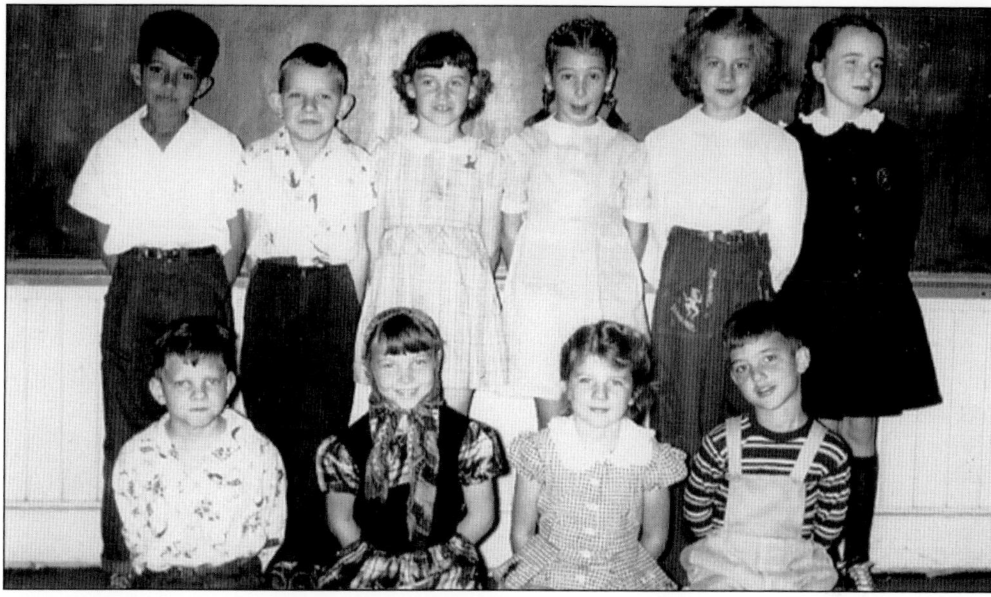

Here is the 1950 chorus of Cove School. From left to right are (front row) Bob Daffin, Kathleen Dennis, Mary Ann Grantham, and Charles Daffin; (back row) Ted Bridges, Bill Cambley, Evelyn Ann Martin, Bonnie Lowery, Wanda Harmon, and Mary Gay Mckenzie.

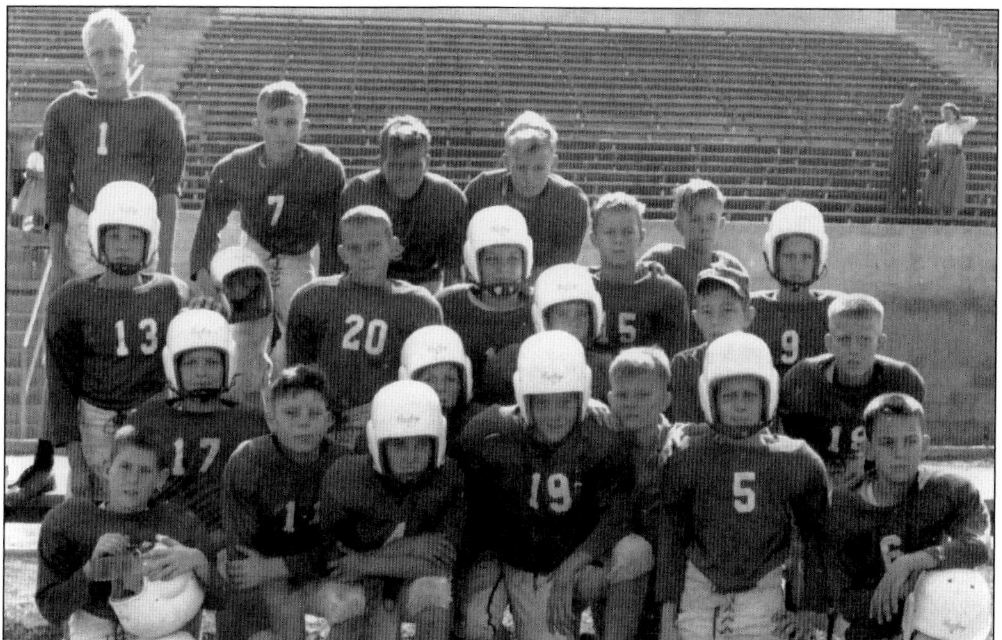

This is a Cove football team in the early 1950s. From left to right are (first row) Dick Scoggins, HB, Pete Bazzel, guard; Stuart Brown, FB, Cecil Smelar, tackle; Frank Pugh, manager; Eddie Cockrell, tackle, and Mike Smith, guard; (second row) Charles McLemore, center; Mark Powell, guard; Gregg Boggs, HB; Charles Lewis, tackle; and Clay Smith, end; (third row) Kit Fairall (sic), center; Lewis Howell, end; Billy Mitchell, guard; Frank Strickland, tackle; and ? Wiley, tackle; (fourth row) Woody Smith, HB; Paul Curry, end; Buster Coleman, HB; John Stoutamire, QB; and Charles Fowler, HB.

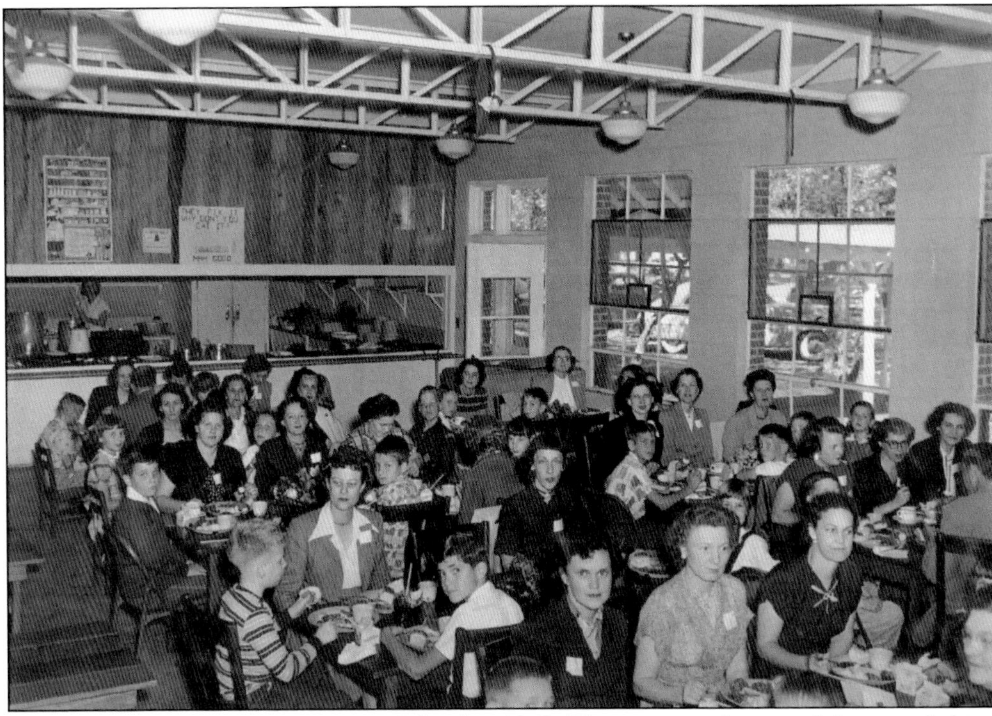

This is the lunchroom scene at Cove School in 1949. The poster in the rear of the room behind the lunch line reads. "They fix it why don't you eat it? Mmm good!"

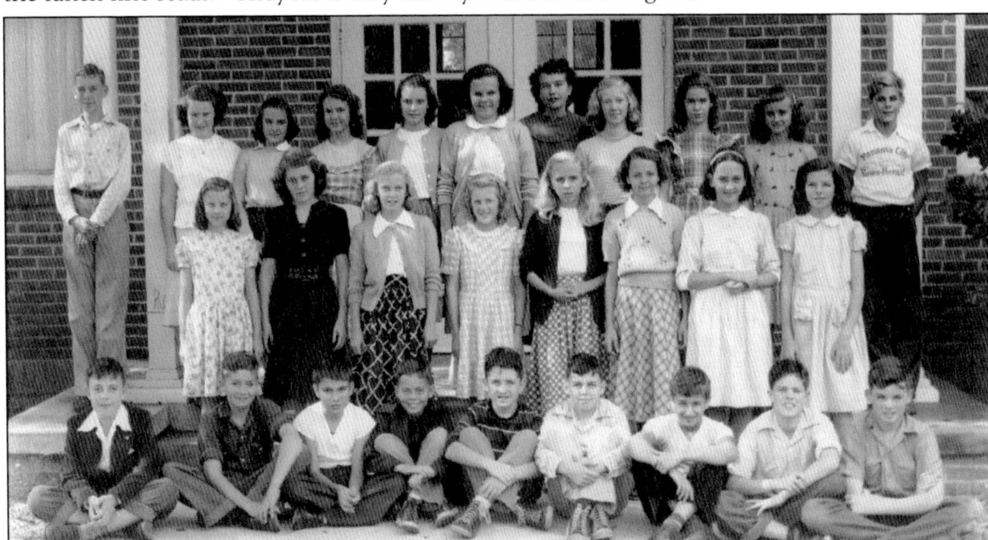

Mrs. Thomas's seventh-grade class is shown here in 1949. From left to right are (front row) Carl Moates, Buzz Leonard, Ronald Sweeney, Harry Prevost, Sidney Daffin III, unidentified, Howard Schneider, Donald Wasson, and Bill Guy; (middle row) Sylvia Goodson, Constance Bounds, Patricia Spiva, unidentified , Charlotte Coonradt, Paul Gray, Marguerite Fleming, and Dorane Louman; (back row) unidentified, Babs Besse, Joyce Crain, unidentified, Linda Peters, Connie Butler, Sarah Grace Thomas (teacher), Lindsey Lou Redmond, Patsy Jones, unidentified, and John Robert Middlemas. (Courtesy John Robert Middlemas.)

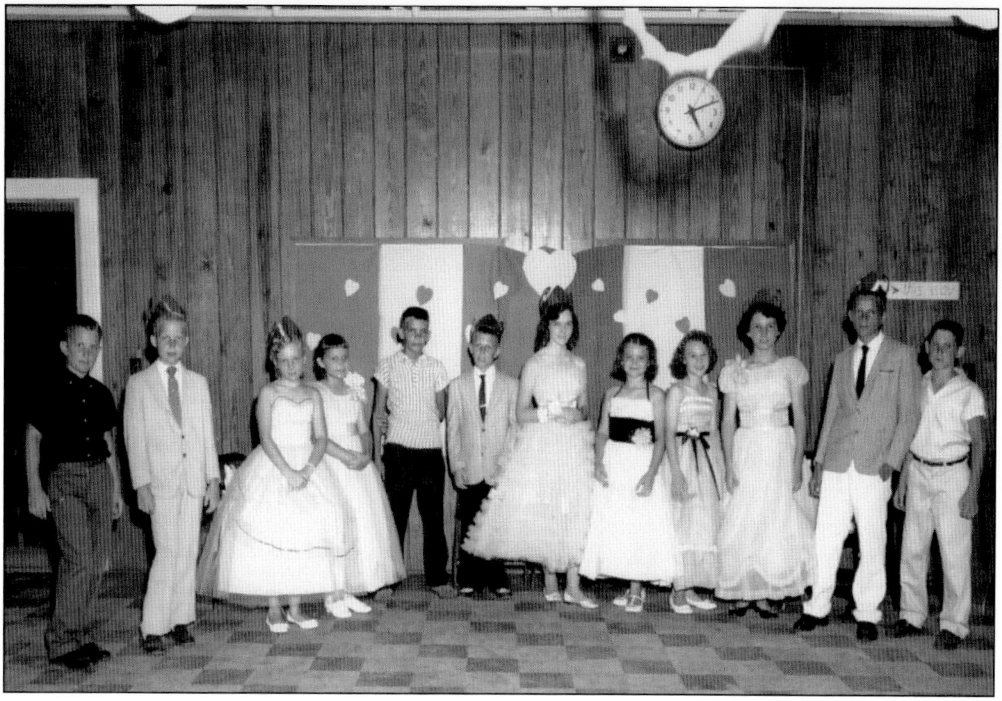

This is the 1957 eighth-grade Valentine's Day program. Lewis Howell (eleventh from left) was the King of Valentines that year.

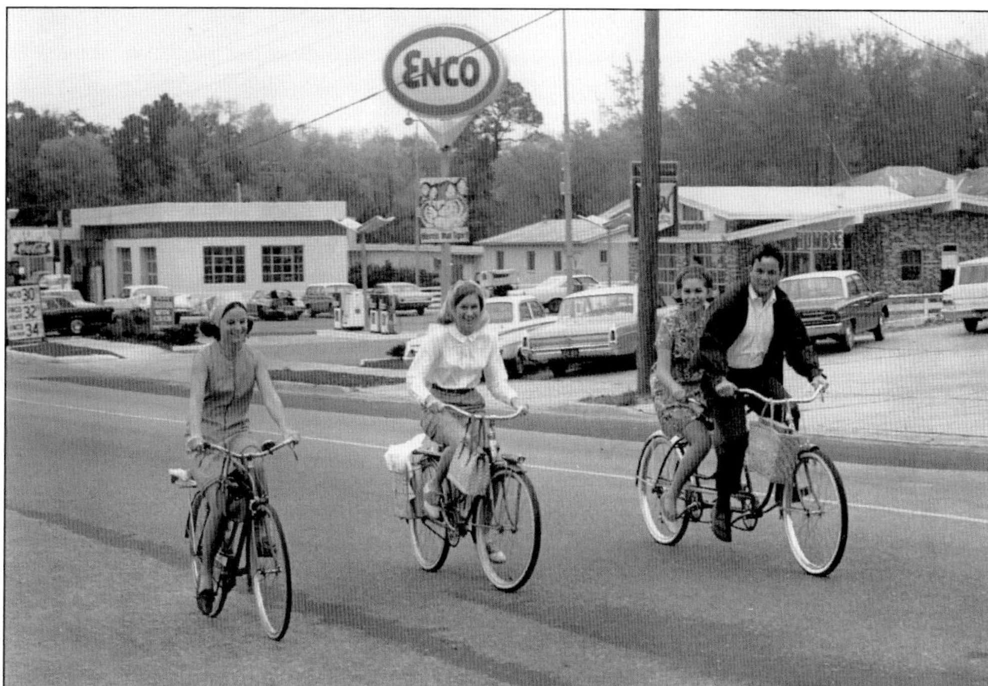

In 1968, Bay County teachers went on strike. Substitutes were hired and these Bay High students decided to bike to school. From left to right are Gwen Howell (O'Rear), Ann Kruse (Percival), Barbara Mitchell (Leonard), and Jim Dickinson.

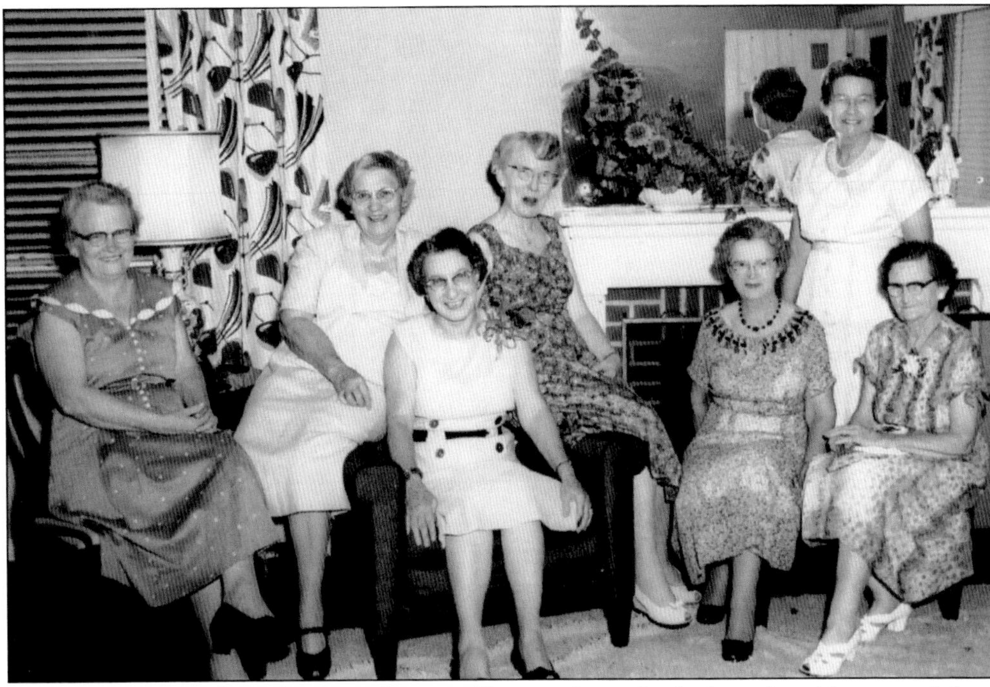

Mrs. Mark Thomas hosted a tea in honor of her mother, who had taught with some of these ladies at Panama Grammar School. From left to right are (top row) Maggie Williams, Wilma McFatter, Patty Culbreth, and Beulah Adams; (bottom row) Ruth Adams and two unidentified women. (Courtesy Sarah Grace Thomas.)

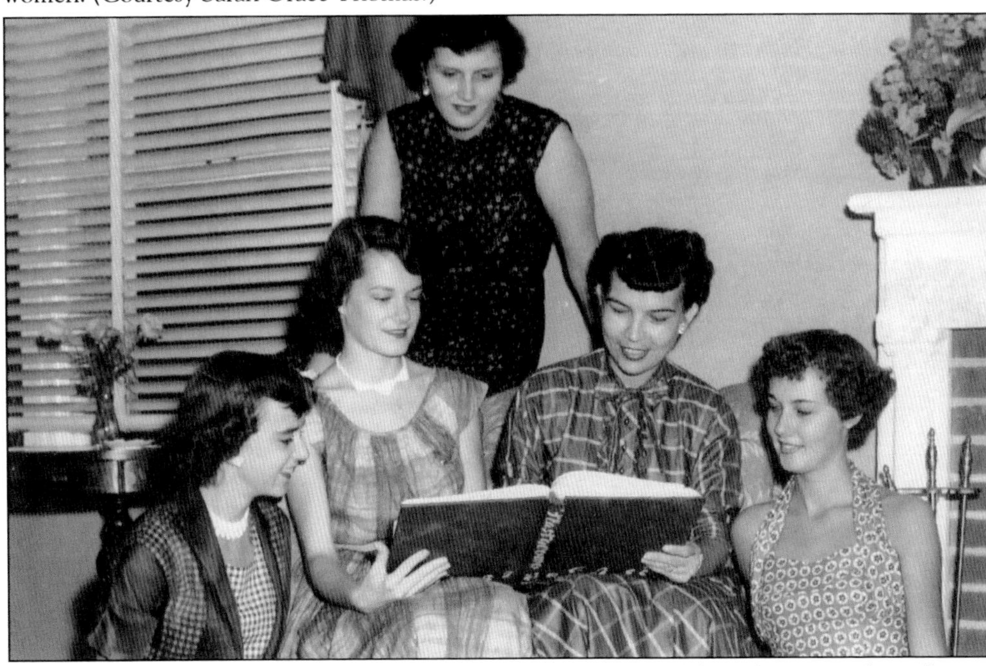

Mrs. Thomas looks back with some former students on the eve of their departures for college in the 1950s. From left to right are June Rowell (Harrison), Adalaide Alinsday (Ware), Barbara Boyd, Sarah Grace Thomas, and Jo Ann Gilbert. (Courtesy Sarah Grace Thomas.)

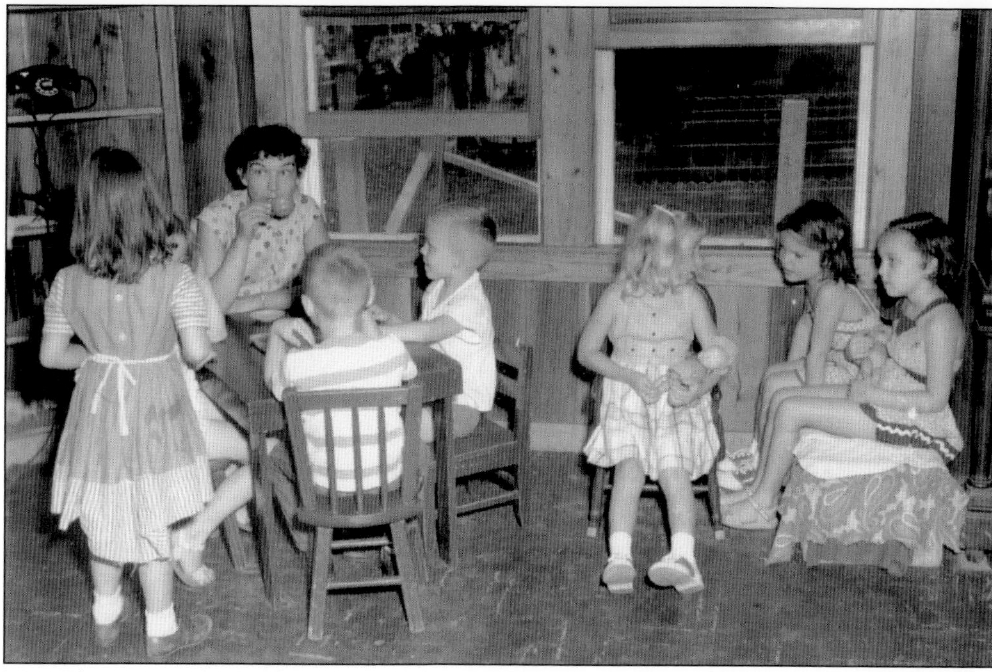

Mrs. Thomas taught kindergarten in the garage of her home on First Court in the 1950s. This was shot during supervised play with students, including Shirley Ellis on the far right. (Courtesy Sarah Grace Thomas.)

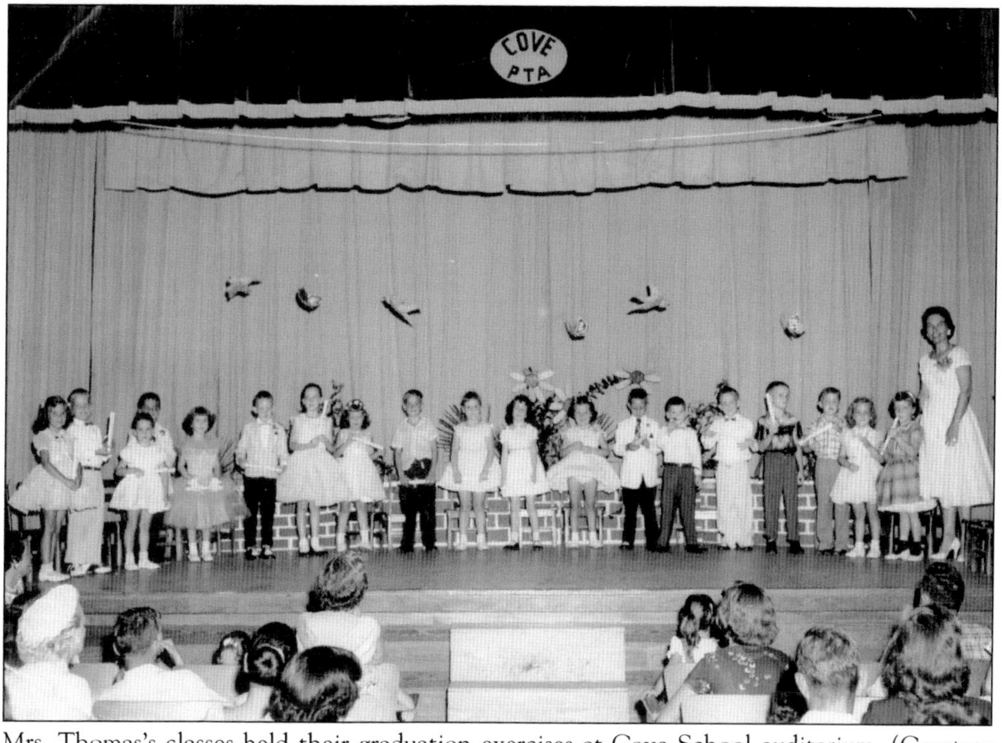

Mrs. Thomas's classes held their graduation exercises at Cove School auditorium. (Courtesy Sarah Grace Thomas.)

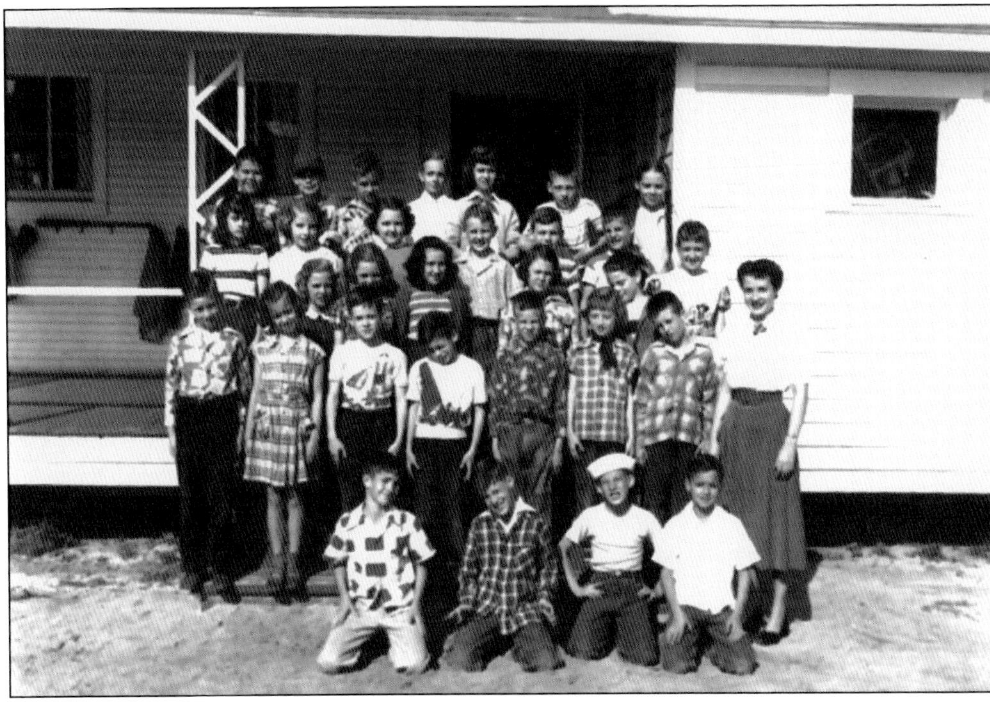

By 1950, Cove School was overcrowded. The new Merriam Cherry Street School was dedicated in 1953 when Tommy Smith was superintendent of schools. In the meanwhile, old barracks were moved to the site of the new school for classrooms. (Courtesy BCPLLHC.)

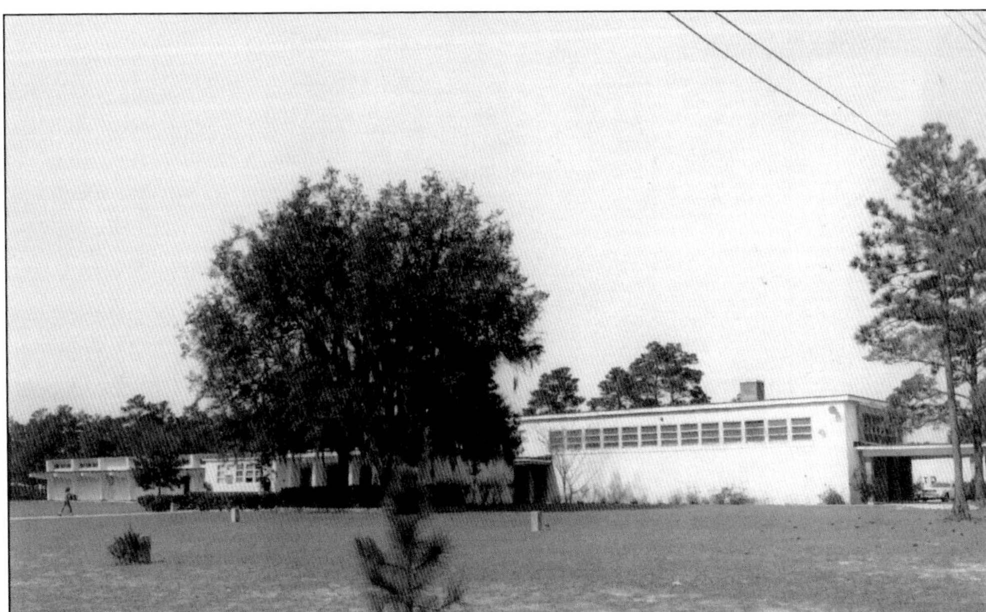

Cherry Street School is seen as it appeared during its first years. (Courtesy Merriam Cherry Street School Media Services.)

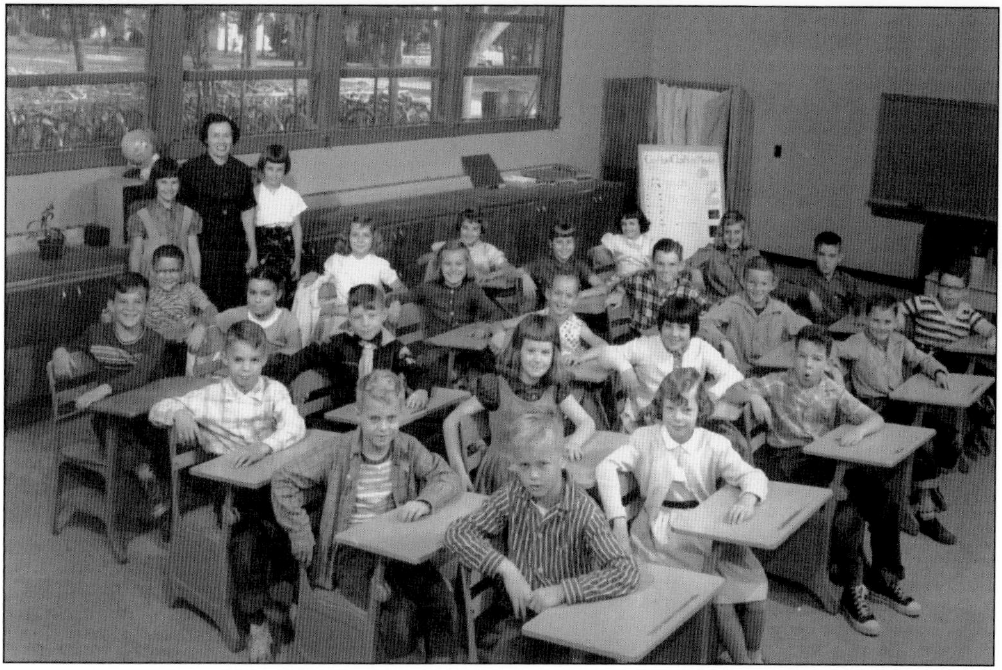

In this photo of an early Cherry Street class, readers will note bicycles that can be seen through the windows. (Courtesy Merriam Cherry Street School Media Services.)

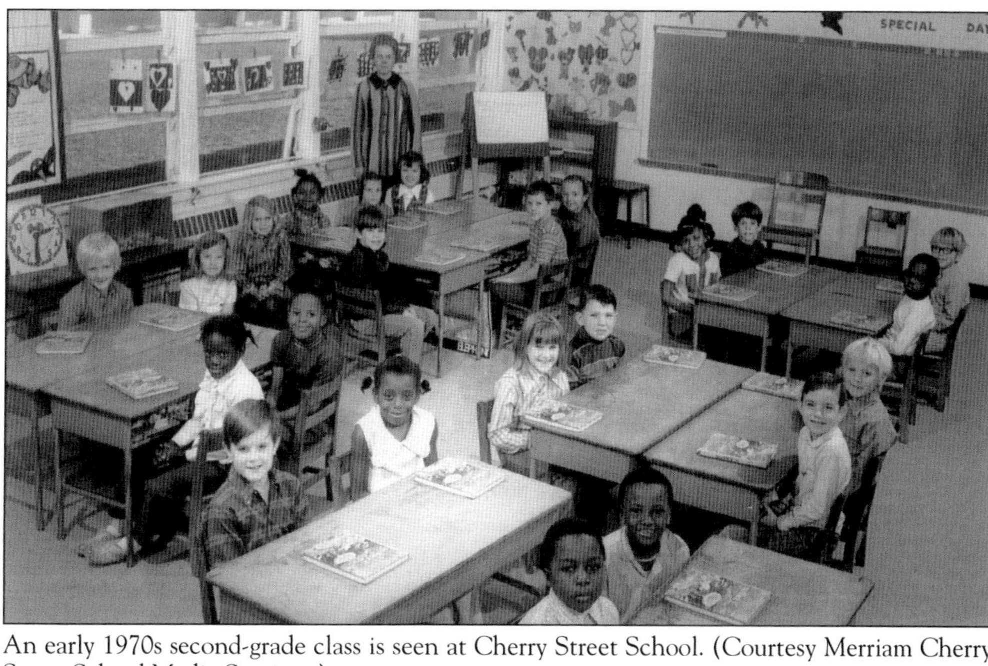

An early 1970s second-grade class is seen at Cherry Street School. (Courtesy Merriam Cherry Street School Media Services.)

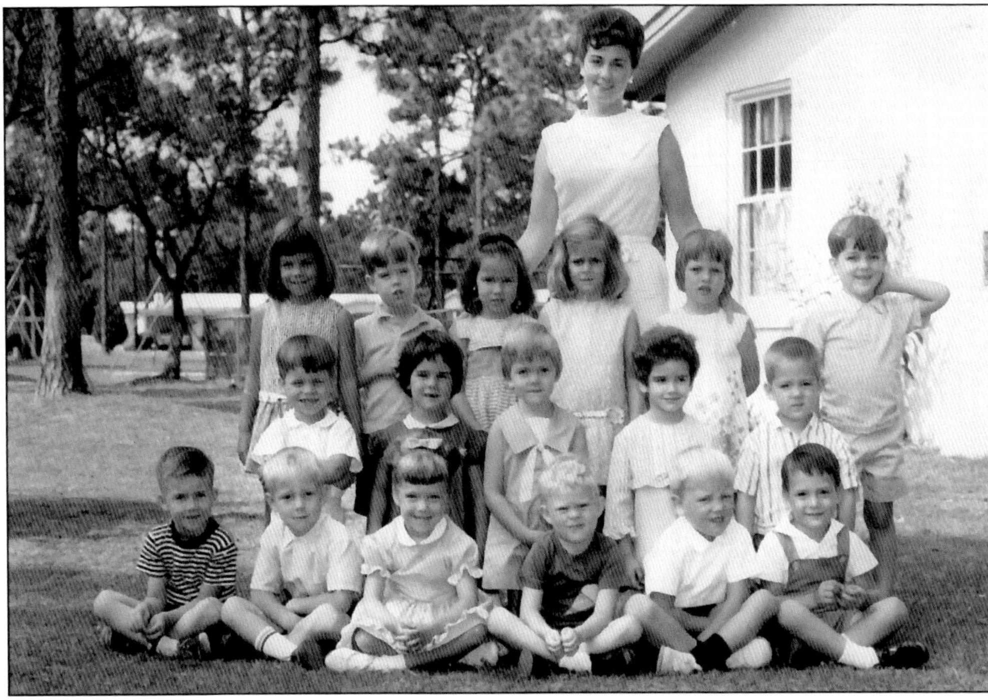

In the first part of the 1960s, Holy Nativity Episcopal church began an education program. This was one of the first classes, a combined four-and-five-year-old class. From left to right are the following: (front row) Scottie Rowe, Sam Bennett, unidentified, G.P. Jessup, Bo FitzSimons, and unidentified; (second row) unidentified, Stacy Smith, Ann Bennett Warriner, Rebecca Sale, and Lee Benoit; (third row) unidentified, Mandeville Smith, unidentified, Mary Middlemas, Carol Lively, and Warren Middlemas; (back row) Ms. Anderson.

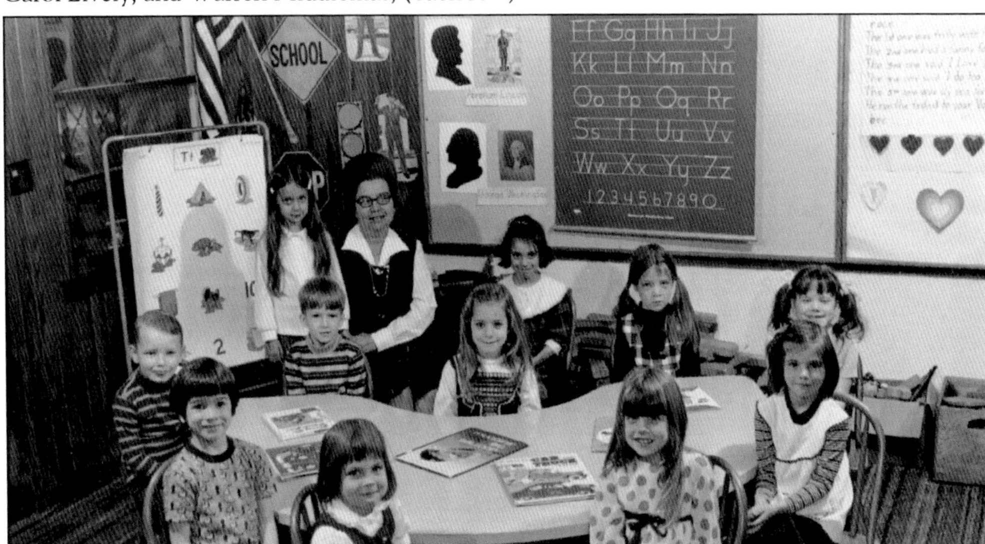

Mrs. Sarah Grace Thomas enjoyed her time teaching at Holy Nativity school. Pictured counter clock wise from the bottom left are two unidentified, Debbie Mason, unidentified, Meg David, Kathy Finlaw, unidentified, Merial Smith, unidentified, Sarah Grace Thomas, Mark Wheeler, and Julie Daffin. (Courtesy Sarah Grace Thomas.)

Eight

Serving the Cove

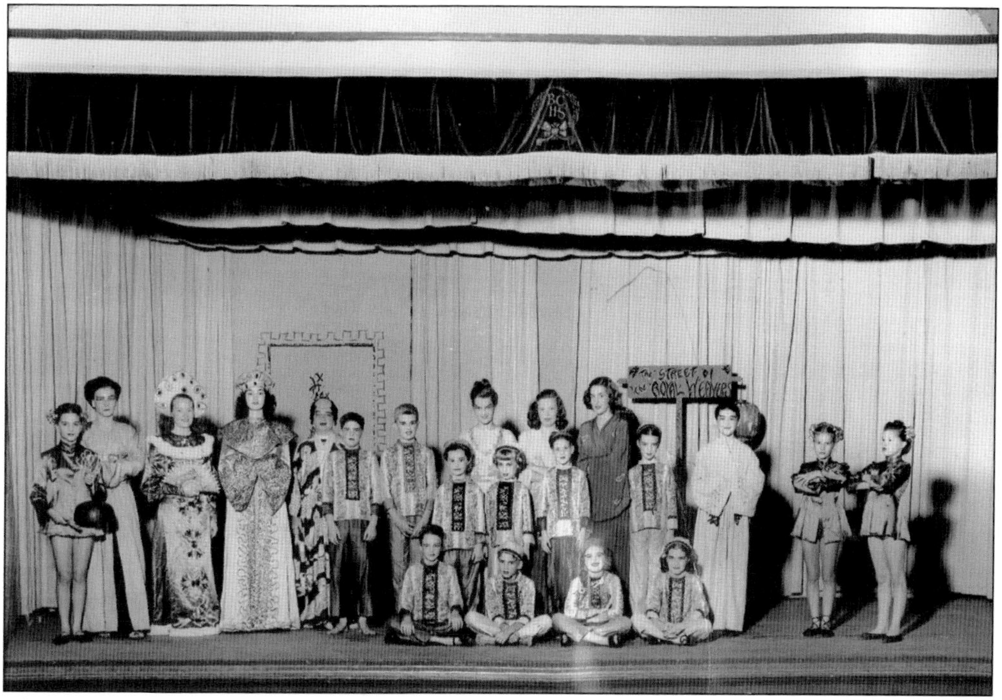

The Three Arts Playhouse, under the direction of Hugh and Margaret Baird (Skipper Laughlin's daughter and son-in-law), performed a piece each year. In 1947 they performed *The Emperor's New Clothes*. Gladys Christo took the part of the Emperor, Salie Allen performed as a snake charmer, and Judy Gore (Lawrence) danced at intermission. Tickets could be obtained at the Old Country Club Log Cabin at "the end of Cherry Street." There was no charge. (Courtesy SBC.)

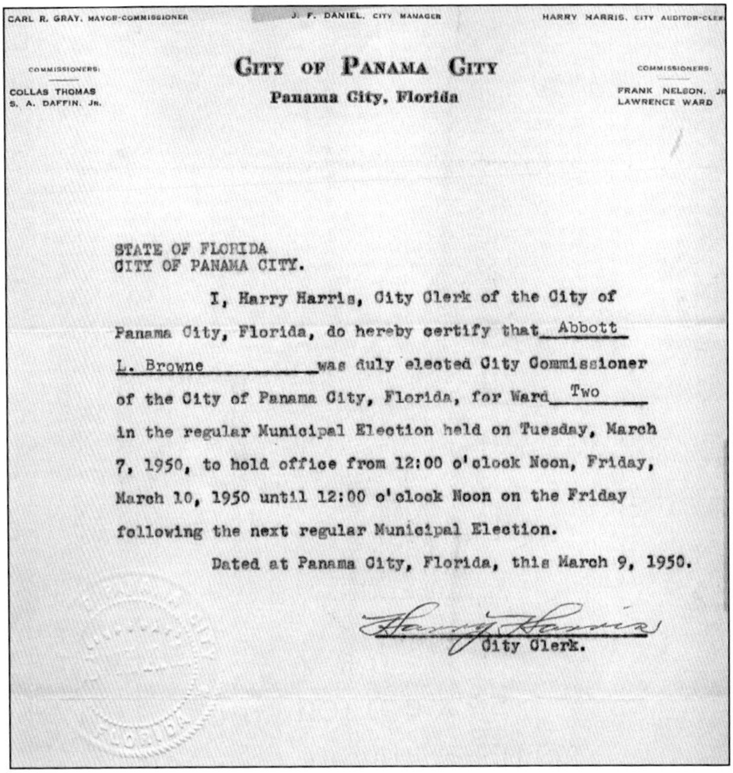

CARL R. GRAY, MAYOR-COMMISSIONER J. F. DANIEL, CITY MANAGER HARRY HARRIS, CITY AUDITOR-CLERK

COMMISSIONERS: COLLAS THOMAS, S. A. DAFFIN, JR.

CITY OF PANAMA CITY
Panama City, Florida

COMMISSIONERS: FRANK NELSON, JR., LAWRENCE WARD

STATE OF FLORIDA
CITY OF PANAMA CITY.

I, Harry Harris, City Clerk of the City of Panama City, Florida, do hereby certify that Abbott L. Browne was duly elected City Commissioner of the City of Panama City, Florida, for Ward Two in the regular Municipal Election held on Tuesday, March 7, 1950, to hold office from 12:00 o'clock Noon, Friday, March 10, 1950 until 12:00 o'clock Noon on the Friday following the next regular Municipal Election.

Dated at Panama City, Florida, this March 9, 1950.

Harry Harris
City Clerk.

In 1950, Abbott Browne was elected to the Panama City Commission. Mr. Browne had a successful real estate business and served The Cove through public office. (Courtesy SBC.)

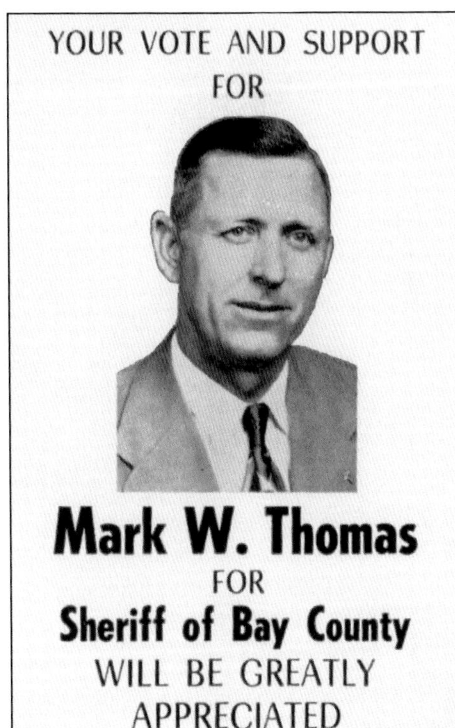

Mark Thomas ran among seven candidates for sheriff in 1952 when the incumbent retired. All were defeated in the May 6 primary except for M.J. "Doc" Daffin, who went on to run unopposed in the November 1952 general election. Other candidates were D.E. Maxwell, Harris McCormick, Coy C. Rushing, John Henry Davis, J.H. Armstrong, and Emory Gay Hobbs. Doc Daffin went on to hold office for the better part of the next two colorful decades. (Courtesy Sarah Grace Thomas.)

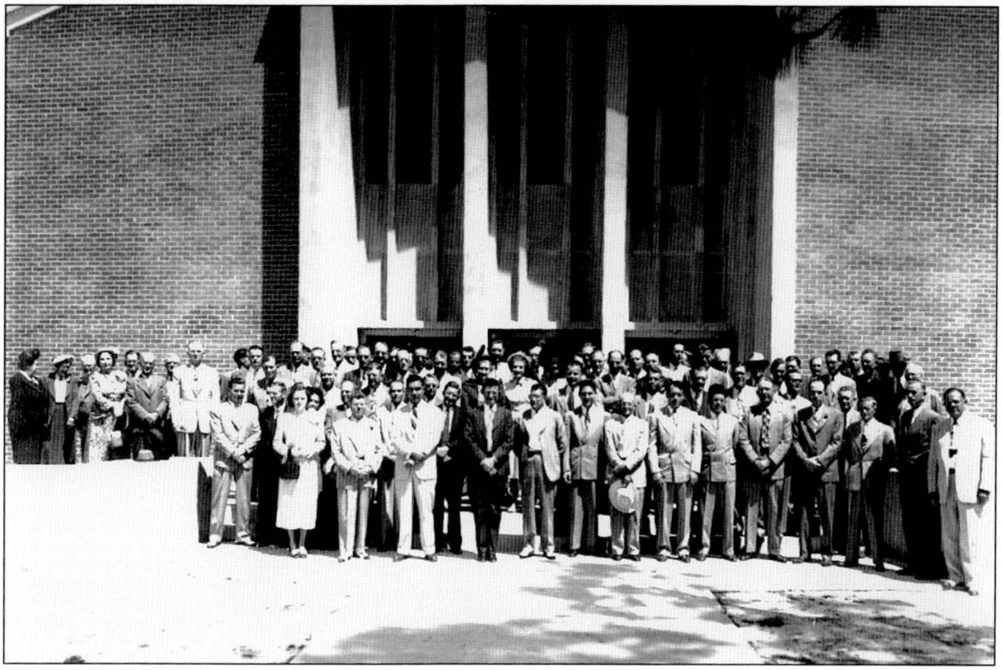

The First United Methodist Church constructed a new building on Sixth Street across from the Church of Christ building in 1950. This photo was taken at the time of the dedication. (Courtesy BCPLLHC.)

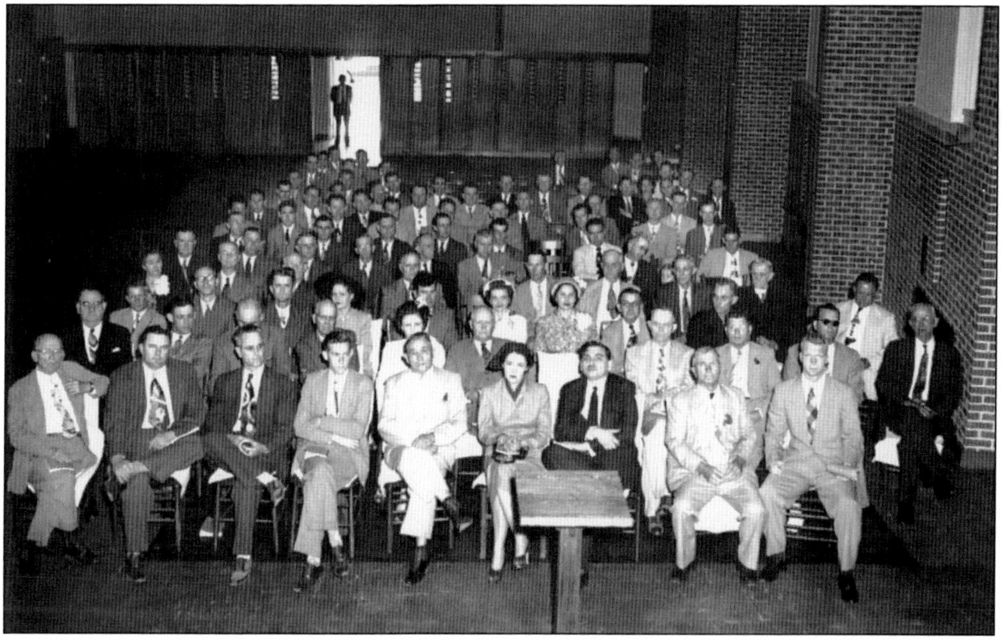

Another group photo was taken at the dedication service for the new First Methodist building. (Courtesy BCPLLHC.)

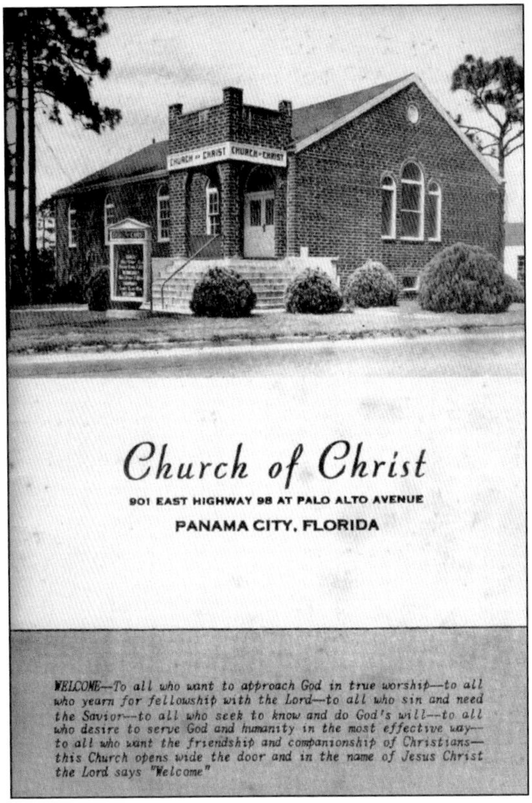

The Church of Christ building was erected in 1946. This building faced Business 98. It was torn down and replaced in 1958 and the new building faced Palo Alto Avenue. Congregations usually refer to themselves by the street where they meet. The group outgrew the facility and built on Highway 231 but retains the name "Palo Alto Church of Christ." (Courtesy Dorothy Wright.)

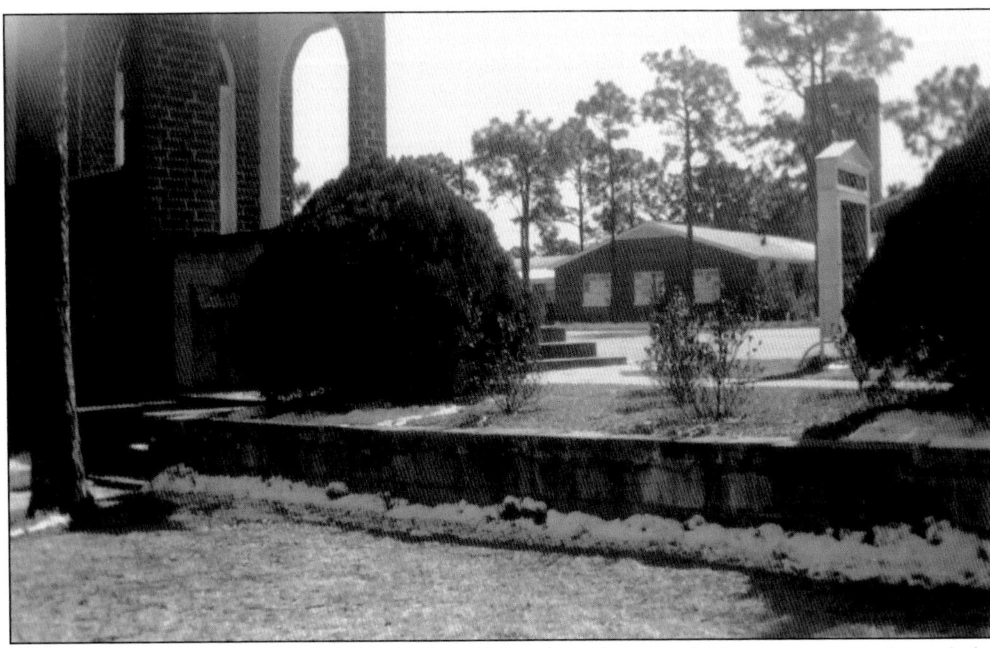

This is a rare view of snow in Florida framed by the Church of Christ on one side and the United Methodist church on the other. (Courtesy Dorothy Wright.)

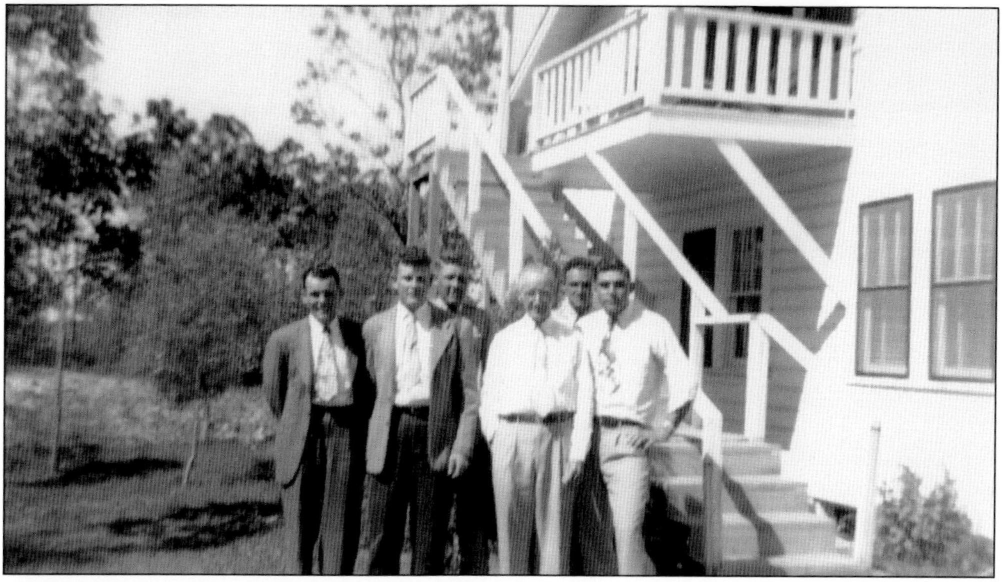

Lonely airmen came alone or with their families to services on Sunday, but rarely did they leave hungry. Mrs. Irrial Wright fed 10 or more as easily as she did the five of her immediate family, so husband Charles collected any airman or other visitor and took them home to feed. (Courtesy Dorothy Wright.)

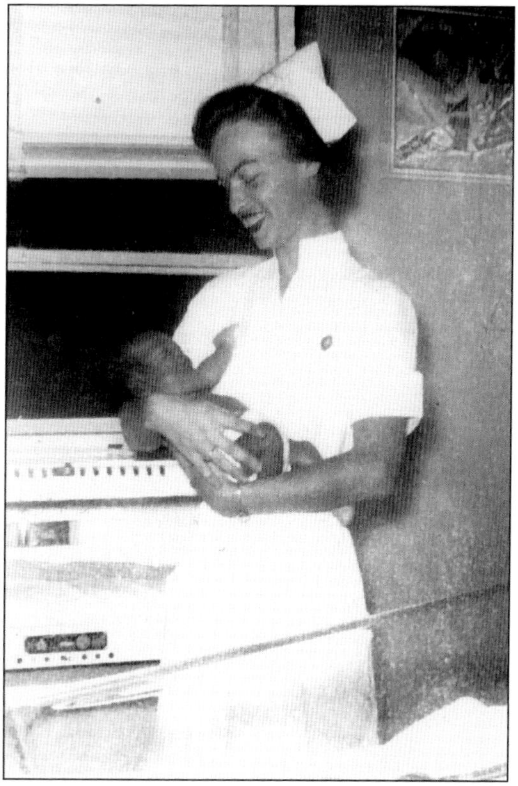

Bette Williams Butler is pictured with a newborn at Bay Memorial Hospital built in 1949 and now Bay Medical Center. This photo is from the early 1950s. (Courtesy BWB.)

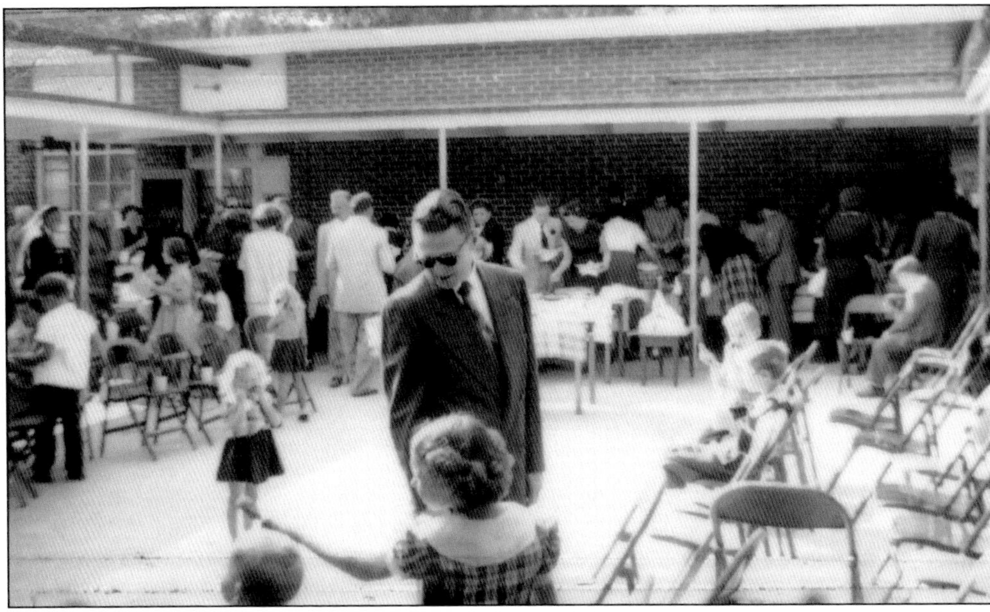

In 1950, Baptists in the Cove area began to feel a need for a new congregation so some of them asked a respected young evangelist and his wife to come and help them start a congregation. Hugh Pyle (standing with sunglasses) accepted and brought his "Queen" Esther and their children to Panama City. They first met in the Cove School auditorium. Mr. Pyle had a radio program called "Echoes from the Cove." (Courtesy Dr. Hugh Pyle.)

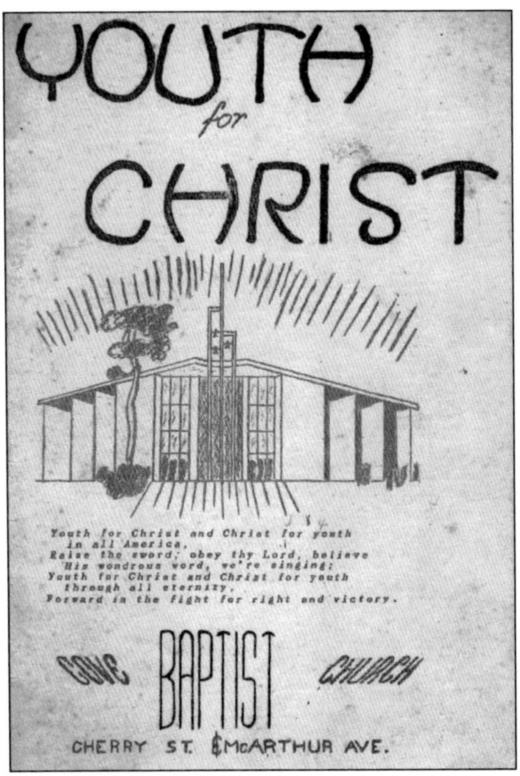

The new Cove Baptists began to make plans for a building, which was built in the early 1950s. This is an artist's rendition of what the new facility would look like when it was built. (Author's Collection.)

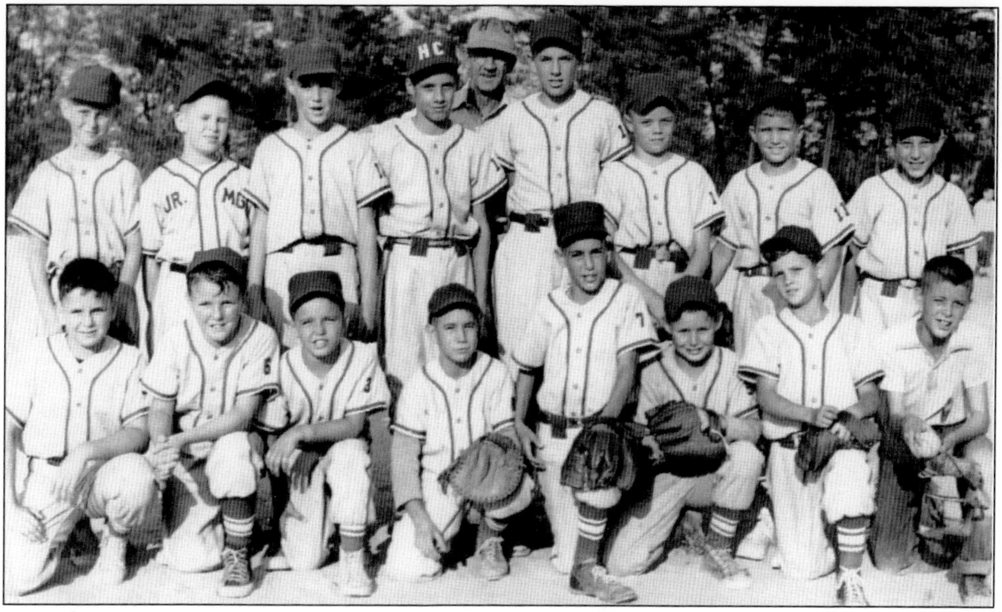

The Howell and Conner team is shown at the Cherry Street Field in the 1950s. From left to right are (front row) Brian King, Jerry Goodman, Bobby Van Hook, Mike Snyder, Johnny Cary, John Stoutamire, Gerald Dyar, and Mike Wills; (back row) David Garret, Ed Story, Charles Albritton, Michael Murfee, Coach Mr. Ray, Rayford Lloyd, Walter Jenks, John Colmont, and Curtis Porter. It was not the team's best season, but Mike Murfee did go to the All-Stars in spite of having been hit by a car while riding his bike by Cove Baptist Church earlier that year. (Courtesy Genear Murfee.)

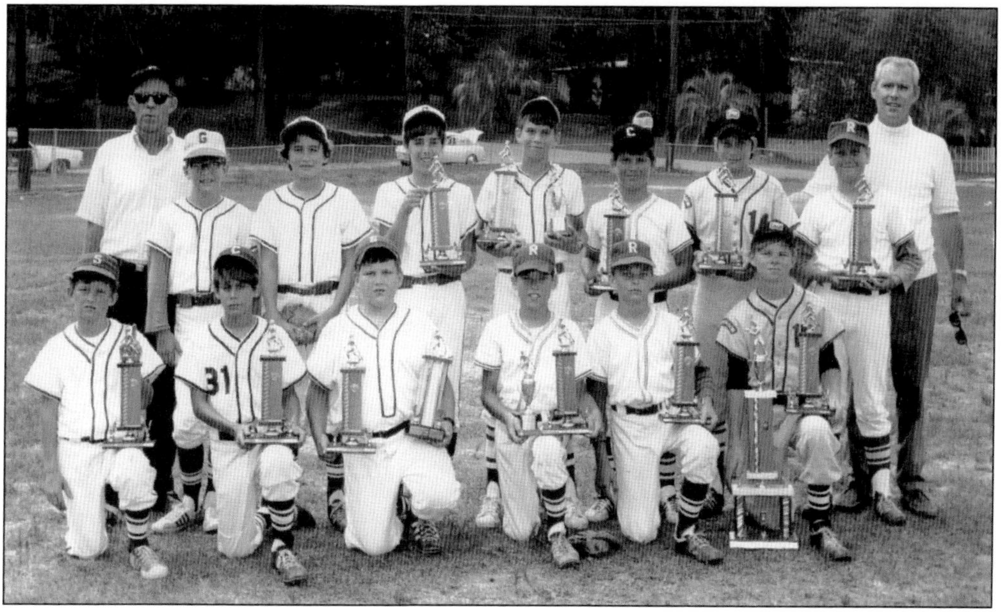

These are the Central League All-Stars of 1971 at Sudduth Park. From left to right are (front row) Paul Thomas, Rob Middlemas, Dickie Simonson, unidentified, Mike Harper, and Eddie Vickers; (back row) Coach Thibodaux, Wayne Ashley, Cyrus McNeil, Tom McAuley, Frank Walker, Bobby French, Ray Williams, George Wheeler, and Coach Leroy French.

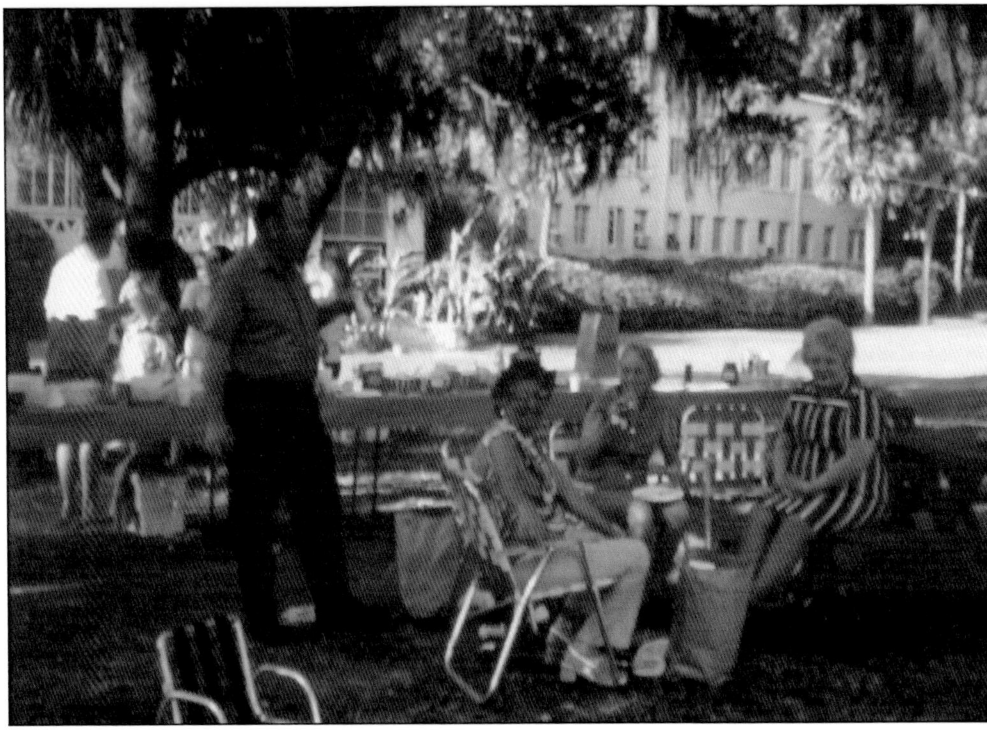

In the early 1970s, St. Andrews Episcopal Church held a Sunday School picnic at the Cove Hotel. (Courtesy Hank Lawrence.)

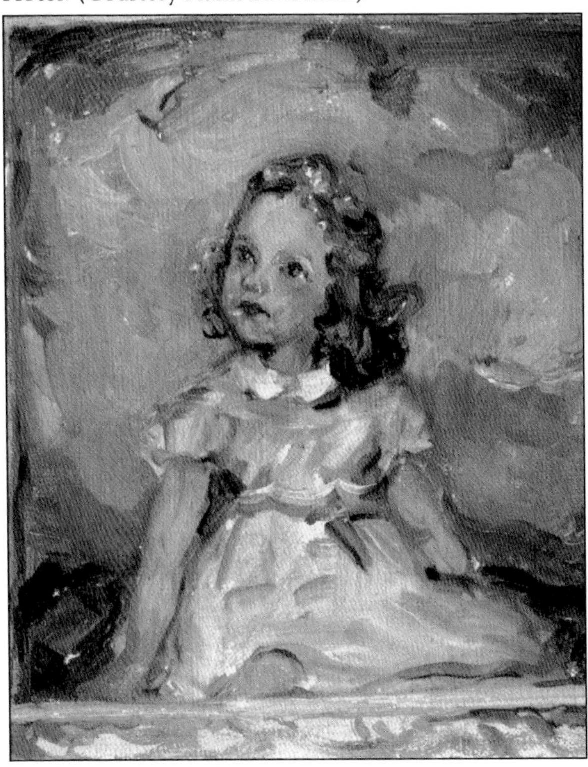

Martha Elliott was a gifted oil painter who came to the Cove in the early 1950s and established a studio at 125 Harmon Avenue, in the building that had formerly housed the Seventh Day Adventists. It had been built in the 1930s as a means of livelihood for Miss Maggie Slicho, who ran a store and lived in an apartment on the south end. Mrs. Elliott later lived across from the yacht club in a cottage built by Carl Browne in the 1930s for his daughter. Ann Percival remembers sitting for her portrait at that house, saying with a smile that it took several sittings. To the right is a cartoon created by Mrs. Elliott in preparation for that portrait. (Courtesy Ann Kruse Percival.)